Knut Papendorf, Stefan Machura,
Anne Hellum (Eds.)

Eugen Ehrlich's Sociology of Law

Gesellschaft und Recht

herausgegeben von

Dr. Dr. habil. Stefan Machura
und Prof. Dr. Klaus F. Röhl

Band 8

LIT

Eugen Ehrlich's Sociology of Law

edited by

Knut Papendorf, Stefan Machura,
Anne Hellum

LIT

This book is printed on acid-free paper.

Bibliographic information published by the Deutsche Nationalbibliothek
The Deutsche Nationalbibliothek lists this publication in the Deutsche Nationalbibliografie; detailed bibliographic data are available in the Internet at http://dnb.d-nb.de.

ISBN 978-3-643-90494-2

A catalogue record for this book is available from the British Library

Klosbachstr. 107
CH-8032 Zürich
Tel. +41 (0) 44-251 75 05
Fax +41 (0) 44-251 75 06
E-Mail: zuerich@lit-verlag.ch
http://www.lit-verlag.ch

LIT VERLAG Dr. W. Hopf
Berlin 2014
Fresnostr. 2
D-48159 Münster
Tel. +49 (0) 2 51-62 03 20
Fax +49 (0) 2 51-23 19 72
E-Mail: lit@lit-verlag.de
http://www.lit-verlag.de

Distribution:
In the UK: Global Book Marketing, e-mail: mo@centralbooks.com
In North America: International Specialized Book Services, e-mail: orders@isbs.com
In Germany: LIT Verlag Fresnostr. 2, D-48159 Münster
Tel. +49 (0) 2 51-620 32 22, Fax +49 (0) 2 51-922 60 99, E-mail: vertrieb@lit-verlag.de
In Austria: Medienlogistik Pichler-ÖBZ, e-mail: mlo@medien-logistik.at
e-books are available at www.litwebshop.de

Contents

Introduction

Stefan MACHURA, Anne HELLUM and Knut PAPENDORF

By 2012, a century had passed since the death of Eugen Ehrlich, one of the main founders of Sociology of Law. His work inspired generations of legal scholars and social scientists, but was always controversial, as he challenged a legal positivist view. This centenary provided an opportunity to take stock of Ehrlich's scholarship and how it has been received. On 2 and 3 November 2012, in the Law Faculty of the University of Oslo, a conference in the Department of Criminology and Sociology of Law was held on *Eugen Ehrlichs' Sociology of Law: its Contemporary Importance for the Current Nordic and International Discourse*.

In preparing this conference, the three editors of this volume wanted to explore the relevance of Ehrlich's concept of "living law" for socio-legal scholarship, focusing particularly on the relationship between centre and periphery. Most theories of law in Scandinavian countries emphasize the close relationship between law and society (Eckhoff 1960, 11). We therefore wanted to explore whether, and to what extent, Norwegian, Swedish and Danish legal scholars had drawn direct inspiration from Ehrlich's scholarship, or whether a parallel development had taken place. We hoped that by looking at the development of legal scholarship in the Scandinavian countries from a centre-periphery perspective we would be able to shed new light on the socio-legal foundation of Scandinavian legal science. We were also interested in exploring how Ehrlich's concept of "living law" features in scholarship addressing local resistance to globalization and the internationalization of law. To address these broad issues we invited socio-legal scholars from Scandinavia, the Netherlands, Wales, Australia and Germany with different disciplinary backgrounds. For us the preparation for the conference, the conference itself, and the editing of the papers have been a voyage of intellectual discovery: we gained a more intimate knowledge of the character and achievements of Eugen Ehrlich, learning about his social and intellectual background, about the early and later reception of his ideas, and considering the strengths and weaknesses of his concepts if applied to today's problems.

Eugen Ehrlich at various stages of his career polemically attacked positions held by scholars defining the main stream of jurisprudence. **Klaus A. Ziegert** in this volume shows how Ehrlich's work in turn was instrumentalized by others to "debunk" rival ideas and to promote a certain perspective. Legal anthropologist John Griffiths criticized Ehrlich for not being anti-state enough. Yet, his ultimate aim was not the Austrian scholar but legal colonialism: western supremacy over indigenous people. Similarly, Japanese scholar Masaji Chiba argued against the imposition of western legal concepts.

In "Beyond 'Living Law': Eugen Ehrlich's General Theory of Law" **Klaus A. Ziegert** draws out the major lines of Ehrlich's work. Ehrlich had planned a trilogy of books: the "Grundlegung der Soziologie des Rechts" (Ehrlich 1913/1967), which is the only book most people are aware of, was to be followed by two volumes on judicial logic and judges' decision-making. The rarely cited "Die juristische Logik" appeared 1918, while the third volume ("Die Theorie richterlichen Entscheidens") remained unfinished when Ehrlich died. **Ziegert** sets his discussion of the "living law" concept within the broader convictions Ehrlich held as a legal scholar. As **Ziegert** shows, Ehrlich disappoints radical advocates of legal pluralism. He did not seek to dissolve state law. Rather, he argued that more account should be taken of the various 'laws' of the associations making up a society. During his life-time, Ehrlich had already achieved an international reputation. **Ziegert** shows how his work was received in the country which still has the strongest Sociology of Law association relative to its size: Japan. It was used for very specific legal-political purposes, as Ehrlich's concept of "living law" could bolster the claim that modern law would have to be finely adapted to meet Japanese cultural needs.

As **Ziegert** points out, it would be misleading to see Ehrlich as someone who wanted to abolish legal scholarship and replace it with sociology. It was rather Ehrlich's aim to provide lawyers with an additional tool: Sociology of Law. He believed lawyers, judges and law-makers needed to develop better practices, informed by empirical legal studies. Accordingly, Ehrlich thought of ways to improve the education of law students and legal practitioners. Sociology of Law had to become part of legal education. However, most German legal scholars rejected Ehrlich's ideas. Only later socio-legal studies were included in the law school curriculum. In the way that had been called for by Ehrlich, social science expertise was drawn on in the process of drafting new laws. **Stefan Machura** tells this story, and describes the view taken of Ehrlich's ideas in introductions to Sociology of Law and by key socio-legal scholars in Germany today. For such scholars Ehrlich's inability to come up with a clear-cut definition of 'law' is a major stumbling block. He cannot meet their expectations, because of the openness of his empirical approach. Critics to this day repeat arguments brought forward by Hans Kelsen (1915/2003) in his controversy with Ehrlich. His "Pure Theory of Law" marks the utmost contrast to Ehrlich's "Living Law" approach. Other aspects of the Bukovina scholar's work have been more warmly received, and legal pluralism is even a focus of recent socio-legal research.

Apart from the Kelsen-Ehrlich controversy, **Machura** introduces other conflicts which have been factors in Ehrlich's legacy. German-speaking jurisprudence also remembers him as a spiritual leader of the 'Free Law Movement'. Though Ehrlich advocated "free finding of law" only when the judge is confronted with a genuine gap in the legal code which cannot be addressed by standard legal interpretation. According to Ehrlich, it is in such circumstances that an empirical method can best help the jurist to find a cautious, 'conservative' interpretation: one that takes into account the interests involved. Nevertheless, Max Weber (1922/1968) argued against Ehrlich on the grounds that law is defined by the existence of a sanctioning apparatus such as the modern state. Modern rational jurisprudence synthesizes law into a cohesive logical system. Allowing judges 'free finding of the law' would ultimately have detrimental social consequences, as it opens the way to arbitrary decision-making. Ehrlich took a more optimistic view of lawyers, and sought to further improve their quality through his educational efforts. Later sociologists of law have commented that Ehrlich when talking about 'free finding of the law' just dared to make explicit what judges have actually always done.

Weber and Ehrlich differed in key aspects. The one wanted to strictly separate jurisprudence and sociology on the grounds they had different logics, while the other advocated sociological jurisprudence: the use of sociological concepts and methods to address legal problems. Legal scholars in the German-speaking world are still divided along these lines. On closer inspection, however, there are plenty of commonalities in the works of the two scholars, which are identified by **Machura**. Both understood that social associations are key ingredients of society and need to be taken into account by anyone contemplating its nature. Where Ehrlich thought that the state had reached the acme of its power, Weber (1922/1968) suspected that its role in society would continue to grow, and he has been proved right by the passage of time. **Machura** finishes his contribution with a discussion of Ehrlich's main thesis: that the bulk of the law would develop in society itself.

According to **Franz and Keebet von Benda-Beckmann**, the most important analytical deficiency of Ehrlich's term 'living law' is that it does not define three core component concepts: law, the relevant associations of communities, and 'living'. Ehrlich, they argue, simply presupposes that law consists of those norms that regulate matters seen as of general social significance, and that it is rooted in certain specific types of action and relationships. Defining the relevant association or community, they point out, poses different problems today than those existing at the time when Ehrlich developed his ideas. Now, in a globalized world linked by the internet, migration, and chains of disaggregated production, a more differentiated conceptual apparatus would be necessary to capture the variations and relative indeterminacy within such communities and associations. A related problem is that, without further conceptual differentiation, the internal norms of associations tend to conjure up an image of unity and consensus and to overlook dissent, differences of opinion, and minority views.

Equally important, according to **Franz and Keebet von Benda-Beckmann**, are the problems that arise when living law changes from a descriptive analytical device into a normative construct, as part of doctrinal and pragmatic application of law. Attempts to convert something that, from an analytical social science perspective, can be called law, into official law often overlook the differences between the perspective of social science and that of law. As an example, **Franz and Keebet von Benda-Beckmann** show the danger in identifying living law with customary law, as is often done. Can we really, for descriptive or political purposes, they ask, say that 'customary law' only deserves the label 'law' if its subjects live in conformity with it, as the legalistic understanding of 'customary law' demands? The problem is illustrated by an example from South Africa, where customary law has largely been perverted or destroyed, with the result that people can no longer live according to its principles and rules because state agents or landowners have made it impossible to do so.

The problems are even more pressing, according to **Franz and Keebet**

von Benda-Beckmann, when one wishes to make use of the term 'living law' in the context of political engagement, particularly in relation to gender issues. In the light of an example from South Africa they argue that, from a social science perspective, it is by no means self-evident that such political instrumentalization of the concept of living law or living customary law would be the most promising way to reach one's objectives: to attain, for instance, gender equality in any kind of law and in social practices. One would need more conceptual sophistication and theoretical analysis to predict whether courts or legislation would be the most appropriate means to bring about the desired social change, or whether the change in conduct and rules of conduct should be stimulated by other, largely non-legal means.

Theories of living law and legal pluralism have in recent years become an ingredient in the diverse body of "post-Westphalian" legal scholarship which moves beyond considering states as the sole actors in international and national law. **Anne Hellum** describes how, in the 1990s, scholars of Scandinavian and African women's law seeking an empirical understanding of women's interaction with the law in contemporary western welfare states and contemporary post-colonial states in Southern Africa, turned to theories of living law and legal pluralism. The overall theme here is how a wide range of theories, ranging from Eugen Ehrlich's early 20th century theory of living law to post-colonial anthropological theory on legal pluralism, have been employed for different purposes. Both in Scandinavia and in Southern Africa, women's law has been defined as a socio-legal discipline that sets out to describe, understand, and change the position of women in law and society (Dahl 1987; Tsanga and Stewart 2011).

To illustrate some lines of development within women's law **Anne Hellum** takes as the basis for her article the women's law research carried out between 1975 and 2000 by scholars at the Faculty of Law in Oslo, at the Faculty of Law in Copenhagen, and at the Faculty of Law in the University of Zimbabwe. Among these scholars are Hanne Petersen, Agnete Weis Bentzon, Julie Stewart, Amy Tsanga and Anne Hellum. She shows how legal scholarship analyzing women as actors in the process of law evolved within a framework whose methodological principle was to start from women's lived experiences and combine it with different theories of living law and legal pluralism. She demonstrates how adopting analytical concepts such as the semi-autonomy of law facilitates studies of women as norm-generating actors in the process of law, rather than as objects of gender-neutral state law which does not respond to women's lived realities. There has been a shift from research addressing the operation of gender-neutral law in a gendered reality to research exploring the multiplicity of norms invoked by women themselves, and other actors in social fields such as the family and the workplace.

Hellum's article focuses on three aspects of the relationship between women's law, legal pluralities and living law. Firstly, it addresses how women's law scholars, in a situation where the prevailing state-centred notion of law blocked engagement with the complex normative situation which was part of women's everyday life, used Eugen Ehrlich's theory on living law as a historical link to a holistic legal tradition. Secondly, it describes how, in order to understand the way women's rights claims were shaped and responded to in a post-war and post-colonial situation, women's law scholars turned to theories exploring law's semi-autonomy in terms of interacting international, national and local norms. Thirdly, it demonstrates how, when seeking to change normative structures negatively affecting women's access to justice and equality, women's law scholars moved beyond a purely descriptive approach to living law and legal pluralism. This normative and value-oriented perspective, **Anne Hellum** points out, calls for careful consideration of the options and limits involved in using living law and legal pluralism as analytical, legal and political tools in diverse and shifting political and legal landscapes. She concludes that any consideration of the use of living law and legal pluralism as a strategy for promoting women's rights must be located and understood within a broader analysis of history, context, power and regimes of governance.

Knut Papendorf's article starts by looking at how Eugen Ehrlich is presented in textbooks of the sociology of law in the Scandinavian countries. The Norwegian situation (Aubert 1968 and Mathiesen 1984/2011) is conspicuous for the absence of Ehrlich, while in the case of Denmark (Dalberg-Larsen 1989/2005) and even more so of Sweden (Stjernquist and Widerberg 1980) presentation and discussion of Ehrlich's theory can be found. But in all the Scandinavian textbooks there is a strong focus on the relevance of the environment of legislation to the effects of law. This is also backed by empirical research – especially in the cases of Sweden and Norway. It is obvious that Dalberg-Larsen's analysis is correct: Sociology of Law in the Nordic countries after World War II was more orientated towards Anglo-American literature, as consequence of the war and the enduring moral disaster Nazi Germany left behind – including that connected with occupation, in the cases of Denmark and Norway. So Ehrlich's absence from Scandinavian textbooks on sociology of law can be seen against this background.

Since this first approach was not in any way exhaustive, **Papendorf** also takes a broader perspective, simultaneously expanding his time frame and including a broader discussion and additional research on issues connected to Ehrlich's suggestions about applying sociological method to legal science. In this regard he starts the second part of his paper with an examination of the famous Danish Greenland expedition of the early 1950s, and of the researchers' findings on the living law situation there (Betænkning 1950).

Then – in the third part of his article – **Papendorf** presents three scholars: Fredrik Stang (1907), Kristian Østberg (1914-1939) and Erik Solem (1933/1970), who all did research on people's traditional legal perceptions in Norway in the first decades of the 20th century. Stang is the most notable: his suggestions regarding customs and practice in trade relationships, where he puts particular emphasis on the practice of established trade organizations, seem to embody Ehrlich's living law concept and research. But Østberg's research on traditional (ancient) law relating to farmers (bonderett) too, is quite close to Ehrlich's methodological suggestions informed by his research on living law. It is also quite close to Ehrlich's presentations of past surveys of living law relating to, for example the leasing of pasture, hay meadows or farmland (Ehrlich 1967, 55). This also applies to Solem and his research on the living law of the reindeer Same.

Hanne Petersen too reflects on the use of the term 'living law' in the work of the Greenlandic Legal Expedition (JUREX), which was appointed by the Danish Government in 1948. Greenland was, as part of the decolonization process, in the throes of political and legal change. The Greenlandic Legal Expedition, made up of Peter Lindegaard, Werner Goldschmidt and Agnete Weis Bentzon, was meant to come up with suggestions for a modern and unified civil, criminal, and family law system. The expedition sailed to various parts of Greenland. The researchers based their work on information about specific cases, and how they had been solved within the local community. Among the expedition's recommendations were suggestions that the new legal system should recognize the local population's understanding of law, and that the courts should be presided over by lay judges who were trusted by local communities and who were familiar with local culture, norms and language. They suggested a local dispute resolution mechanism called the Arctic Peace Model should become part of the official legal system, the idea being that peaceful coexistence should take precedence over the requirement for people to behave in the same way and in general be in conformity with each other. This was not the highly modern approach to a unified legal system, which (parts of) the administration might have expected. The report presented by the members of the expedition, was never published, unlike other reports by other commissions.

What was the attraction of Greenland for Werner Goldschmidt and Agnete Weis Bentzon, and what were its academic, legal, social and personal influences? To cast light on their insistence that the norms and values of the Greenlanders should be recognized as part of the official legal system **Hanne Petersen** points to the fact that the members of the expedition had themselves experienced exile in Sweden as political refugees during the Second World War. She also draws a parallel between the life situations of Werner Goldschmidt and Agnete Weis Bentzon, and of Eugen Ehrlich: they all lived and worked on the legal situation of marginalized groups on the 'edge of empires'.

It is clear from the writings of both Bentzon and Goldschmidt that they were unaware of Ehrlich's work on 'living law' around the time of the expedition, and that they drew their inspiration from other academic sources. In their doctoral dissertations, which analyzed the field work experiences of the expedition, most of the academic references were to American legal realists, with the exception of some to the German sociologist Theodor Geiger's 'Vorstudien zur Soziologie des Rechts'. This reflects a general trend for Scandinavian academics after World War II.

Agnete Weis Benzon lived for almost a generation longer than Verner Goldschmidt. The last section of Petersen's article discusses the way she came to absorb and integrate this experience at the end of another era – after her formal retirement in 1988, not least during the post-communist era after 1989, when a new period of activity for her – and for living law – began in the Nordic countries. It became clear, especially in her later works, that the concept of 'living law' was very useful to describe some of the experiences of the members of JUREX in 1948-49. In the 1990s, when she became involved in research cooperation with Southern African scholars (Bentzon et al. 1998), her Greenlandic post-colonial experiences were further developed through comparisons between living law and legal pluralism in Greenland and Mozambique.

Like his contemporaries Durkheim and Weber, Ehrlich used the existing wealth of historical and ethnographic literature as a source for case-studies and examples. He was Professor of Roman Law, and paid close attention to the findings of early ethnographers who had swarmed over the Balkans and Eastern Europe. Some of these exhibit similar ideas to Ehrlich in their descriptions of how law and legal practice developed among the various communities. In this book **Olga Litvinova** and **Stefan Machura** apply some of Ehrlich's insights, and the findings of his Eastern European colleagues, to the law of the Don Cossacks. The Cossacks first had to generate institutions and rules for their initially fiercely independent community. Later, they succumbed to the imperial forces of neighbouring Russia. Their 'living law' is still important as a point of reference for Ukrainian and Russian culture, an example being the "Maidan" legacy of direct democratic decision-making.

Ehrlich does not only argue for his "living law" theory by pointing to the example of legal pluralism in his native Bukovina. **Litvinova** and **Machura** identify another strand in his argument: historically, states had come to recognize the principle of the "nationality of law", with people being treated differently according to their macro-social background. It is the modern-type territorial state which imposes its universal law on all. Imperial Russia was a prime example of the principle of nationality of law at work and **Litvinova** and **Machura** demonstrate how this applied to the Don Cossacks. But how did Ehrlich define nations? He did so in terms of their culture and a common feeling of connectedness. Facing dangerous conditions on the margins of Europe, the Don Cossacks developed this kind of bond. Ehrlich even envisaged a world society, where people are bound together by common sentiment, as **Machura** mentions in his article on Ehrlich's legacy.

Despite the social optimism which makes itself felt in Ehrlich's work, he did take power and the abuse of power into account. In their contribution, **Litvinova** and **Machura** apply Ehrlich's insights to the history of the Don Cossacks, whose freedom and democratic organization of life fell victim to the ever-tightening grip of the Russian Tsar and the Orthodox Church. A ruling aristocracy was formed. Only under the ultimate threat of the Bolshevik army did the Don area return to its more egalitarian and democratic traditions.

Eugen Ehrlich's living law concept addresses the fault line between state law that is not applied by the people – dead letter law – and those legal rules which associations develop to self-organize. **Monika Lindbekk's** contribution highlights conflicts within associations about the content and the application of legal rules. The author's chosen example, the struggle over marriage and divorce laws among Orthodox Copts in Egypt, has been made more prominent by the tactic of legal reformers to appeal to state institutions in an attempt to overcome the resistance of conservative forces within their church. The reader learns of various ways in which individuals can escape the strict morals of their church. This article is a fascinating description of the positioning of politically minded actors amidst the turbulent events of the 'Arab Spring'. The Orthodox Church feels threatened by secularist and Islamist developments, and is reverting to a narrowly defined religious dogma that does not allow divorce, except for adultery.

As in the preceding article, we find an example of the – in this case Egyptian – state accepting the legal status of individuals as defined by their associations, which means in this case their religious affiliation. However, the official adoption of 'Islamic Law' by the state of Egypt creates a tension which Orthodox campaigners wanting to benefit from more liberal rules on marriage and divorce attempted to exploit. The state's judges are Muslims and apt to interpret Orthodox Christian rules according to Islamic legal principles. In her concluding remarks, **Lindbekk** therefore highlights the fact that Ehrlich's "treatment of state law contains a significant element of agency from litigants and adjudication by judges".

Social norms which discriminate against women and that are common to Orthodox Christians and Muslims influence the decisions of the courts. In the last analysis, Islamic law and its view of the nature of marriage proves to be the most decisive force. The prospect of being subjected to Muslim laws made the Orthodox Christian reformers finally turn back to seeking to influence their own Church's policies from within.

According to the 2012 Corruption Perceptions Index, Uzbekistan is one of the most corrupt countries in the world. **Rustamjon Urinboyev's** and **Måns Svensson's** paper aims to explore the multifaceted meaning, logic, and morality of informal transactions, in order to better understand the social context that informs the meaning of corruption and bribery in Uzbekistan. They argue that Western-centric interpretations cannot satisfactorily explain the nuances of corruption in Uzbekistan, and that there is a need to consider the 'living law' of everyday life under which informal transactions are carried out. A theoretically-founded hypothesis is that informal transactions in Uzbek society reflect different cultural and functional meanings to a greater degree than is the case in most of the Western world.

Their paper is based on three periods of field research carried out between 2009 and 2012 in the Ferghana Province of Uzbekistan. During the research they observed eight wedding ceremonies that were hosted and attended by different social groups, ranging from local elites to ordinary farm workers. During second and third field trips they conducted two informal interviews with a traffic policeman and a minibus driver.

The paper then examines previous research on 'corruption'. Part three provides the theoretical framework of the study, which is based on Eugen Ehrlich's concept of 'living law'. In part four, the authors present the results of their ethnographic fieldwork. They use evidence from the wedding ceremonies to show the local relationship to money and how this could undermine Western-centric interpretations of corruption. Their aim is to show the underlying social norms, moral codes, and local perceptions of a society where corruption occurs.

Urinboyev and **Svensson** summarize their results by making three points: (1) informal transactions are deeply embedded in cultural practices; (2) not all informal transactions are corrupt; (3) when talking about, or measuring, corruption, social norms, moral codes, and local perceptions should be considered. By exploring informal transactions in both non-state and state arenas in the light of Ehrlich's concept of 'living law', their research differs in one respect from that of other researchers. By utilizing this concept, they underline the importance of understanding the 'living law' of the society in which corruption is being discussed and/or measured. Their study claims that informal transactions that are considered to be corruption in a Western-centric interpretation have little to do with abuse. Rather, informal coping strategies are incorporated into Uzbek culture as a rational way of 'getting things done'.

Our last article, in which **Olga Litvinova** writes on the social significance of ornamented textiles takes us back to the Bukovina, Ehrlich's home province. Some of the traditions described in this chapter were encountered by our author when she was growing up in a Ukrainian peasant culture. It is still the case that traditional textiles are a key element of Ukrainian national self-definition. Hitherto we have known little about Bukovina culture, as most previous literature concentrated on the legal debates Ehrlich had with German-speaking scholars, Ukrainian and Russian sources which Ehrlich knew intimately, and the social background of the 'living law' concept in his home province are less understood. **Olga Litvinova** examines Ehrlich's personal interest in the traditional textiles of the Bukovina, which he collected. Even today, these are famous for their extraordinary artistry. Leading art museums exhibit this folk art. In Ehrlich's time, they were already being collected by wealthy members of the European elite. But more crucially, the textiles were part of everyday traditional life and gave their owners an identity. Special textiles featured prominently in traditional marriages and funerals, as well as in such things as agricultural rituals. Embroidered patterns identified and distinguished the associations to which individuals belonged. They made visible what, according to Ehrlich, makes up a society: associations like neighbourhoods or ethnic groups. Ehrlich grew up in his parents' Jewish house amid Bukovinian cultural pluralism, and later chose to formally convert to Catholicism. The daily spectacle of people making their affiliations obvious must have influenced his sociological imagination.

As a legal scholar, Ehrlich devotes much of his energy to pointing out how the actual legal practices predominant in associations have to be understood as law. Rational organizations such as modern factories also develop laws to facilitate commercial interaction. Ehrlich's "living law" should not to be misunderstood as a splendid portrayal of a dying traditional world. **Litvinova's** article makes clear that Ehrlich focused in his analysis on phenomena that were relatively rational and modern. It is the more arcane and often superstitious behaviour of country people which is described in this chapter of our book. Ornamented textiles were believed to help against all kinds of bad fate, including misfortune in the courts.

The cover picture of this volume is part of a woodcut from a 16th century book whose title was "The Good Judge", and the inscription under the woodcut explains further the point that was also at the heart of Ehrlich's oeuvre:

> "Look how the 99 degree angle is applied to all sides of a piece. Often, the meaning of a written law is hidden deep within and is wholly in the hands of the judge. In different cases he has to interpret it differently and not always follow one and the same basic rule."[1]

---

1 Costalius 1555, reproduced in Prinz 2009. The editors would like to thank Stephan

Our endeavour would have been impossible without the support of several institutions. The Norwegisch-Deutsche Willy-Brandt-Stiftung, the Department of Criminology and Sociology of Law, Law Faculty, University of Oslo (IKRS), and the research centre Rights, Individuals, Culture and Society, University of Oslo (RICS). We are especially indebted to Daphne Day, Llanfairfechan (Wales), for proof-reading the manuscripts with extraordinary care.

When organizing the conference, it was natural to invite Franz and Keebet von Benda-Beckmann. With their decades of joint research and scholarship, both exemplify the combination of Sociology of Law and Social Anthropology. They presented a well-prepared paper that set off an important discussion regarding the relevance of Ehrlich's concept of 'living law' in the context of globalization and the internationalization of law, both at the conference and in the papers presented in this book. We all remember the conversations with Franz round the table later on the first day. He was as witty as ever and in good spirits. None of us knew of the illness he was battling with. We were surprised and extremely sorry to hear of his death only two months later. He will be very much missed.

References

Aubert, Vilhelm. (1968), *Rettssosiologi*. Oslo: Universitetsforlaget.

Bentzon, Agnete W., Hellum, Anne, Stewart, Julie E., Ncube, Welshman and Agersnap, Torben (1998), *Women's Law: Pursuing Grounded Theory. South-North Experiences in Developing Women's Law*. Oslo/Harare: TANO/Mond Books.

Betænkning afgivet 6. september 1950 af den juridiske ekspedition til Grønland 1948-1949. Volumes 1-6. (cited: Betænkning).

Chiba, Masaji (1997), Japan. In: Poh-Ling Tan (ed.), *Asian Legal Systems – Law, Society and Pluralism in East Asia*. Sydney: Butterworths, pp. 82-123.

Costalius, Petrus (1555), *Cum narrationibus philosophicis*, Lugduni: Apud Matthiam Bonhomme, reprinted in Prinz 2009.

Dahl, Tove Stang (1987), *Women's Law: An Introduction to Feminist Jurisprudence*. Oslo: Norwegian University Press.

Prinz for permission to reprint the picture. The original German text reads: "Sieh, wie an allen Seiten eines Werkes stets der rechte Winkel gelegt wird. Oft ist der Sinn eines geschriebenen Gesetzes tief im Innern verborgen und liegt ganz in der Hand des Richters, Dieser muß ihn in den verschiedenen Fällen, unterschiedlich auslegen und nicht immer ein und derselben Grundregel folgen."

Dalberg-Larsen, Jørgen (2005), *Lovene og livet. En retssociologisk grundbog*. 5th edition. København: Jurist-og Økonomiforbundets Forlag.

Eckhoff, Torstein (1960), *Sociology of Law in Scandinavia, Rettferdighet og Rettssikerhet – Justice and the Rule of Law*. Oslo: Johan Grundt Tanum Forlag, pp. 9-42.

Ehrlich, Eugen (1913/1967), *Grundlegung der Soziologie des Rechts*. 3rd edition, Berlin: Duncker & Humblot.

Ehrlich, Eugen (1918), *Die juristische Logik*. Reprint Tübingen: Mohr, 1925 and Aalen: Scientia-Verlag, 1965.

Ehrlich, Eugen (1967), *Recht und Leben*, edited by Manfred Rehbinder. Berlin: Duncker & Humblot.

Geiger, Theodor (1947), *Vorstudien zur Soziologie des Rechts*. Aarhus: Universitetsforlaget.

Griffiths, John (1981), What is Legal Pluralism? Paper prepared for delivery at the 1981 Annual Meeting of the Law and Society Association at Amherst College, Amherst, Mass.

Kelsen, Hans (1915/2003), Eine Grundlegung der Rechtssoziologie. Reprinted in: Klaus Lüderssen (ed.), *Rechtssoziologie und Rechtswissenschaft*. Baden-Baden: Nomos, pp. 3-54.

Mathiesen, Thomas (2011), *Retten i samfunnet*. 6th edition, Oslo: Pax forlag.

Østberg, Kristian (1914-1939), *Norsk bonderett i 12 bind*. Kristiania/Oslo: Grøndahl: Cappelen.

Prinz, Stefan (2009), *Juristische Embleme*. Munster: Lit, DVD supplement.

Solem, Erik (1933/1970), *Lappiske rettsstudier*. 2nd edition, Oslo: Universitetsforlaget.

Stang, Frederik (1907), *Handelskoutumer*. Kristiania: Særtryk af Tidsskrift for retsvidenskab.

Stjernquist, Per, and Widerberg, Karin (1989), *Rätten i samhällsbyggandet*. 3rd edition, Stockholm: Norstedts Förlag.

Tsanga, Amy, and Stewart, Julie (eds., 2011), *Women and Law. Innovative Approaches to Teaching, Research and Analysis*. Harare: Weaver Press.

Weber, Max (1922/1968), *Economy and Society; an Outline of Interpretive Sociology*, translated by Ephraim Fischoff et al., edited by Guenther Roth and Claus Wittich. New York: Bedminster Press.

Ehrlich's Legacy

Beyond "Living Law": Eugen Ehrlich's General Theory of Law

Klaus A. ZIEGERT

The art of debunking

It is quite common in academic and even scientific[1] debate to "pick a fight" as part of a strategy for promoting one's own ideas. Such sharper, adversarial heightening of the differences between one's own propositions and those of the opposition is not only helpful for working out a comparatively "more accurate" proposition, but it also allows for a dramatisation or even "scandalisation" of the debate that turns into a moral condemnation of the "enemy". This lifts the matter in question from a mere methodological mistake, or weakness in theoretical concepts or a simple failure to achieve "good science" to the moral sphere of "false thinking" and "wrong" ideology. As a consequence, it is often not quite clear what the objective of such an adversarial strategy is, and whether it is, indeed, scientific discovery or a public outing and shaming of the "enemy". It appears to be, first of all, a good marketing strategy to attract attention but it is more difficult to say whether the arguments which are put forward ultimately compel an audience or divide it even further.

So, for the strategy to work, much rides on picking the right, "useful enemy" (*Niels Christie*), generally referred to in the plural. "They" must be sufficiently concrete and yet, at the same time, not too clearly delineated in order to leave ample room for fictitious, and most importantly, moral embellishment. However, a continuing academic and scientific debate – and all

[1] It should be noted that in (native) English language use "science" and "scientific" relate to the natural science(s), unlike the Nordic and German terms "vetenskap/Wissenschaft". Therefore, the quite conventional concept of "rättsvetenskap" does not translate as "legal science" but translates normally, and unless further specified, as "law". It is important to keep this distinction in mind when reading this chapter, which turns on the issue of lawyers accusing the "opposition" of having a "wrong" concept of science, and therefore a "false" concept of law, as part of their scientific strategy; the lawyers under review in this paper "think" in three different languages (US-English, Japanese, German) and in at least two different knowledge paradigms, law and sociology.

academic and scientific debates continue and are never settled completely – draws the "battle lines" between "us" and "them" more distinctly. In this way the "enemy" becomes more useful and makes it much easier to distil and present compellingly what one claims to be better informed about. This is the art of debunking.

This art seems to have been particularly cultivated by and in the US-American school of Critical Legal Studies. As indicated by the choice of the word "cultivated", we acknowledge a long historical heritage of debunking designed both to normatively dismiss a scientific point of view (whether or not those supposed proponents call it scientific) and to devalue a moral point of view (whether or not those who are supposed to exhibit this point of view actually do so). This cultural heritage is evidently not restricted to academic or scientific debates in the United States. However, the purpose of this chapter is not to discuss this heritage of "dialectical" critical thinking, or its cultivation in the law schools in the United States. Nevertheless, it is remarkable, and perhaps not accidental, that this heavily rhetorical adversarial academic style is nurtured in the common law environment through common law culture and ideology. However, the strongly rhetorical adversarial academic style is also alive in the cognitive "grey" areas of the history of ideas between law and social sciences everywhere in the world. This last observation is not irrelevant for our discussion but has to remain on the sidelines of the "case" that this chapter wishes to make.

The case is this: when we discuss the approaches of the three scholars under review here, we find connections between them and similarities and dissimilarities which are not immediately evident. Only the deliberate selection of the three authors, out of many scholars in the field of "law & society", explains the connection between them as the similarity in their approach – *John Griffiths, Masaji Chiba* and *Eugen Ehrlich* are all scholars who can be called socio-legal scholars with a primary professional socialisation in law or Rechtswissenschaft, and who are associated in the literature with concepts of "legal pluralism". All three authors reject the concept of a "state-centrist" law, and that is often taken as synonymous with legal pluralism. And all three authors make use of the art of debunking in order to make their voices heard in the academic community. Following the "logic of scientific discovery", however, it is only by pointing out the dissimilarities (differences) between these scholars and their use of "debunking" that we can find the true objective of their similar approaches. And it is in such an assessment, then, that we can more fully understand and appreciate the contribution of *Eugen Ehrlich* and the implications for sociology of law today. In other words, this chapter argues that Eugen Ehrlich used the concept of "living law" as a debunking strategy in his contemporary historical context of doctrinal law to put on notice the established state-centrist ideology of jurists and lawyers (or *Rechtswissenschaftler*) of his time, and to prepare the ground for his "truly scientific" approach to law (legal science). What he was interested in was a scientific general theory of law (*gemeine Jurisprudenz*), thus a sociological theory of law. His alleged association with ideas of legal pluralism is based on myths which need to be debunked.

This clarification of the main objective of this chapter clearly stakes out the structure of this chapter, in spite of its appearance of a "dog's curve". In order to understand Ehrlich's debunking strategy, we must first briefly discuss John Griffith's approach to legal pluralism as a way to promote legal anthropology, an approach he explains most clearly and succinctly (Section II). Secondly, we must compare Griffith's take on legal pluralism with the debunking approach taken by Masaji Chiba to promote the concept of legal pluralism in order to promote a proper understanding of Japanese law (III). It emerges from these discussions that the debunking approach of Eugen Ehrlich under the label of "living law" is not designed to promote legal pluralism, but to promote his own concepts for constructing a "scientific" general theory of law (IV). A summary of all the discussions yields the insight that Ehrlich cannot be blamed for explaining poorly what he did not set out to explain (living law). Instead his work, with his theoretically radical, but methodologically sound, concept of a strict separation of law and state in a scientific approach to law is still relevant for contemporary sociology of law. This is particularly the case in Nordic societies which are faced with increasing problems of demographic change of the kind that attracted the attention of Eugen Ehrlich's inquiry more than 100 years ago (V).

John Griffiths – a descriptive (empirical) theory of legal pluralism

"Legal pluralism is the fact. Legal centralism is a myth, an ideal, a claim, an illusion". With this straight-shooting statement John Griffiths (1981, 4)[2]

2 This paper was written for presentation at the 1981 Annual Meeting of the Law and

opens the attack on, presumably, doctrinal law, and certainly on a certain state of mind of lawyers, an ideology. This ideology is "legal centralism" and it "has had such a powerful hold on the imagination of lawyers and social scientists that it has been successfully able to masquerade as fact, and it has formed the foundation stone of social theory" (ibid.). Many questions are raised by such a simple statement of "fact", but Griffiths quickly diffuses any attempts at scientific scrutiny by pointing out the purpose of his statements and of the paper that contains them. "In short, part of the burden of this essay is simply a debunking one, as the necessary prolegomenon to any clear empirical thought about law" (Griffiths 1981, 4-5).

The discussion announced as a "prolegomenon" that follows in Griffiths' paper is far from being only a simple obligatory introduction to the "main piece". It reveals rather clearly the adversarial positions, or better oppositional pairs, that the author has in mind. These are "legal pluralism vs. legal centralism" and "empirical thought" vs. "ideology". While legal pluralism plays the empirical-factual part in an advertised "powerful descriptive theory" (ibid., 4) as evidenced by "the relative frequency in a social field of behaviour pursuant to more than one legal order" (ibid., 1)[3], legal centralism plays the part of the normative-ideological "villain", and is defined as "the assumption that the state and its law are the centre of the legal universe" (ibid.). We could pretend to be – methodologically – surprised by such unevenly matched pairs – assumption vs. behaviour, ideology vs. empirical thought, the latter probably referring to empirical testing of theoretical thought, since otherwise "empirical thought" would be just another ideology. But the "prolegomenon" is openly announced as destructive polemic and so we know, such is the art of debunking, that the dice are loaded and that there is to be no level playing field for seriously descriptive concepts. Nevertheless, even if we can understand the polemic message of the exercise, it is not easy to suspend – for the time being – questions such as: what if legal centralism was the fact, and legal pluralism the belief, what if legal centralism was the behaviour and legal pluralism the assumption, or

Society Association at Amherst College, Amherst, Mass., U.S.A., June 12-14 1981 and for discussion by an audience which at the time was as yet largely uninformed about theoretical concepts of legal pluralism beyond legal anthropology classics and post-colonial nation-building literature. The references and quotes used here are from a draft copy which was given personally by John Griffiths to the author in November 1987.

3 This is the working definition for legal pluralism for John Griffiths.

ideology, of law everywhere in society, and what if the "powerful hold of legal centralism on the imagination of lawyers" (Griffiths, 4) is explained by the legal reality of the modern state; and what if the theoretical concept of legal pluralism cannot succeed because it is an ideal, a claim, an illusion?

But, first and before we answer such heretical questions, the task of the "destruction" of the concept of "legal centralism" has to be completed: "Lawyers, but also social scientists, have suffered from a chronic inability to see that the legal reality of the modern state is not at all that of the tidy, consistent, organised ideal; it is rather a pluralistic mess of inconsistent and overlapping parts, lending itself to no easy legal interpretation, morally and aesthetically offensive to the eye of the liberal idealist, and incomprehensible in its complexity to the would-be empirical student" (ibid.,3-4); and "by way of false comparisons... the theory of law in "primitive" society has also suffered..."(ibid.,4). As, ever so slightly, the target of "destruction" shifts from law, and perhaps never was law, to the state's law and finally the state, and in particular the colonial state, Griffiths' disciplinary identification with social anthropology is revealed and it explains the absence of definitions of law in the debunking exercise and the presentation of behaviour in a social field as law in its stead. The information that Griffiths has a social-anthropological perspective may or may not be relevant for understanding the arguments of Griffiths' paper, but the polemic delivery of these arguments raises the suspicion that it is relevant. Obviously, legal centralism – whether ideology or fact – is the collective trauma of legal anthropology, its status as a science, its colonial or anti-colonial credentials and the academic heritage of legal anthropology.

With the foe of legal centralism shamed but unexplained, Griffiths turns to the construction of a powerful "descriptive theory of the variability of pluralistic social fields" (ibid., 2). If we were interested in such a theory we would follow Griffiths in his lengthy discussion, but we are not. Instead, we are interested in the "building blocks" that Griffiths seeks to retrieve from existing research on legal pluralism or something like legal pluralism[4]. It is in this latter group that we find reference to Eugen Ehrlich, together with

[4] Griffiths (1981, 39 ff.) classifies two groups of scholars who provide in his view a valid descriptive accounts of legal pluralism, with either explicit definitions and analyses of the concept of legal pluralism (Hooke, Gilles, Vanderlinden), or with "implicit" descriptive theories of legal pluralism (Ehrlich, Pospisil, Smith, Moore).

other scholars such as Pospisil (1971), Smith (1974) and importantly and most influentially Moore (1978).

Griffiths associates the work of Eugen Ehrlich with legal pluralism because he identifies Ehrlich as one of the "writers [who] have contributed to the development of an empirical concept of legal pluralism although that was not their (primary) objective" (Griffiths 1981, 39). Griffiths assumes that the "central contribution of Ehrlich's work (1936)[5] to the sociology of law is a descriptive theory of law that he developed in reaction to the legal centralist ideology (often referred to as "legal positivism") of his day" (ibid.); and he argues that the "key" to Ehrlich's descriptive theory was the distinction between "rules for decision" and "rules for conduct" (ibid.). This description leads Griffiths to align Ehrlich's description of law with his own view on legal centralism, namely as if Ehrlich defined law from the point of view of an official of the state. Griffiths follows Ehrlich in his laborious efforts to distinguish between the two sets of normative realms (conduct vs. decision-making) and makes the most of Ehrlich's hazy definitions of "conduct", while missing all along that the decision-maker that Ehrlich is talking about is not the state but the judge, and that the effort that Ehrlich expends on describing the efficient ordering of society beyond the law is for the purpose of demonstrating what lawyers are missing out on because they – unlike architects, engineers and other practitioners of a trade – do not have a science or scientific approach to call on. Lawyers are stuck in their traditional way of thinking and arguing because for them law is not a science but a trade. Ehrlich takes the "sociological turn" more or less by default (Ziegert 1979) because his sociology is a conscious but rather speculative extension of the writings of a nationalist school of German legal historians around the legal scholar Otto Gierke (Ehrlich, 1936, 23, in Griffiths 1981, 41) who tried to show the true existence of a Germanic law in the spirit of the people versus the attempts of the strictly doctrinal "Romanist" school of the Pandectists who tried to resurrect the alleged conceptual purity of Roman law. Gierke insisted that the organisation of small groups (*Genossenschaften* = associations) exhibited the spirit of such a people's

[5] Griffiths refers to the US-American translation of Ehrlich's 1913 work on sociology of law under the auspices of the Dean of Harvard Law School, Roscoe Pound. All the following quotes from Ehrlich (1936) are taken from Griffiths' rendition of Ehrlich (1936) in order to keep them in context.

law.[6] It is interesting in this context, that Ehrlich's famous contemporary, the scholar and co-founder of the German Sociological Association, Ferdinand Tönnies,also develops his concept of norms with reference to Gierke but with the goal of a truly sociological definition of the social dynamics of norms. He provides with his definition of *Gemeinschaft* and *Gesellschaft* the foundation for the sociology of primary groups and, almost synonymous with primary groups, social control. Ehrlich's sociology, however, is not based on sociological or empirical descriptions of small groups[7]; he never mentions Tönnies or any other sociological scholar with the notable exception of Herbert Spencer (Ziegert 2002), even though he introduces empirical research methodology in his teaching programmes (Ziegert 1979). But the empirical concept of the "inner order of associations" provides us with the requisite evidence for the key to *Ehrlich*'s work – in contrast to what Griffiths holds as being the key to *Ehrlich*'s theory – namely the insight from his historical empiricism that the dynamics of law ("centre of gravity of legal developments") are not found in legal propositions, legal decisions, legislation or, in fact, any legal texts whatsoever, but in society itself (*Ehrlich* 1913, Vorwort). And this is why *Ehrlich* makes sociology the scientific base for his legal science.

Griffiths is evidently not aware of the historical origin of *Ehrlich*'s concept of "the inner order of associations" and so, in his quest for a descriptive theory of legal pluralism, he has to take *Gierke's* mainly philosophical legal-theoretical concepts of the normative structure of associations, recorded by Ehrlich as "legal norms", as a descriptive concept. Even if this concept of a "legal norm" – as against a "legal proposition" – lacks empirical validity, it does not stop Ehrlich making it the cornerstone of his sociological construct of "living law" – indeed it facilitates such a speculative conception because of that lack of sociological precision. Living law, as an order "which dominates life itself even though it has not been posited in le-

---

6 In this context it is also uncertain whether or not the German concept, and sound, of the word 'Recht', especially when used in the Germanic-nationalist context and as used by Gierke and Ehrlich, is properly translated by 'law'; this problem is shared, with similar semantic connotations of "folk och rätt", by Nordic legal scholars at the time. This intense discussion of socio-legal history in Germany at the beginning of the last century resurfaces in Nordic sociology of law before WW2 without referring to Ehrlich in particular. See the contribution by Knut E Papendorf in this volume and his observation of the "absence" of Ehrlich in Nordic sociology of law before Per Stjernquist (1912-2005).

7 For further discussion of *Ehrlich's* primary group concept, see below, section IV.

gal propositions" (Ehrlich 2002, 493) functions on its own terms and does not require lawyers or, generally, legal decision-making to get involved; however, when lawyers do intervene they should be scientifically informed rather than just following precedent in the comfort zone of legal reasoning. Griffiths underestimates the strategical, "debunking" mission of "living law" in Ehrlich's conceptualisation; he should have taken the lack of empirical validity as a warning that Ehrlich's theory is not adapted to a project which tries to establish a descriptive theory of legal pluralism. Ehrlich's associations and their inner order are not separate legal microcosms – they do the job of installing normative expectations and are thus the law "not yet formulated"; and it is always law in the singular. There is only one law – the law of society's legal norms, and lawyers have to learn to see and recognise them.

It is not surprising then that Griffiths is not really happy with Ehrlich's descriptions of living law or the lack of them. Griffiths cannot see a clear "independent criterion of "the legal" (Griffiths 1981, 46), or an indication as to "how an association might be identified" (ibid.), or an adequate description of the "inner order" (ibid.); he is unhappy about Ehrlich's "curious lack of interest in processes within associations" (ibid.) and about the fact that Ehrlich "had little more than generalities concerning borrowing and imitation. . . " (Griffiths 1981, 47). Worst of all, "Ehrlich has nothing to say about . . . the connection of his theory with a theory of individual legal behaviour" (ibid.). With such naïve expectations that were so thoroughly disappointed, it is likewise curious that Griffiths chose Ehrlich in the first place for his line-up of candidates for an implicit descriptive theory of legal pluralism. The myth of "living law" as debunking legal positivism must have had a sufficiently strong appeal in the circles of critical legal scholars, and in the Law & Society Association, to revive interest in Ehrlich's writings, something not reflected in the European sociology of law of the time. This myth must have been so strong that it escaped the attention of everybody concerned that the "legal centralism" that Ehrlich debunked was the ideology of lawyers; its centre was not the state but legal decision-making by judges, and there is nothing in Ehrlich's theory – if his "legal science" can be called a theory – which suggests that he had any idea of or interest in describing a "pluralist" legal order.

Masaji Chiba – a fair understanding of Japanese law and society

The "useful enemy" for Masaji Chiba is quite generally the conception of law of Western legal scholars, exemplified – as in the Japanese experience – "by the transplanting of a modern legal system into a traditional system" (Chiba 1997, 82). This "Western understanding" of modern Japanese law includes the concept of legal pluralism as a concept of a dual structure – a transplanted law from a "Western country to a Non-Western country" (ibid.) –in following Gilissen and Moore as "two or more legal systems" coexisting in the same social field (ibid.). "From an East Asian perspective this kind of analysis is superficial and lacks real insight into the people and the culture" (Chiba, 1997, 82). Though there is – according to Chiba –, because of the intense "Western" interest, or rather curiosity, regarding Japanese law, a large literature about Japanese law in general, "advocates of a non-Western perspective are rare in the world of legal science, raising the question who observes whose law. The author's scheme of legal pluralism, which may allow non-Westerners to observe their own law, requires these questions to be answered" (Chiba 1997, 83). Evidently, a "rare non-Western perspective" – such as Chiba's – assumes a stand against both "state law monism" and the relationship between state law and legal pluralism (ibid.) – or, a stand for a legal pluralism with Japanese characteristics.

What are these Japanese characteristics? "Japaneseness" has been and still is the problem which pervades all discussions of social structure, including law, in Japan.[8] It is a problem because it is not just a fascination of "Westerners" with the "otherness" of Japanese social organisation, but a core issue for the image that a traditional society tries to present to the world while having been, throughout its history, never sure what that image is (Ziegert, 2008). While it is a truism that there is no truly autochthonous culture, and peoples generally adjust to "strange", i.e. foreign forms of innovation, the Japanese organisation of society seems to transmit particularly strongly the ambiguity of its elites' envy of the cultural achievements of neighbouring societies (there are only China and Korea) coupled with fear of "contamination" of the firmly grounded social (normative) order through contact with foreigners and foreign thought. In this form, social or-

8 I.e. the issue of Japanese uniqueness (McCargo 2004:5-6,219) and Patrick Smith's observations of Japanese society (Smith 1997).

der becomes the self-defence mechanism of the elites, which, as the power of dynastic families never changes, while dynasties come and go, is rejuvenated through social mobility facilitated by wealth and military prowess. This social order was institutionally locked in early in the previous millennium, and it is path-dependent in the insular, small group society (Ziegert, 2008). This form of social order reached its full, undifferentiated ascendancy in the rule of the military in the shogunates of the Tokugawa period and its "fortress Japan" mentality which lasted for 200 years of isolation from mainland China and Korea and the rest of the world[9]. Even the shock of the realisation at the end of the 19th century that the world had moved on, and that the military strategy of bunkering down alone would not save Japan from contamination, did not essentially change the time-honoured, and politically enforced, patterns of normative order. The elites just changed their policies and carried out reforms, as they had done before and did again whenever these "shocks" occurred.[10] Ironically, Japanese elites, in order to

[9] As usual, "totalitarian" control is not hermetic and the elites managed to have their supply of arms and luxury goods secured by allowing a trading post exclave on Kyushu (on the outskirts of Nagasaki), the island which is furthest of the five main islands of the Japanese archipelago from the main centres of power. Notably, this trading post was run by Dutch merchants, i.e. an association close to the Japanese concept of association and not a state organisation; it was also through this Dutch link that the first introduction to a Western legal code was engineered, during the Tokugawa period (1852); this Dutch civil code was translated by a team of a Dutch and Japanese legal academics; the translation "disappeared" however with the change of governments in 1869 (sounds familiar). The Meiji government started its projects to translate the Prussian and later the German Civil Code from scratch (Verwajen 1996).

[10] The more notable incisions in recent times occurred in 1868 and 1947. The end of the Tokugawa and beginning of the Meiji governments in 1868 opened the way to reforms of industrial and legal technology following mainly UK and Prussian examples, in response to the "face-losing" exercise of the "unfair treaties" with Western powers after the US Navy had pried open ports with "canon boat tactics", though leaving the normative order largely untouched by sidelining the military leadership through a restoration of the emperor (and the associated bureaucratic imperial court elite) to full power. The capitulation of the Japanese army in1945 to mainly US-American troops and the ensuing occupation by the United States opened the window of opportunity for at least a formal democratisation for only a short moment (1945-47) after which the incoming US administration (government) in a switch to cold war mode reversed reform policies ("reversed course") and made Japan in essence a US protectorate, stalling the prosecutions of "war criminals" and restoring the old elites and social order, thus choosing stability over "democratisation" (Smith 1997, passim) and using Japan as a security buffer and naval base for its cold war strategy.

avoid colonisation, imitated the dual regime of colonial law by applying a "modernised", i.e. "western" formal normative layer on top of the traditional order, and continued to rule in the usual patrimonial fashion under the veil of "modern law". While Chiba can claim that this is a superficial, clichéd Western view of the historical consistency of the normative orderliness of Japanese society, it has been largely the official historical writing and re-writing[11] of Japanese history by Japanese scholars which has contributed considerably to evoke and sustain this image. In this context, Chiba*'s* efforts to debunk Western misconceptions about Japanese law and society with the help of his own brand of legal pluralism are slightly ambiguous as they appear as just another rehabilitative rewriting of Japanese legal history.

Chiba's "scheme of legal pluralism" (Chiba 1997, 83), while following empirical concepts from legal anthropology – Merry's proposition of two or more legal systems coexisting in the same social field (Merry 1988 in Chiba 1997, 83), von Benda-Beckman's suggestion of "different levels of socio-legal entities (quoted in Chiba 1997, 85) – is not applying or exploring a descriptive legal theory but is an attempt to validate his taxonomic scheme of law with the help of Japanese legal history. In turn, the taxonomic grid of legal pluralism allows it to be seen, according to Chiba, that there has been law in Japan on many levels and in many forms throughout Japanese legal history, contrary to the superficial "Western view" of barbarian Japanese culture. These attempts at identifying "legal facts outside state law" as the "main aim of legal pluralism" (Chiba 1997,84) in the form of the co-existence of other "system(s) of law co-existing with state law" yield a triple structure of "minor law, state law and world law" (ibid., 85). When Chiba applies his nominal concept of law as "a kind of social norm, which designates the specified qualification for entitled behaviour patterns as right, and the corresponding responsibility for obliging behaviour patterns as duty, being supported by a particular set of values and ideas on the one hand, and by the legitimate authority of a certain socio-legal entity on the other" (ibid., 87) he arrives at the (hierarchical?) levels of "official law, unofficial law, indigenous law, transplanted law, legal rules and legal pos-

[11] More recently, US academics were employed to euphemistically praise the "good world citizen behaviour" of Japan and help to cover up Japanese war crimes and atrocities, especially in Korea and China during WWII (Smith 1997).

tulates (e.g. religious law), and the identity postulate" (ibid., 86-89) which he then can support with examples from the legal history of Japan.

The problem with Japanese historical records is the absence of writing until the 7th century AD, though Chinese characters were known, the earliest records being allegedly Chinese descriptions of Japanese society under a shaman-queen of the name Himiko or Pimiko (Chiba 1997, 90; Smith 1997, 319). But eventually Japanese society adopted Chinese cultural and technical forms either directly or through Korea on the base of its tribal and clan structure. Chiba describes this structure as a "primitive legal pluralism of (imperial) court and clan law" (Chiba 1997, 91) on the basis of a shamanistic belief system which grew into the powerful religious organisation of Shintoism with its altars and temples everywhere in the country. Shintoism has preserved its dominant position as a pervasive normative order for the whole society until today and together with the superstructure of Confucianism and Buddhism imported from China and Korea under the legendary Prince Shotoku (593-622), has locked in this religious amalgam as an institutional norm base. With the Prince's legendary law reform, we can see the "traits of legal pluralism as the prototype of the Japanese legal system" (Chiba 1997, 91), or alternatively, as the foundation for the path-dependency of the political and social order in Japan that has existed up to the present (Ziegert 2008). "Reform" from now on always means, in line with the Shotoku model, importing the tools of governance (penal law – *ritsu*, administrative law – *ryo*, imperial edicts) from China and Korea. When these tools, given the superior industrial and military strength of the European powers, seem no longer to be working, civil, penal, and constitutional law have to be imported from powerful Western nations. However, beneath all formal reform, the normative order of the families, the clans, the tribal organisations, the associations, the *buraku*[12], the *zaibatsu*[13] and *keiretsu*[14], *the boryoku-dan*[15] *and* the *tenno* dynasties and their Shinto shrines prevails and persists. All these organisational forms are permeated

[12] I.e. village or hamlet.

[13] I.e. larger industrial and/or financial conglomerate.

[14] I.e. communication network of business-related companies.

[15] I.e. "mafia" organisation, ironically mostly with Korean members; the better known term 'yakuza' denotes individuals (i.e. worthless person) and not the criminal organisation; see Schloenhardt 2010.

by the normative principles of *iemoto*[16] the fictitious relationship structure of the extended family (Chiba 1997, 115), which resists any attempts at change or reform. In this way, any reforms of the corporate structure in Japan lead nowhere, in contrast to the more successful Korean reforms of the inherited[17] Japanese *zaibatsu* system. Likewise any attempt to destroy the criminal organisational structure of the *boryoku-dan* is doomed to be a "mission unaccomplished" (Schloenhardt 2010), which may shock the German criminal law researcher, but does not surprise the Japanese legal pluralist. The *boryoku-dan* are too well integrated into the family structure of the Japanese order and are even respected for their good work in their "dirty togetherness" schemes[18] and for keeping the streets free of crime and violence (Chiba 1997, 115). In summary Chiba can state that "indigenous religious law has an unofficial role to play in comparison with the official workings of transplanted law which is based on Judeo-Christian tradition" (ibid. 114). Would Eugen Ehrlich agree with that view of living law?

Eugen Ehrlich – a general theory of law

We do not know, because Ehrlich does not seem to have commented on Japanese law – in contrast to his contemporary and fellow jurist Max Weber (see especially Breuer 1984). But a surprisingly large number of Japanese legal scholars seem to appreciate Ehrlich's work, as is evident from the wide interest in Japan, beginning with his first publications and extending to modern sociology of law in Japan today (Vogl 2009), so much so that the most comprehensive collection of study materials on Ehrlich in the world was collected in Japan[19]. Of course, such a – comparatively – warm reception accords with the period of highest admiration for and learning from

16 Derived from the Japanese concept of a headmaster of a school of traditional arts and performances (Chiba 1997, 118).

17 After winning the war of the conquest of Korea in 1910, the military-industrial leadership of Japan embarked on a ruthless programme of annihilating Korean culture by forcing the assimilation of Japanese social organisation on Korean society. Japanese rule in Korea ended with the capitulation of Japan at the end of WWII in 1945. As a consequence, the usual East Asian distinction between social organisation ("the inner order of associations") *li* and the bureaucratic (penal) law *fa* has the further twist that in Korea the official law is associated with Japanese rule and rejected the more strongly.

18 Adam Podgórecki (1973) uses this useful sociological description to define corruption.

19 Stefan Vogl (2002, 41) claims that the Japanese scholar Rin-itsu Kawakami provided the most comprehensive collection of material on Eugen Ehrlich in 1989; Vogl (2002)

German "legal science" in the Meiji restoration years and beyond; visiting Japanese scholars must have gathered up everything that they could find in German research institutes and faculties of law. It is not surprising, though, that Chiba,who must be aware of the reception accorded to Ehrlich in Japan, does not mention Ehrlich in the context of his "scheme of legal pluralism" – in contrast to Griffiths' efforts at a descriptive theory of legal pluralism. Japanese legal scholars appreciate, as an appropriate expression of their Japanese law experience, Ehrlich's concept of the "inner order of associations" and the relative unimportance of state law in view of the normative strength of the social order of the families in Japan on the one side and the partisan disturbance of that order through state law on the other side. They must also have liked the fact that Ehrlich assumes that the social structure of the family normative order is, as much as Gierke's "Germanic" spirit of association for German law, an expression of the unity of Japanese law and not just a "parallelism" of "legal systems" in the same "social field" as Griffiths and Chiba hold.

However, as Griffiths has correctly observed[20], Ehrlich is not interested in descriptive "snapshot" analyses of the organisation of social and behavioural control in primary groups. He uses for his debunking strategy the "telescopic lens" of history in order to unsettle the complacency of established legal reasoning or doctrinally normatively closed juridical logic (*juristische Logik*). Ehrlich is aware of the dynamics of society and of dynamic change not as a distant academic observer, but as a "hands-on" legal politician[21], particularly under the guidance of his eminent socialist teacher and law professor Anton Menger in Vienna (Vogl 2002, 81), one of the hubs of European demographic and social change at the time. He is therefore keenly interested in the role of law and lawyers in such a dynamic environment, and turns to historical research and evolutionary theory, and importantly, evolutionary sociological theory (Herbert Spencer). In contrast, he finds that legal knowledge production (Ziegert 1998) is not up to the challenges that law faces in contemporary society. Consequently

built his own dissertation on this material and must be considered now as the most authoritative source on Ehrlich's life and work to date.

20 See Griffiths 1981, and above section II.

21 Stefan Vogl (2002, 75-98) makes a distinction between the work of Ehrlich at the University of Vienna as more politically oriented and the work in Czernowitz (Bukowina) as professor of Roman law which is more scholarly and theoretical.

he develops his idea of an empirical legal science which could challenge the artificial normative construction of doctrinal legal decision-making and the blind execution of the legislative programmes of state law. A first step towards identifying the reasons for the functional insufficiency of legal education, legal practice and legal decision-making is a historical and evolutionary analysis of the development of legal ideas and legal reasoning. But in order to "send a powerful message" to the opponents of his idea of finding law without doctrinal restrictions *("freie Rechtsfindung"),* he has to unveil law as something that lawyers cannot see unless they "lift their eyes from the texts": the living law. This view is provocative and may be speculative but it is certainly spectacular in challenging the social reality of norms, especially legal norms to which lawyers adhere in their thinking, or, as Masaji Chiba *put it*: whose law are lawyers observing? Through pitting the counter-intuitive "living law" against their counter-factual doctrinal law, Ehrlich has a "circuit-breaker", an opener to begin the debate on the sociological enlightenment of lawyers and legal decision-makers, even if he has not yet got a ready-made sociological theory of law on offer. Judging by the irritated responses to this single volume on preparing the ground for a legal science[22], mainly from lawyers but also, as we have seen, from legal anthropologists from his own time until our own, Ehrlich certainly achieved his desire to incite debate. Significantly, sociologists are absent from this debate[23], or, at least, mainstream sociology does not mention Ehrlich or his work.

In the total output of Eugen Ehrlich[24], the sociology of law with its corresponding realist-empirical substratum of living law accounts for only a minor part of his writings, and even in the trilogy planned as the core

22 Again translation problems abound: the German "Grundlegung" (Ehrlich 1913) changes to "Fundamental Principles" (Ehrlich 1936, 2002) in the Harvard-led US-American translation. This may explain the possibly greater disappointment of an English-speaking audience with Ehrlich's lack of specificity on sociological detail than that felt by a German-speaking audience, which has the added benefit of not being restricted to the translation of just one piece of work by a (prolific) author; see infra.

23 Max Weber (who does not consider himself as a sociologist) is probably the only exception but he criticises Ehrlich not on his historical-sociological concepts, which he welcomes, but for his polemical attacks on positivism and the "resubstantivation" of positive law through an allegedly murky "ideological" concept of people's law (living law), see Ziegert (2004).

24 See the careful bibliography in Vogl 2002. Vogl counts 10 major works (books) and more than 40 more or less major contributions to journals and newspapers.

of his general theory of law (Ehrlich 1918, 313)[25], the "*Grundlegung*" is only, quite in the sense of Griffiths' "prolegomenon", the debunking exercise involved in erecting his theoretical architecture on "raised ground". Nevertheless his sociology is not just a quickly sketched collection of *superficial* arguments but a thoroughly observed and long considered conceptualisation of scientific methodology applied to law. In this light, the lack of specificity or clarity in his sociological definitions is not necessarily a weakness of Ehrlich's theory but an expression of the level of abstraction which he has in mind. As seen above in connection with the historical account of the development of Japanese law, the inner order of associations is concrete data on the structural design and function of social relations, which is not seen when individual "behaviour" is observed in a social field; only this structure reveals the options that individuals have, or do not have, and which they chose, or do not choose. This is a robust sociological argument, confirmed by primary group research and historical research and, has – as far as I can see – never been refuted. The evidence of Japanese history as regards the extraordinary solidity but also adaptability of the familial normative order, enabling it to keep law at arm's length for centuries exactly reflects the functional statement of Ehrlich; it also allows him to draw a functional line, again empirically grounded, between the realms of normative order and legal decision-making. His terminology in doing so could be seen as unfortunate, and certainly can only be fully understood in the context of the ideological battles of his time; today it is merely confusing. Attributing to the normative order of groups and associations "legal norms" and to the legal decision-making (only) "legal propositions", he evidently expressed his value-preference for legal reality in the face of the empirical impossibility of identifying the quality of a norm other than through its source, i.e. the ordering and organising effect of "real" norms, i.e. legal norms, versus the merely norm-evaluative effect of legal propositions. But this functional division of norm-labour also allowed Ehrlich to make further accurate observations and robust empirical arguments as to the effectiveness or ineffectiveness of the impact that law can have on norm-use for the inner order of associations. In attributing to the norms of the associations

[25] The planned trilogy were the volumes of the *Grundlegung der Soziologie des Rechts* (Ehrlich 1913) and *Die juristische Logik* (Ehrlich 1918, 1925). He produced fragments of the third volume (*Die Theorie richterlichen Entscheidens*) but died in 1922 before completing it.

a legal quality, as if law is the expression of the normative effectiveness of social organisation, and not the political power-structure of social control, Ehrlich misses the opportunity to distinguish between the normative order of associations as social control operations maintaining traditional power-relations on the one hand, and on the other, legal decision-making producing rules for decision in order to produce more rules for decision. Such a distinction would also have helped legal pluralism to distinguish more accurately between social control and legal decision-making, or between norms and norm decision-making for the purpose of maintaining order and norms and norm decision-making for the purpose of making normative decisions. Even if, particularly in largely undifferentiated society, such distinctions are difficult to make, that does not justify attributing to them a parallel legal plurality that they do not have in the empirical reality of society. Finally, a clearer distinction would help to understand the increasing "pull to the centre" in its historical development. According to Ehrlich this centre of legal norm selection is not the state – which is just another social association occupied with social control and worried about maintaining "the inner order" – but the institutions of the judge and of the (judicial) court organisation.

A sharper focus on legal decision-making is also the objective of the second volume (Ehrlich 1918, 1925) of the trilogy. He elaborates there the major tenets of his general theory of law. Significantly, Ehrlich drops the concept of living law from the discussion and, for that matter, any mention of sociology of law, and concentrates on meticulous, empirical-historical research into the development (or differentiation) of legal reasoning from earliest times to his own time of pervasive legislation and a receding but not negligible input of lawyers' law. The sometimes tediously long, but always informative, discussions of his legal-realist observations confirm his suspicions that judicial decision–making at the beginning of the 20th century has deteriorated into a largely mindless, automatic, industrial production of court-decisions which, in their self-referential isolation, by-pass social reality on two fronts: they cannot achieve in society what they normatively proclaim to achieve, and they idealise in their doctrinal purity what actually happens in courts and court-communication (Ehrlich 1925, 290). Ehrlich calls it the value (German: *Wert, ibid.* 289-315) of legal reasoning in question. Law, especially penal law, cannot and certainly does not "evoke social forces which are not given by society; every penal law can only work with what is already available in the collective psychology of the people ... What distinguishes the legal administration of justice is always the endeavour to decide on a balance of interests" (ibid., 291). However, doctrinal-normative decision-making is poorly equipped for such a performance: "The juridical logic (legal reasoning) has nothing in common with logic (reason) except its name. It is not logic at all but a technique" (ibid., 299). This technique consists of a "crypto sociological" operation "to first decide on justice and then find the proper sources for supporting this decision afterwards" (ibid., 296).

Ehrlich sums up his historical analyses of the specialisation of legal decision-making "away" from society and its organisational norms in three points (see Figure 1).

1. A just judicial decision is a decision which assesses the interests of parties in a conflict correctly; whoever is in charge of assessing interests in society and of deciding which of these interests deserve support, is entrusted with part of the governance of society. The effective governance of society depends on a knowledge of the forces which are at work in society (ibid., 309-310);
2. In modern society, work on the judicial norms of decision-making is differentiated into three different legal roles: the legislator, the legal academic or teacher, and the judge (ibid., 313);
3. It will be the task of the general legal theory of coming generations to show the way as to how the findings of the social sciences can be used in legislation, legal literature and the administration of justice (ibid.).

Modestly, Ehrlich concludes that his three volumes of a general legal theory "are only the beginning of a scientific foundation of a general theory of law. Probably only the legislators, jurists and judges of coming generations will stand on truly scientifically secure ground. However, even a beginning needs to be begun" (Ehrlich 1918, 313).

Implications for Nordic Sociology of Law

Ehrlich justifiably relativises his work in view of the enormity of the task before him. But he is optimistic. With the benefit of hindsight over the past 100 years, we can safely say that the triumph of science over legal doctrine has not materialised, or not quite in the way Ehrlich imagined. His under-

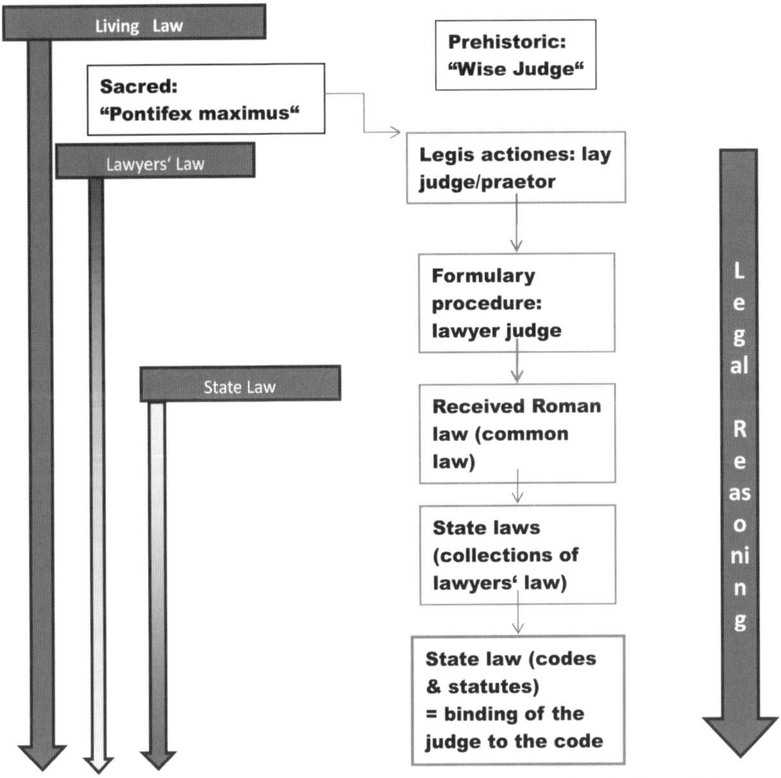

Figure 1: Differentiation of legal reasoning according to Eugen Ehrlich. The initial creativity of lawyers' law decreases as legislation promoted as state law increases.

standing of the "forces working within society" was just not differentiated enough to foresee what modern society would undergo in the hundred years following his publications. But few legal scholars at the time could foresee this, and he did better than most other legal scholars. Most of the dissatisfaction with *Ehrlich's* work arises from the focus of the discussion being based on just one book, and for the English-speaking audience, a translation of one book, that is preparing the ground for the promotion of his idea of legal science with the polemical concept of living law. With his subsequent legal-realist analysis of legal reasoning he provides corrections for misconceptions forming around his "*Grundlegung*", and also confirms descriptively the overall robustness of his sociological arguments as to the structure and function of law.

This minimalist-realist position of the legal science of Ehrlich,i.e. avoiding building "grand theory" but allowing for sufficient abstraction of his concepts to make them universally applicable, resonates with the Nordic legal culture. The foundation and development of the Rättssociologiska Seminariet in Lund in the Seventies and Eighties of the last century could have been taken from a blue-print designed by Ehrlich for the purpose. Certainly, Eugen Ehrlich'*s* sociology of law (the book) was among the basic "classics" for teaching and research under Per Stjernquist[26].In his social-anthropologically oriented study of the organisation of the Swedish forestry industry (Stjernquist 1974) he was able to apply Ehrlich's formula of living law in its entirety. But also more generally, Ehrlich's realist approach is particularly suited to socio-legal research on the "enabling law" approach (Rosefielde and Hedlund 2009) of the Nordic model of governance. However, there is a fine line between living law as normative guidance for doing things safely and properly on the one side, and the socio-technical lure of instrumentalising the organising effect of law for conditioning the behaviour of citizens which can easily mislead research. For instance, it would be a misunderstanding of Ehrlich's findings on living law if one declared the use of speed camera traps and penalisation as an exercise in a "living law of safe driving". We can safely, with Ehrlich, say that the overwhelming majority of car drivers are sufficiently socialised, competent, and safe drivers. However, all that the remaining 10% or so of "deviant" drivers learn from the existence of radar traps is aversive behaviour – as is the political effect of all authoritarian-punitive education: drivers comply with the demands of the camera but do their speeding somewhere else where it won't be seen.

Ehrlich does not give ready-made recipes for socio-legal research. But his basic advice that there should be better scientifically informed governance of society through law is still a good starting point for socio-legal research in pragmatist Nordic society – if one can avoid the pitfalls of "living law" and manage to read perhaps more than just the polemical prolegomena to his general theory of law.

---

26 See also the chapter by Knut Papendorf in this volume.

References

Breuer, Stefan (1984), Feudalismus und "Rechtsstaat" in Westeuropa und Japan. In: Stefan Breuer and Hubert Treiber (eds.), *Zur Rechtssoziologie Max Webers*. Interpretation, Kritik, Weiterentwicklung. Opladen: Westdeutscher Verlag, pp. 112-151.

Chiba, Masaji (1997), Japan In: Poh-Ling Tan (ed.), *Asian Legal Systems – Law, Society and Pluralism in East Asia*. Sydney: Butterworths, pp. 82-123.

Ehrlich, Eugen (1913), *Grundlegung der Soziologie des Rechts*. München and Leipzig: Duncker & Humblot, transl. Moll (1936), *Fundamental Principles of Sociology of Law*. Cambridge, Mass.: Cambridge University Press, reprinted with new introduction by K. A. Ziegert (2002), New Brunswick: Transaction Publishers.

Ehrlich, Eugen (1918), *Die juristische Logik* (The Juridical Logic). Tübingen, reprint Tübingen: Mohr, 1925 and Aalen: Scientia-Verlag, 1965.

Gilissen, John (1971), Introduction à l'étude comparée du pluralisme juridique. In John Gilissen (ed.), *Le pluralisme juridique*. Bruxelles: Université de Bruxelles, pp. 7-18.

Griffiths, John (1981), What is Legal Pluralism? Paper prepared for delivery at the 1981 Annual Meeting of the Law and Society Association at Amherst College, Amherst, Mass.

Hooker, Michael B. (1975), *Legal Pluralism – An Introduction to Colonial and Neo-Colonial Laws*. Oxford: Oxford University Press.

Merry, Sally E. (1988), Legal Pluralism. *Law and Society Review* 22:869?896.

Moore, Sally F. (1973), Law and Social Change: The Semi-Autonomous Social Field as an Appropriate Subject of Study. *Law and Society Review* 7:719?746.

McCargo, Duncan (2004), *Contemporary Japan*. Basingstoke: Palgrave.

Podgórecki, Adam (1973), *Law and Society*. London: Routledge & Kegan Paul.

Pospisil, Leopold (1971), *Anthropology of Law: A Comparative Theory*. New York: Harper and Row.

Rosefielde, Steven and Stefan Hedlund (2009), *Russia since 1980*. Cambridge: Cambridge University Press.

Schloenhardt, Andreas (2010), Mission Unaccomplished: Japan's Anti-*Bôryoku-Dan* Law. *Journal of Japanese Law*. 29:123-136.

Smith, Michael Garfield (1974), *Corporations and Society*. London: Duckworth.

Smith, Patrick (1998), *Japan – A Reinterpretation*. New York: Vintage Books

Stjernquist, Per (1973), *Laws in the Forest*. Lund: Gleerup.

Vogl, Stefan (2002), *Soziale Gesetzgebungspolitik, freie Rechtsfindung und soziologische Rechtswissenschaft bei Eugen Ehrlich*. Baden-Baden: Nomos.

Vogl, Stefan (2009), Eugen Ehrlich's Linking of Sociology and Jurisprudence. In: Marc Hertogh, ed., *Living Law. Reconsidering Eugen Ehrlich*. Oxford: Hart Publishing, pp. 95-123.

Vanderlinden, Jacques (1971), Le pluralisme juridique: Essai de synthèse. In: John Gilissen, ed., *Le pluralisme juridique*. Bruxelles: Université de Bruxelles, pp. 19-56.

Verwajen, Frans B. (1996), Early Reception of Western Legal Thought in Japan 1841-1868, Doctoral Dissertation, Leiden: University of Leiden.

Ziegert, Klaus A. (1979), The Sociology behind Eugen Ehrlich's Sociology of Law. *International Journal of Sociology of Law*, 7:225-270.

Ziegert, Klaus A. (1998), Eugen Ehrlich and the Production of Legal Knowledge. *Sydney Law Review* 20:108-125.

Ziegert, Klaus A. (2002), Introduction to the Transaction Edition. In: *Eugen Ehrlich, Fundamental Principles of Sociology of Law*, transl. Walter Moll (1936). New Brunswick: Transaction Publishers, pp. xix–xlx.

Ziegert, Klaus A. (2014), Max Weber (1864-1920). *Zeitschrift für Europäisches Privatrecht* 22:97-115.

Eugen Ehrlich's Legacy in Contemporary German Sociology of Law

Stefan MACHURA

"The word is a highly imperfect instrument of thought, and no-one has yet succeeded in holding sway over things through words."

(Eugen Ehrlich 1903/1967, 192, translated)

Eugen Ehrlich profoundly influenced the history of the Sociology of Law, and this influence extended beyond the German-speaking countries. He was also studied by American academics at a key moment in the development of the study of law and society. The texts assembled in this volume show his effect on Sociology of Law in yet more nations. The contemporary German Sociology of Law has more or less arrived at an agreed view on his merits and contemporary relevance. This article deals with Ehrlich's legacy in Germany. But first, who was Ehrlich, and how are the person and his work related?

Eugen Ehrlich was born as Elias Ehrlich 1862 in Czernowitz, then the Bukowina Province of the Austro-Hungarian empire, now part of Ukraine, the son of a Jewish lawyer (Rehbinder 2007a, 271). Polish was his mother tongue (Rehbinder 1986, 20). He chose the route of radical assimilation, adopting the name of Prince Eugen, who he adored (Rehbinder 1986, 27; 2007a, 272), and even formally converted to Catholicism. Ehrlich felt passionate about the Habsburg Empire and its cultural and political accommodation of the utmost social and ethnic pluralism (Vogl 2003, 101-103). From 1899 until 1914, when the first occupation by Russian troops (Rehbinder 2007a, 273) heralded the end of his world, Ehrlich worked as Professor of Roman Law at the University of Czernowitz.

As a scholar of considerable international reputation, Ehlich might have secured a chair at a more elite law faculty. His career was hindered by opponents (Vogl 2003, 92), and this, together with the fact that his works were profoundly misunderstood by many legal scholars (Rehbinder 1967, 9), makes him a tragic figure. Another view, however, can be offered. In Czernowitz, and at the local university, Ehrlich was at home in more ways than one. To start with, the professor, who never married, lived with his elderly mother in his native city. Ehrlich relished its melange of different cultures and his hobbies, apart from foil fencing, were collecting local traditional carpets and embroidery (Rehbinder 1986, 17; 2003a, 210; Ehrlich 1922/1992, 2), also testifies to this. Embroidery patterns even today serve as a form of cultural memory, and reflect life in the local ethnic communities of Ukrainians and Romanians[1].

Czernovitz's built environment alone offered a fantastic variety of styles: modern designs and various versions of traditional architecture[2]. The city was also home to a number of intellectuals and academics still remembered today. Czernovitz University was founded to serve as an agent of Austro-German culture in the far east of the Habsburg realm. German speaking students, however, were not a majority, but the largest minority, and for more than half of them, Yiddish was actually their mother tongue (Rehbinder 2008, 200). Fifty percent of students were Jewish, Ehrlich (1916/2007, 147) himself remarked, with Jews forming 10% of the local population. Ehrlich (1916/2007) classed the barely industrialized Bukowina Province, with its economically struggling inhabitants, among the poorest countries. Life was not harmonious (Ehrlich 1912/1967b, 77), as was evidenced by the frequent violence of Romanian nationalists against Jewish students (Rehbinder 2008, 211).

Eugen Ehrlich was not only a widely known legal author, whose opinion was sought on the reform of the court constitution by the Association of German Judges, and on the reform of legal training by the German *Juristentag*, he also represented his university as rector in 1906/1907 (Rehbinder 1986, 16 and 20). The University of Groningen, on the occasion of its tercentenary, bestowed an honorary doctorate on him (Rehbinder 1986, 22). If one adds his ridicule of Hans Kelsen in their famous controversy (to be discussed below) and his evident celebrity, to be seen in the fact that a local paper reporting on a charity sports event, noted his passionate style of fenc-

1 See Olga Litvinova's article in this volume.

2 Lüderssen 2003, VII–VIII. The website of the Czernowitz-L Discussion Group "concerned with genealogy and the history of the Jewish community in the Czernowitz-Sadagora area", shows period photography and cards: http://czernowitz.ehpes.com/, last accessed 12 September 2012, also the site: http://chernivtsi-history.cv.ua/index.php/halereia/zobrazhennia/stari-photo-chernivtsi?page=1#category, last accessed 21 December 2013.

ing (Rehbinder 2007a, 279), Ehrlich, until the outbreak of the First World War, may well have been at the top of his game.

His fall from fortune was dramatic (Rehbinder 2003a). Ehrlich spent his last years in exile, unable to secure a stable position. With the break-up of the Habsburg Empire, the Bukowina became part of an enlarged Romania. In 1922 Ehrlich died in Vienna, after years of hardship in which the opposition of local Romanian nationalists prevented his return to Czernowitz. It was to no avail that Ehrlich had been able to mobilize support in Bucharest and seemed set to accommodate with the new state and teach in Romanian.

One can't fail to recognize the similarities between Ehrlich's life and his Sociology of Law. The man, who defends the multi-ethnic state and collects folk embroidery, studies legal pluralism and conducts empirical field work. These two key elements of his teachings are expressed in what is regarded as his main work: *Grundlegung der Soziologie des Rechts*, 1913. It is a key publication advocating sociological jurisprudence: lawyers are advised to approach legal problems with sociological knowledge. An English translation by Walter L. Moll, with a foreword by the eminent jurist Roscoe Pound, was published in 1936 by the Harvard University Press. Articles had already been printed by the Harvard Law Review (Ehrlich 1915/1916; 1922). In his lifetime Ehrlich had attracted interest from Japanese scholars[3]. In German-speaking countries Ehrlich's ideas proved very controversial and legal scholarship generally developed away from sociological jurisprudence. On top of this, Czernowitz, the Bukowina and German-Jewish cultural relations were all but completely destroyed by the National Socialists.

After 1945 it took decades for Eugen Ehrlich to be rediscovered in Germany. Sociology of law eventually became a fashionable subject in the 1960s and, in search of ideas, a new generation turned to Ehrlich, Marx and other thinkers. Later the subject suffered severe setbacks, due to political circumstances and budget crises (Machura 2012). Today, however, students in Sociology of Law lectures will invariably hear about Eugen Ehrlich and his concept of "living law".

What follows will focus on Ehrlich's influence within contemporary German Sociology of Law. As a consequence of the topics German soci-

3 Rehbinder 1986, 22-24 and 2005b, 143. See also the article of Klaus A. Ziegert in this volume.

ologists of law have chosen to discuss, the article will deal mainly with German and Continental European law and the corresponding political and social phenomena. This leaves out social-anthropological and other scholarship on countries in e.g. Asia and Africa[4].

We will mainly concern ourselves with what students and faculty preparing to teach Sociology of Law are likely to learn about Ehrlich. The Ehrlich vs. Weber debate therefore needs to be discussed. We will consider how Ehrlich is dealt with in recent introductions to Sociology of Law. The genre of introductions is important, as they are read by students and they also inform the teaching of a subject. In German jurisprudence, there is a distinction between *Lernbücher* – written for students and not too wide-ranging – and *Lehrbücher*, voluminous treatises which provide an overview of a subject, similar to large legal commentaries (Langer 2004, 67 f.). Both types of book will be covered. We will not concern ourselves with a number of older introductions which are unlikely to be used nowadays, except for very specific purposes[5]. The same applies to edited books[6].This leaves the following field:

- Manfred Rehbinder's introduction to Sociology of Law which has already appeared in a seventh edition (2009, I will be using the 5th edition, 2003).
- Hubert Rottleuthner's 1987 introduction is out of print, but he also deals with Ehrlich in his *Foundations of Law* (2005) and other publications.
- Klaus F. Röhl's *Rechtssoziologie* of 1987 is also out of print, but as an online-document is now probably the most accessible of all. Its author also intends to continue developing the chapters. Further publications by Röhl will be included because they might also be read by students and their teachers to learn about Sociology of Law, and because they provide a strong critique of Ehrlich.
- Thomas Raiser's widely read *Grundlagen der Rechtssoziologie* (2013, I am using a previous edition of 2007), which hails back to an early edition in 1987, too.

---

[4] But see the article of Keebet and Franz von Benda-Beckmann in this volume and Röhl/Machura (2013).

[5] Such as Geiger (1947/1987), Ryffel (1974), Girtler (1976), Dux (1978), Hirsch (1984), Kißler (1984a, 1984b).

[6] E.g. the once very influential Hirsch/Rehbinder (eds., 1967), or Röhl (ed., loose-leaf edition).

- The pocket book introduction to the sociology of state and law by Zippelius (3rd ed. 2012), is still in print – it seems to have developed from a predecessor of 1980.
- Hesse's Sociology of Law appeared in 2004 and most of its chapters deal with aspects of the state-law relation.
- The most recent introduction mentioning Ehrlich would be that of Susanne Baer (2011) and is very much influenced by political perspectives on law[7].

Ehrlich's living law

In the Bukowina, according to Ehrlich, local life was not determined by the law of the Austrian-Hungarian State, but rather by the law of the different ethnicities inhabiting the area. This law could be traditional, but might also be newly developed. The full extent of the Bukowina's ethnic diversity becomes apparent when Ehrlich (1912/1967a, 43) lists the peoples living there: Armenians, Germans, Gypsies, Hungarians, Jews, Romanians, Russians, Slovaks, and Ukrainians. Lawyers would have to learn about the "living law": the law which actually guides actions within the social associations that people form, and that cannot just be found in legal codes. Instead of, exclusively studying legal texts and perhaps their history, as had been their practice hitherto, lawyers should also turn their attention to legal documents, to interviews and legal actions. Law-making and jurisdiction should be based on empirical facts[8].

Ehrlich has a particular theory about where law develops, his "origination thesis", to use an expression coined by Röhl and Röhl (2008, 208). At all times the main developments of law will take place in the sphere of the' 'living law", the law of the social associations making up society

[7] Among recent introductions, Gerhard Struck (2011) decided to follow a different concept and did not deal with classics of Sociology of Law. Personal communication, 3 October 2012.

[8] Ehrlich 1936/2002, 486-488, 491-493, 498 and 1920/1921/2007, 191-200. At this time there were many scholars conducting ethnographic research in various countries (see for example the article on Russia by Litvinova/Machura in this volume). Ehrlich (1911/1967, 41) himself mentions for example a systematic survey of the traditional law used by local courts in the Russian empire. The Croat Valtasar Bogišić combined empirical and historical research with legal scholarship and came close to Ehrlich's endeavour, but was not interested in Sociology of Law (Rehbinder 2013, 42).

(Ehrlich 1936/2002, Foreword and 493). The state may produce law that exists in the legal code but is not actually used ("dead letter", Ehrlich 1922, 142). Certainly, some law is used, and as such it will become part of the living law. Yet, as Ehrlich sees it, social life will develop its own laws much more quickly than the state. Some of it may go against state law, and some may alter its meaning or surpass its content. In idea way reminiscent of Durkheim Ehrlich sees society as made up of associations (and/including ethnic groups)[9], ranging from families to organisations, such as factories with their own regulations. Living law does not rely on statutes or legal documents, but can be found in folkways that are taken for granted. Law organizes life (Ehrlich 1911/1967, 39). According to Ehrlich (1912/1967b, 77), in contrast to codified law, which is mainly territorial, the living law is "personal", defined by the "circles" to which people belong.

In Ehrlich's view, law can best be studied by observation of daily legal interactions, by systematic interviews, and by reading legal documents, such as contracts and wills. If he had been asked about the most important qualities for a lawyer to have, Ehrlich would have replied: "Eyes to see and ears to hear" (Ehrlich 1920/1921/2007, 200). With a seminar for lawyers (*Praktikerseminar*, Rehbinder 2005c, 136), Ehrlich went to do field work in the vicinity of his university. In other words, Ehrlich formulated not only a theory of the law's relation to society, but also a method that he perceived to be better for lawyers. Sociological jurisprudence would be the "truly scientific" study of law (Ehrlich 1936/2002, 505).

Sociological jurisprudence approaches legal cases with the help of sociology. The initial historical context of this was the *Freirechtsbewegung* (Free Law Movement) which attracted some support among lawyers at the turn of the last century. According to Rehbinder (1986, 21-22), Ehrlich was known as the "spiritual head" of this movement, to which he gave a name with his publication *Freie Rechtsfindung und freie Rechtswissenschaft* (1903/1967). The movement concerned itself with finding the law where the legal code leaves gaps – unlike orthodox academic legal teaching of

[9] Ehrlich 1912/1967b, 77. See the article by Litvinova/Machura in this volume for Ehrlich's concept of the "personality in law" in the context of ethnicities ("nationality in law"). The Habsburg Empire was not a modern nation state, but rather a conglomeration of different entities held together by readiness to accept the monarchy. Seen from this perspective Ehrlich's universe of living law also reflected a political reality (Eppinger 2009).

the time, which insisted on a seamless system of abstract legal rules. The *Freirechtsbewegung,* according to Max Weber (1922/1968, 888 f.), one of its critics, aimed at an emancipation of lawyers from the legal code and from strict political-bureaucratic control by the state machinery. Lawyers did not want to be reduced to a cog in a giant legal machine.

Terms, however, can be misleading. The way Ehrlich presented his ideas must bear part of the blame for misunderstandings well-meaning legal scholars argue (Barta 2013, 25 f.; Hagen 2013, 50; Broucek 2013, 99). The Austrian civil code already allowed "free finding of the law" (Ehrlich 1903/1967, 190). Ehrlich, though, missed out on the chance to cite the exact paragraph which might have opened the eyes of his German critics (Barta 2013, 25 f.). Paragraph 7 of the Austrian civil code ABGB stipulates that if it is impossible to decide a legal case from the "natural" meaning of the paragraph, similar cases covered by the code and the intention of other related laws are to be taken into account. If the case were still in doubt, it is to be decided with regard to the carefully established and thoroughly considered circumstances and according to the "natural" principles of law[10].

In essence, Ehrlich only advocated the "free finding of law" where there is a genuine gap in the legal code which cannot be addressed by standard means of legal interpretation, and even then, he recommends a cautious, "conservative" interpretation[11]. Decision-makers should be aware of the stakes involved in a case, namely, the weighing up of interests by the legislator and the actual interests of the parties to the dispute (Vogl 2003, 333-334, Broucek 2013, 98). And in this kind of interpretation, lawyers would be best served by an empirical method.

10 "Läßt sich ein Rechtsfall weder aus den Worten, noch aus dem natürlichen Sinne eines Gesetzes entscheiden, so muß auf ähnliche, in den Gesetzen bestimmt entschiedene Fälle, und auf die Gründe anderer damit verwandten Gesetze Rücksicht genommen werden. Bleibt der Rechtsfall noch zweifelhaft; so muß solcher mit Hinsicht auf die sorgfältig gesammelten und reiflich erwogenen Umstände nach den natürlichen Rechtsgrundsätzen entschieden werden." (http://www.jusline.at/7_ABGB.html, accessed 25 August 2013).

11 Rehbinder 1986, 96-98; Ehrlich 1916/2007, 179 f., 1903/1967, 187. "The free finding of law is conservative as every freedom, as freedom means personal responsibility (...)", Ehrlich (1903/1967, 193) stated.

Ehrlich versus Weber

German students are likely to learn about Ehrlich in connection with Max Weber's ideas. The comparison usually starts with the different definitions of law offered by the two founders of legal sociology. Where Ehrlich emphasized the living law of associations, Weber (1922/1968, 34) made the existence of a sanctioning apparatus key to differentiating between "law" and *Konvention*. Ehrlich would accept Weber's definition as that of "state law". "The state brings law into existence by creating institutions through its power of compulsion (in the last analysis military) and provides them with a legal regulation" (Ehrlich 1922, 137). But generally law is much more for Ehrlich: "the organization of state, social and economic life" which would be in a bad way if it depended on coercion exercised by agencies (Ehrlich 1911/1967, 39).

In his *Rechtssoziologie*, Weber (1922/1968, 886-895) responds to the Free Law Movement and to what he calls socialist "legal intellectuals", offering a defence of formal-rational jurisprudence. He describes that Continental European Law had been developed by lawyers into a system of abstract legal principles. It is technically superior to other legal systems. As such, it produces reliability, especially calculability for economic interests. "Free finding of the law", to Weber is a recipe for insecurity in legal matters, especially when informed by ideals of "material justice" that aim to change society. The wealth-generating motor of capitalism needs security for investment.

In his analysis Max Weber encounters the "England-Problem" (Treiber 2011, 49): the most advanced capitalist country of his time had a different, case law system based on the rulings of judges. Weber (1968, 886-892) addresses this problem in the following way: the decisive element is the calculability of law, and English law serves the capitalist interest perfectly, as it is based on class justice. Lawyers are pivotal here. The education of English lawyers lies in the hands of the legal profession, which mainly serves the dominant economic forces. The moneyed classes form the lawyers' clientele. As a consequence, the law has been developed to serve their interests and practical legal thinking is channelled in this direction. Furthermore, English judges, idealized by some proponents of the Free Law Movement (including Ehrlich 1903/1967, 195), are, argues Weber (1968, 892), appointed from the top ranks of these lawyers. Finally, according to Weber the local lay judges are prone to irrational decisions. In Weber's eyes Continental European state law is clearly superior. Strict legal logic, with its restrictions on judicial decisions, and the disciplining of (academically trained) judges as career bureaucrats limit arbitrary decision-making. Under conditions in which political leaders are elected and have to vie for the public vote, a codified law system with career legal officials does not disadvantage the lower classes more than the alternative (Weber 1968, 893 f.). Weber extends to lawyers his doubt that German judges had the personal, ethical and professional qualities to deal on their own with challenging social issues (Weber 1895/1993, 533 f.). Judges would be all too happy to be mere judicial automata. Weber was not alone among the early socio-legal scholars in this analysis. Tellingly, the academic and social democrat politician Hugo Sinzheimer, favoured a formal development of labour law and opposed more freedom for judges. According to Sinzheimer, people did not trust the judges (Rottleuthner 1986, 6 and 1987, 29 f.).

Typically, the teaching of Sociology of Law focuses on the differences between Ehrlich and Weber. Weber defines law in the context of his general theory of societal development towards increased rationalization, which also means the separation of spheres, while Ehrlich is interested in researching manifestations of law (Miribach 2013, 215-217). But, although they define "law" differently, with Ehrlich emphasizing the acceptance of law by the people, and with Weber "law" being a social order guaranteed by a staff of people that enforces the law (*Rechtsstab*), on closer inspection there is some overlap between them. In his theory, Weber (1922/1968, 31 f.) insists that those "social orders" will be most stable that are believed to be "legitimate". Among the pure types of legitimate order, Weber (1922/1968, 36 f.) mentions the legal-rational type, which can for example be based on mutual agreement on a set of rules, and he lists a "traditional" pure type based on belief in the venerable dignity of the old ways. As law is only a special type of social order, legitimate law – the law that will be most stable – according to Weber's theoretical concepts easily takes the shape of what Ehrlich observed as "living law". Ehrlich's analysis of existing legal pluralism, exemplified by the various layers of living law in the Bukowina, also finds a parallel in Weber's sociological approach. Max Weber planned to publish his sociology as *Die Wirtschaft und die gesellschaftlichen Ordnungen und Mächte* – The Economy and the Social Orders and Powers.

Further similarities to Weber can be listed when close attention is paid to Ehrlich's position. For both, legal education, social legislation and rules favouring economic activity were important. Ehrlich advocated a reform of legal education to enable lawyers to study the living law. We have to ask: what for? Surely for judges to function better within the (Austro-Hungarian, later Romanian) legal system! For the development of state law, the availability of well-trained lawyers would be one of the crucial factors (Ehrlich 1936/2002, 144 f.) and here he agrees with Weber[12].

But there is a special undertone in Ehrlich's thought. Every application of a legal rule would "necessarily pass through a person" (Ehrlich 1903/1967, 194). Therefore, Ehrlich (1912/1967b) aimed at improving legal education and practice. He was bound to do so, as he believed that the highest guarantee of justice, was not provided by the hierarchy of courts or by panels of professional judges but by the "personality of the judge" ("Persönlichkeit des Richters", Ehrlich 1903/1967, 188).

Another, lesser known aspect of Ehrlich's thinking was devoted to social reform legislation. The law-giver should base his policies on a sound empirical survey of the living law, making use of social science methodology. In his short treatise on state and law, the legal scholar Reinhold Zippelius (2012, 86 and 152) emphasizes that Ehrlich, like Roscoe Pound, saw the lawyer as a "social engineer". In the industrial society, law needs to be set carefully to realize certain objectives. The law's effectiveness follows from a general acceptance of the social orders by the people and when the law and the social orders by which people live are reconcilable (Zippelius 2012, 105 f. and 152 f.).

This, then, would point to Ehrlich's "conservatism": he sought to make sure that codified law and legal decisions are not at odds with the living law. Importantly, however, Ehrlich's ideas differ from those of the many authors of his time who collected folk law, which they saw "not as the germs of new law, but, – in a spirit of backward-looking romanticism – as the dying remnants of past forms of law" (Rehbinder 1986, 18, my translation). When it comes to contemporary society, "living law" is by definition modern law, one that is unfolding at present.

Despite the fact that Ehrlich defined law as acceptance of the social order of an "association", or group, he stressed that these may have a legal

---

12 Apart from this, advocates were seen by Ehrlich as part of society and the "law" they found, or developed he saw as part of "social" in contrast to public law (Porsche-Ludwig 2011, 29).

order of their own, and sometimes their own law enforcement apparatuses (Rehbinder 1995, 239 f.). This is pretty close to Weber, as Weber's definition of "law" also covers non-state orders in so far as they have their own law enforcement apparatus (Weber 1922/1968, 35). Churches or organisations with statutory internal arbitration could serve as examples. Furthermore, Ehrlich distinguished between "first order norms", or "rules of conduct" on the one hand, and "second order norms", or "decision- and administration rules" on the other. The latter can be enforced by jurists and the state, and can influence the former (Rehbinder 1995, 239 f.). As Ziegert (1998, 115) explains: "For Ehrlich, all rules are rules of conduct, that is social norms, and the notion of 'rules for decisions' only specifies further the locus of operation, namely a historically differentiated legal decison-making system, including legal practice, jurisdiction and legislation."

To conclude, there is evidence of plenty of common ground between Weber and Ehrlich when it comes to understanding law, and more generally, normative rules, in society. Where they profoundly differ is in their basic definitions of law. They also have opposing views on the virtues of dogmatic jurisprudence, which turned Weber into a figure-head for legal positivism and Ehrlich into the godfather of its critique. In a lesser known book *Juristische Logik* (Ehrlich 1918) published later than the "Grundlegung der Soziologie des Rechts", Ehrlich however moves somewhat closer to mainstream jurisprudence, and combines dogmatic and sociological jurisprudence (Hagen 2013, 50, Broucek 2013). Ehrlich and Weber typify two different ways to reconcile Jurisprudence and the Sociology of Law. Weber (1922/1968, 311 f.; 1913/1988, 439 f.) insisted on a separation of the two, on the grounds of their different logic, one being dedicated to the abstract system of law, while the other analyses any type of actual behaviour influenced by law (even circumventing or breaking law). In contrast, Ehrlich advocated more of a fusion of the two subjects as he (1912/1967b, 70) aimed to "rebuild" jurisprudence on the basis of the social sciences.

Ehrlich's legacy according to Rehbinder

In a monograph first published 1967, Manfred Rehbinder set out to correct a misleading picture of Ehrlich's work found in post-war jurisprudence that amounted to outright "libel" (Rehbinder 1986, 12). Rehbinder edited volumes containing Ehrlich's sociological and political essays. After the fall of the Soviet Empire, Rehbinder could access local archives and add to what was known about Ehrlich.

In his introduction to Sociology of Law, Manfred Rehbinder draws only infrequently on Ehrlich, which is surprising, because more than anyone else, Rehbinder had reintroduced Ehrlich to the German discussion. However, he appears rather sceptical about key aspects of Ehrlich's theory. The following outline of his position uses additional publications, and not Rehbinder's introduction alone. To start with, "living law" is understood differently today. "Law itself" could only be studied by analysing the behaviour of the *Rechtsstab*, those professionally responsible for lawgiving, and the application and enforcement of law (Rehbinder 2008, 217). The actual behaviour of those governed by law serves only as an indicator of the law's effectivity (Rehbinder 2008, 217). The key to understanding law would be not the acceptance of the law by those subject to it, but their compliance with it (Rehbinder 2008, 217). Today's Sociology of Law thus has decided against Ehrlich's concept (Rehbinder 2003, 50). When it comes to matters of detail, the population even is a stranger to the law (*Rechtsfremdheit*, Rehbinder 2003, 50). Rehbinder adds further doubts about Ehrlich's success in shaping jurisprudence: Legal scholars were not convinced by Ehrlich's idea of Sociology of Law as the only science of law – studying the living law – in contrast to jurisprudence as merely practical legal scholarship (Ehrlich 1922, 143 f.). But importantly, Rehbinder regards him as having made "the first attempt at an encompassing sociological theory of law" (Rehbinder 2008, 217). This judgement may well be true, as predecessors like Marx and Engels had only studied law from particular angles, Durkheim's treatment of modern law stayed rather abstract and Weber's *Rechtssoziologie* was only published posthumously and later than Ehrlich's *Grundlegung der Soziologie des Rechts*.

Rehbinder's treatment leaves it unclear why today's students should pay any closer attention to Ehrlich. The co-founder of sociological jurisprudence would be merely a topic for specialists.

Hubert Rottleuthner and the Kelsen-Ehrlich debate

"Ehrlich is and was always a good companion", Hubert Rottleuthner states, but he prefers Hans Kelsen's acumen (personal communication, 19 October 2012). Since his practical concern was to fill the information deficit in a narrowly conceived dogmatic legal practice and jurisprudence, Rottleuthner sees Ehrlich as a representative of a "compensatory Sociology of Law" (Rottleuthner 1986, 4; 1987, 26 and 30). Rottleuthner counts the "compensatory role" as one of the main functions of the academic subject (Rottleuthner 1986, 17). The Free Law Movement, according to Rottleuthner, only had the courage to express what judges largely practised, making it hard to understand why it has been so vigorously rejected (Rottleuthner 1986, 9).

Ehrlich is placed by Rottleuthner in a category of legal thinkers that includes Marx and Geiger, who assume that law follows from facts. This assumption is strongly criticised by Rottleuthner (2005, 137). The "facts of law" listed by Ehrlich (1936/2002, 35 f.): usage, domination, possession, declaration of will (contracts, wills) were already "shot through with norms, i.e. normative expectations, obligations, transgressions, and sanctions" (Rottleuthner 2005, 137). Therefore Ehrlich's assumption (e.g. Ehrlich 1922, 138 f.) that law derives from social practices and is then moulded by judges and legal scholars as norms for decision, and eventually codified by the state legislator as "legal proposition"[13], is put into question (Rottleuthner 2005, 137). Although Ehrlich had advocated a "substantive theory of legal development" with law as the structure of social associations, he nevertheless chose to define law psychologically (Rottleuthner 2005, 143). For Ehrlich (1916/2007, 105), the legal order emanates from the rules people follow, their actions and the "ideas, feelings and emotions" which accompany them. He also states that laws once derived from the social order will in turn shape it (Ehrlich 1916/2007, 105). This suggests that for Ehrlich, there is a main perspective on the relation between life and law and a sidelight as well.

Rottleuthner (1986) offers a careful analysis of a key debate between Ehrlich and Hans Kelsen[14] as representative of a synthetic jurisprudence. Jurisprudence and Sociology of Law are irreconcilable; Ehrlich confused Is and Ought claimed Kelsen[15]. In his attempt to logically separate jurispru-

---

13 "Legal Proposition" is the term Ehrlich uses for codified legal rules.

14 The controversy started with a long review essay devoted by Kelsen to Ehrlich's *Grundlegung der Soziologie des Rechts*. The debate extended through the 1915 to 1917 volumes of the Archiv für Sozialwissenschaft und Sozialpolitik (reedited by Lüderssen 2003).

15 Kelsen 1915/2003, 4-7, 26, 54. On closer reading, Kelsen (1915/2003) left open the

dence as dealing with what ought to be, and sociology, which investigates social facts, Kelsen misses the point that sociology can also treat the validity of legal norms in real life (Rottleuthner 1984).

The question of the difference between Is and Ought which Kelsen and many other legal scholars turn against Ehrlich, is taken as point of departure by Rottleuthner (1981, 194-203) to introduce different uses of the contrast. Some of these may be useful in understanding Ehrlich's and Kelsen's discussion. The following is a slightly simplified version of Rottleuthner's (1981, 202 f.) dimensional analysis:

1. From a sentence like: "A pays B" (Is), the sentence "A should pay B" (Ought) does not follow logically.
2. A norm can be described in words to provide information (Is), the same words can also be used as a command, or prescription (Ought), depending on the situation.
3. A sentence can express how much a behaviour does or does not conform to a norm (Is), or can formulate the norm (Ought). The logical relation would be congruence or non-congruence.
4. A legal text can be seen as a formulation of will, the lawgiver has decided to establish this norm (Is), or its meaning can be explored to find out what has to be done (Ought).
5. Conditions can be specified under which a law becomes relevant (Is) in contrast to a discussion of the validity of a norm under these conditions (Ought). There is no logical implication between them.
6. Law can be discussed as it is described in legal propositions (Is), but it also can be discussed as it should be (Ought). One gives information about a law "as is", the other evaluates law from a higher position, perhaps from a moral view.

---

possibility that there could be a Sociology of Law in its own right, albeit with a reduced remit, certainly not as part of what Kelsen saw as "jurisprudence" (Rottleuthner 1984, 545-548, Dobler 2013, 181). According to Rehbinder (1986, 119 f.), Kelsen's critique and the reaction of legal scholars who sided with him have hindered the development of the Sociology of Law for a long time. Kelsen is reported to have regretted in the 1960s that he had obstructed the acceptance of Ehrlich's work and of Sociology of Law (Rehbinder 1986, 120, and the destructive effect of this is also noted by Rottleuthner 1981, 31). For Austria, however, Barta (2013, 20) puts forward the view that Kelsen was not alone responsible for the exclusion of Sociology of Law and points to influential Private Law scholars.

It becomes clear that the abstract talk of "Is" and "Ought" glosses over important differences and is bound to lead to misunderstandings. Even a strict social science in Weber's tradition that largely excludes value-judgements by the investigator, will at least find it legitimate to describe various manifestations of "Oughts".

Kelsen (1915/2003, 33-35) also raised objections against the criteria Ehrlich suggested for determining whether a rule counts as "law" or as "moral norm". Ehrlich searched for an empirical trait that would distinguish law. The solution he offered was that breaking the law arouses stronger feelings. Walter L. Moll's English translation (which is certainly clearer in its choice of words than the German original) of the relevant paragraph reads:

> "The various classes of norms release various overtones of feeling, and we react to the transgression of different norms with different feelings. Compare the feeling of revolt that follows a violation of law with the indignation at a violation of a law of morality, with the feeling of disgust occasioned by an indecency, with the disapproval of tactlessness, the ridiculousness of an offense against etiquette and lastly with the critical feeling of superiority with which a votary of fashion looks down upon those who have not attained the heights which he has scaled. Peculiar to the norm is the reaction for which the jurists of the Continental common law have coined the term *opinio necessitatis*." (Ehrlich 1936/2002, 165)

Kelsen correctly disputed this notion[16], because violating a moral norm might in many cases make people more upset than breaking a law. Ehrlich was not even able to label the supposedly categorically different emotional reactions in a conclusive way. How do we tell apart *Empörung* involving law from *Entrüstung* involving moral norms? The leading online-dictionary Beolingus currently translates both German words as "outcry", or "indignation"[17]. To be fair, Ehrlich only claimed that these criteria would usually work well (Ehrlich 1936/2002, 164 f.). But: what would be the statistical cut-off point to decide when a norm can no longer be labelled as law (Rottleuthner 1987, 160)? Ehrlich's attempt to operationalize "law" with the feelings of disapproval still does not work. To talk about *opinion necessitatis* also is hardly conducive (Rottleuthner 1984, 544). "Does not the

[16] Kelsen (1915/2003, 33 f.). And, of course, later authors like Rehbinder (e.g. 2003b, 50 and 2005a, 229), Röhl (1987, 216: "practically completely useless"), or Rottleuthner (1987, 160 f. and 2005, 24).

[17] http://dict.tu-chemnitz.de/, accessed 17 November 2012.

moral law also carry the character of necessity?", Kelsen (1915/2003, 35, my translation) asked. For Kelsen, Ehrlich's attempt to define law without recourse to the state blurred the distinction between law and society (Kelsen 1915/2003, 49, Rottleuthner 1984, 542). Rottleuthner ends his discussions with the sentence: "In sum, as Kelsen put it, Ehrlich has exposed himself with his definitional attempt to *ridiculousness* without transgressing a norm of *etiquette*"[18].

For Rottleuthner (2005, 24), Sociology of Law needs to define law by taking into account the actions of the state, in particular, the validation of law through the state. Ehrlich's failure to offer an alternative would only exemplify that law cannot be sufficiently understood without referring to the state. Rottleuthner (1981, 174-175) also points out that Ehrlich's interest was mainly focused on ways in which private legal autonomy is used and how effectively binding it can be. As a consequence, behaviour subject to criminal law, where a higher, state authority punishes wrongdoers, is barely addressed in Ehrlich's work[19]. As we will see, other critics also noted a lack of attention to political phenomena and to criminal law.

"Practically useless" according to Hesse

In a further introduction to the Sociology of Law, Hans Albrecht Hesse (2004, 20) states that for Germany, Weber and Ehrlich could be seen as starting points of the theoretical Sociology of Law which had many more predecessors. Extending the discussion around the concept of law, Ehrlich, according to Hesse (2004, 28) did not distinguish strictly enough between "law" and "other norms", and therefore his concept of law was "practically useless". Hesse prefers a definition which focuses on the courts as decision-makers defining "law", but also allows popular understanding to count as law insofar as it can be seconded by the courts (Hesse 2004, 25 f. and 28 f.). Hesse's (2004, 25) definition reads:

"Law should be understood as the totality of rules meant to serve as standards for an evaluation oriented towards the legal-illegal-scheme of facts, actions and

[18] Rottleuthner 2005, 143, referring to Kelsen 1915/2003, 34, italicisation in the original.

[19] Rottleuthner (2014, 202-203) has traced where Criminal Law is mentioned in Ehrlich's writings. According to Rottleuthner, it is strange that Ehrlich did not discuss a "bottom-up" development of Criminal Law, following the public's desire to have certain crimes punished.

failures to act, and which are seen as law by state courts or could be seen as such." (My translation, SM)

Like other authors, Hesse states that defining "law" is not a question of "truth" but of "usefulness", and the "understanding of law" today is "primarily" professional and academic (Hesse 2004, 23 f.). While lay people are not necessarily sidelined, law nevertheless is ultimately and primarily in the hands of legal practitioners and scholars. As a consequence, Hesse does not devote much space to a discussion of Ehrlich's work.

Thomas Raiser: living law, judge-made law and codified law are equally important

In contrast to Hesse, Thomas Raiser devotes a whole chapter to Ehrlich, complete with a photo in the early editions. Such prominent treatment is otherwise only given to Marx and Engels, Durkheim, Weber, Geiger, Luhmann and Helmut Schelsky[20]. Earlier editions of Raiser's book were even titled *Das lebende Recht*. Nevertheless, the reader finds a critical discussion of Ehrlich.

According to Raiser (2007, 83) Ehrlich's social science positivism by now seems somewhat outdated. And indeed, Ehrlich went about his fieldwork without the methodological finesse of later generations. Current epistemology would tend to emphasize how unlikely it is that one can just detect socio-legal facts, and would emphasize the fact that theoretical assumptions and the methods chosen exert a pivotal influence on "findings". In defence of Ehrlich, however, it can be said that sociology as a proper academic subject did not really exist at his time (Hagen 2013, 56; Ehrlich 1912/1967b, 61 and 67). Even today, social scientists still occasionally declare they can approach fieldwork without theoretical prejudice and that their analysis will be guided solely by their observations. Ehrlich (1936/2002, 506) indeed concludes his "Fundamental Principles" with an acknowledgement that methods will always continue to evolve.

Relations of dominance and possession do appear in Ehrlich's work: law can be based on these as well as e.g. on voluntary agreement, but such

20 Schelsky became an extremely influential social democratic intellectual after 1945, and later morphed into an "anti-sociologist", prosecuting left-leaning sociologists of law that he thought were attacking the foundations of society (Schelsky 1975).

ideas are less developed (Raiser 2007, 83 f.). The darker sides of law which attract a great deal of attention in public debates and socio-legal scholarship are indeed not stressed by Ehrlich. An optimistic, perhaps even sympathetic, undertone is felt in many of his discussions of the living law. He aimed to alert lawyers to "the steady ordered walk of life" (Ehrlich 1912/1967b, 69).

While Ehrlich's ideas were rejected by German lawyers, according to Raiser they nevertheless influenced jurisprudence "on the quiet" (Raiser 2007, 85). Legal decision-makers on a daily basis approach "legal gaps" by filling them with their own knowledge of the social context. However, they rarely acknowledge this. For Raiser (2007, 295), living law, judge-made law and codified law are equally important. As a teacher of Labour and Business Law, he could easily arrive at this conclusion. When it comes to the criteria for the validity of law, Raiser advocates that acceptance and coercion should both be employed (Raiser 2007, 295). In this his view reflects the teachings of both Weber and Ehrlich. Not surprisingly, Raiser comes to the conclusion that Sociology of Law and legal dogmatics "need each other and are also the equally important complementary elements" of an encompassing legal science (Raiser 1986, 1).

Susanne Baer: every-day legal pluralism

The latest introduction comes from Susanne Baer, now a judge at the Federal Constitutional Court. Her book is intended to serve as an invitation to students to learn about those subjects that might be a foundation for Critical Jurisprudence, such as Feminist Studies, Social Anthropology, Queer Studies, or Law and Literature. She settled for the book title "Sociology of Law" as this is a well-established brand[21]. In the context of questions such as: What is law?, What is Sociology? What are facts of law?, Baer (2011, 28-30 and 32 f.) introduces the Kelsen-Ehrlich-debate. She agrees with Ehrlich that jurisprudence inevitably mixes "Is and Ought" (Baer 2011, 34).

Baer's introduction departs from the usual weary discussion of legal pluralism among German legal scholars which so negatively affects the response to Ehrlich's work. To start with, Ehrlich is set in the context of a

[21] Book presentation at the conference "Der Kampf ums Recht", Vienna, 1-3 September 2011.

broad discussion of legal pluralism, which includes Teubner, Engle Merry, Podgórecki, Sorokin and others (Baer 2011, 88 ff.). Baer (2011, 100) strikes an almost sympathetic chord when she emphasizes "every-day legal pluralism" (*alltäglicher Rechtspluralismus*). Furthermore, she offers students an example likely to be close to their daily experience. With the pullover gift example, Baer (2011, 95) speaks of remedies for dissatisfied customers offered by different non-state regulations. Soon after this, she discusses the rules which are routinely used by legal decision makers to deal with legal pluralism (such as subsidiarity, Baer 2011, 101 f.). All these seem, however, examples of legal pluralism which could be effortlessly subsumed into "monistic" (in contrast to "pluralistic") legal thought (Röhl and Machura 2013, 112).

Finally there is discussion of developments in Baer's book which would have been unheard of in Ehrlich's time. One of these is the widespread use of patterns of practice (e.g. *Musterverträge*) which are developed by lawyers. In addition, large international law firms wield huge influence in the world of law (Baer 2011, 100). Ehrlich had assumed that "at all times" most laws developed in society itself, rather than being made by lawyers in a separate sphere. We will turn to this assumption in the concluding chapter.

Klaus F. Röhl's critique of "Ehrlich's panjurism"

Klaus F. Röhl's *Rechtssoziologie* stands out from other German introductions to Sociology of Law because of the sheer depth of content covered, and because it aimed to reflect the international state of the subject. For Röhl, law has severed its links with its social basis and has become an instrument of the state, even "an aspect of the state", and is understood as such by the people (Röhl 1987, 32 f. and 219 f.). In a later publication Röhl argues:' 'Law is no longer based on the experiences and consciousness of the public. It is created and administered by a political elite working with a legally trained bureaucracy" (Röhl 1991a, 471, my translation). He agrees with Weber: Law under the influence of a legally trained administration has become an independent system separated from social morality and from the economy (Röhl 1991b, 474).

Ehrlich had a "distorted" view as to the ability of the state to implement law: it could actually be very successful in this undertaking. Furthermore, the state does not necessarily need to resort to coercion. Ehrlich himself would have correctly said that in daily life a lot of law is generally followed without problems (Röhl 1987, 33 and 533-535; Ehrlich 1936/2002, 162 f.). The validity of norms results from sanction-validity as well as from behavioural validity (Röhl 1987, 215). Thus, the state may enforce its law, but that is only part of what is happening.

Ehrlich's main thesis is seen as "tautological", and results in *Panjurismus* (Röhl 1987, 216). The concept of law loses its distinctive power as jurisprudence becomes the science devoted to all the social orders. Ziegert (1998, 123) mentions Röhl's critique and reiterates that panjurism would be a consequence of Ehrlich's view of law as the inner order of associations, which requires lawyers to take this into account. But Ehrlich would not have had a theory of social differentiation.

According to Röhl's *Rechtssoziologie*, a pluralistic concept of law is wrong as it excludes so little (Röhl 1987, 219). In addition, there have been key developments over the decades. Today law changes much more quickly than in Ehrlich's time, and it is less in conflict with customs and morals (Röhl 1987, 275). Furthermore, the amount of customs that are practiced ("cake of customs") has been reduced under the influence of the law (Röhl 1987, 275).

The German economist Adolph Wagner famously declared that the modern state would play an ever-growing role, taking over more and more responsibilities. Max Weber (1917/1968, 1403) uttered gloomy formulations such as: "In view of the growing indispensability of the state bureaucracy and its corresponding increase in power, how can there be any guarantee that any powers will remain which can check and effectively control the tremendous influence of this stratum?" According to Röhl (1987, 550), Ehrlich mistakenly assumed that the highpoint of state expansion had been already reached or even passed (Ehrlich 1936/2002, 139).

Röhl later drafted a general jurisprudence *Allgemeine Rechtslehre* (recently in its third edition co-authored by Hans Christian Röhl). The book is written from a classic liberal perspective. It covers the law of the modern territorial state and how it has changed because of Europeanization and Globalisation (Röhl and Röhl 2008, 7). It "takes the point of view of official law, and thus from the outset makes no attempt to incorporate legal subcultures, and what has been called social law by Eugen Ehrlich" (Röhl and Röhl 2008, 7, my translation). To be more precise, what is adopted is the perspective of the courts. They are at the centre of the law and therefore their perspective is the perspective of the law (Röhl and Röhl 2008, 8).

Ehrlich tried to replace jurisprudence with social science and – the perennial problem of sociological jurisprudence – confused "Is and Ought" (Röhl and Röhl 2008, 639 f. and 256). In his *Rechtssoziologie*, Röhl (1987, 73) suggested that lawyers typically ask "What should we do?", whereas Sociology of Law has to concentrate on empirical analysis and on theoretical understanding. Max Weber's (1914/1973) idea of "value-free science" emphasising the difference between value-driven decisions and scientific research could have informed this view.

Röhl and Röhl (2008, 209) have no problem with Ehrlich's concept of "soft legal pluralism" – as they call it, to distinguish his approach from more radical ones – a concept which can be regarded effortlessly as a delegated state definition of law, or as "private legal ordering". They (2008, 211) agree with Ehrlich that law can be different from what actually happens, and also, that state law often takes its content from society. In recent years, the state has as a matter of policy allowed and facilitated the growth of private legal regimes (Röhl and Röhl 2008, 213). Greater legal pluralism appears as a political strategy. Commemorating the centenary of the publication of Ehrlich's *Grundlegung der Soziologie des Rechts*, Röhl emphasized that the debate on legal pluralism would be central to Sociology of Law today and this would be the legacy of Ehrlich (Röhl and Machura 2013). There would be no turning back, though some interpretations of legal pluralism would clearly overstate their case.

According to Röhl and Röhl (2008, 211), constructing the unity of the legal order would be the main purpose of jurisprudence. This task is becoming ever more difficult. In a recent manuscript Röhl (2012, 9) argued that in the process of social modernisation the legal system would have to "deal with the idea of equality"[22] and would have to shape itself to work as the infrastructure for the economy, and as an instrument of control for government and administration. Furthermore, ideas about universal rights are institutionalised on a global level. Locally, however, these developments would be accompanied by a "return to national, indigenous or religious legal traditions" (Röhl 2012, 15). Yet, "social law" would "often be reac-

[22] Rehbinder closes his own treatment of legal pluralism with the remark that law, when it comes to its ultimate meaning, is directed towards "order and equality" (Rehbinder 1995, 251).

tionary, discriminatory and undemocratic" (Röhl and Röhl 2008, 211 and 215). These remarks reflect a wider concern that has been voiced in public debates. Analysing the situation in South Africa, Nadine Gordimer (2012) for example, speaks about "barbaric elements" in traditional law.

Conclusions

In the latest volume commemorating Ehrlich, it is said that the founder of the Sociology of Law unfortunately remained "largely an unknown" (Barta 2013, 17), that his achievements "had fallen into oblivion" (Rehbinder 2013, 43), and that "at least" in Austria, he remained "on the periphery of the academic bustle" (Hagen 2013, 45). This is certainly not the whole picture, though it characterizes general and applied jurisprudence. But Ehrlich's key insights have become part of the canon of topics mentioned in Sociology of Law introductions and his ideas are also taught in Sociology of Law lectures in German law schools. The emphasis is certainly put on the concept of "living law". "Conservative legal scholars" take exception to Ehrlich's definition of law and his understanding of jurisprudence. By "conservative", I do not refer to party political inclination, but rather to a sense of pride in the advances of German legal dogmatic scholarship. This was challenged by Ehrlich at the beginning of the 20th century and one can still sense a degree of hostility, if not against Sociology of Law as a whole, then against Ehrlich. The man has become a symbol as has his home province. Tellingly, Gunther Teubner (1996) attracted world-wide attention to his systems-theoretical account of legal pluralism by using the expression "global Bukowina". Ehrlich's name and the place symbolise a challenge to a strand of legal thought that assumes a unified and codified law of the nation state, administered by legal professionals.

Generally, Ehrlich stands accused of illicitly mixing Is and Ought. He may actually be guilty of this. It may have been a consequence of law, morals and every-day practice not being separated outside of the state-law-sphere. It might therefore have been inevitable that Ehrlich's research into the social orders of associations would not produce clear-cut terminology. Furthermore, discussion of Is and Ought can become very unclear, and these terms can refer to very different things, as Rottleuthner pointed out in striking detail. However, at the heart of the accusation is the insistence of almost all legal scholars on a state-centred definition of "law". This has the advantage of drawing relatively simply a line between law and non-law. Law is laid down in codes, and is what the state courts accept as legally valid. For the modern nation state and its outliers on the transnational level, the definition works. It allows for a large area of private legal ordering and of other living law to be included. In daily practice, judges and other legal decision-makers use a truncated version of the solution that Ehrlich suggested for "genuine gaps in the codified law". They certainly do not conduct a systematic field survey or call in sociologists as expert witnesses, but they use their knowledge of the underlying social constellations to the best of their ability. Just occasionally systematic surveys are commissioned, for instance in disputes about brand copyright, but that's far from being routine. Legal decision-makers do occasionally dwell in the grey areas between the supposedly clear-cut categories of Is and Ought.

The social sciences and jurisprudence have grown beyond recognition since the times of Ehrlich, Weber and Kelsen. Mega-trends in law include a differentiation into more and more specialised areas, as well as a closing of the gap between Continental-European and case-law systems. Social and human rights have been integrated into law on an unprecedented scale, both by parliaments and national courts and by inter- and transnational actors. Legal training and the practice of law have to deal with the ever more complex sets of rules. Elements of Sociology/Social Science now form part of general education and even – to varying degree – legal education. Legal professionals and the courts have become specialised, and with this specialisation comes the expectation of a clearer view of the problems underlying a dispute. Training comparable to Ehrlich's field seminar for practitioners would however still be hard to find. The participation of lay judges and expert lay judges, as well as the recruitment of personnel from wider social backgrounds may also be counted as strategies to provide the legal system with a better knowledge of the living law.

For decades, justices in the German Federal Constitutional Court have often been recruited from the ranks of *Rechtssoziologie* teachers in law faculties. At any given time over the last decades there have been a group of them in the most powerful German court. Other higher German courts also have judges with credentials in Sociology of Law. Even if the courts do not usually explicitly make social science arguments in their rulings, sociological jurisprudence is not a stranger to legal institutions in Germany.

The legislature has widely conformed to Ehrlich's advice to study the living law to improve the codified law. The political machinery holds in its arsenal a wide array of procedures to draw in knowledge prior to legislating and to allow those affected a degree of participation. Expert social science and legal knowledge is systematically called in when laws are being drafted. Political decision-makers, including ministerial staff, themselves often have a high degree of expertise in their areas of work.

With only one exception the introductions to Sociology of Law were written by the "old guard", who are now retired. They are all lawyers and almost all of them qualified as career judges at a time when the nation state was not questioned within jurisprudence. The combination of generation and of traditional legal training might in part explain why most have little sympathy for the concept of legal pluralism. And indeed, it can be argued that no substitute for the state has been found to institutionally guarantee legal order in the last instance. Younger socio-legal scholars are more in favour of legal pluralism and this is reflected in the book by Susanne Baer. At her institute in Berlin she collaborated with junior members of staff and a postgraduate network (Berliner Arbeitskreis Rechtswirklichkeit) and for years they have organized talks on legal issues related to internationalisation and multiculturalism (Machura 2012, 518-519). Her book suggests that legal pluralism is already part of every-day life and that German law has developed ways to deal with conflicts resulting from it. Similarly, according to Klaus F. Röhl and others, "soft legal pluralism" à la Ehrlich constitutes no challenge for 21st century legal doctrine (Röhl and Röhl 2008, Röhl and Machura 2013).

Finally, what about Ehrlich's thesis in the *Foreword* of his living law book, that the bulk of law is at all times developed within society, that is, not by the state (and not by lawyers)? Does this still apply? Admittedly, it is difficult to answer this question unless one uses a narrow, state-centred definition of law. An attempt to operationalize Ehrlich's seemingly straightforward hypothesis encounters numerous problems. To begin with, who would have the necessary information? How would one take account of different countries with their particular legal cultures and different legal institutions? Certainly, life today in the "developed countries" appears much more influenced by professional legal actors. Since Ehrlich's time, the number of lawyers has multiplied, especially if one counts all those with some sort of legal training who are employed in numerous functions and sectors of society. As a new phenomenon, large law firms have developed, operating world-wide, and they shape the contracts people need to enter into when, for example, using software. They are also increasingly involved in drafting laws. Specialised lawyers work with NGOs and international institutions within global legal regimes. Landlords, on-line retailers, and high street-shops have their customers sign complicated terms which have been drafted by legal advisers. Ehrlich (1936/2002, 497-498) knew about similar contracts at his time but characteristically insisted that it is more important "to deal peacefully with people", to get on with the other party than to execute contracts rigidly. Where would the dividing line be between professional legal influence and legal doctrine on the one hand, and what one might call "autochthone" living law emanating from the "associations" on the other? Admittedly, non-lawyers still often decide whether there should be professional legal action broadly conceived and thus shape law (Fuchs 2013, 125-131). The introductions discussed in this article have by no means exhausted the consequences of cultural globalisation (Machura and Ulbrich 2001). Avid viewers of TV series and law films are confronted with legal matters and problems from very different legal systems and unfamiliar social worlds. The way people think about law and how they conduct legal dealings can be changed by all of this. Finally, with the spread of internet media it is apparent that society has become what Luhmann (1993, 571-572) called "world society" based on communication, and what Ehrlich (1912/1992, 10) called a "society encompassing the whole mankind" based on cultured sentiments.

References

Baer, Susanne (2011), *Rechtssoziologie*. Baden-Baden: Nomos.

Barta, Heinz (2013), Einleitung in die 5. Tagung "Rechtstatsachenforschung? Heute", 14. und 15. Juni 2012. Erinnerung an Eugen Ehrlich. In: Heinz Barta, Michael Ganner and Caroline Voithofer, (eds.), *Zu Eugen Ehrlichs 150. Geburtstag und 90. Todestag*. Innsbruck: Innsbruck University Press, pp. 17-36.

Broucek, Miriam (2013), Eugen Ehrlich und sein Vorwurf an die eigengesetzliche "juristische Logik" der Pandektistik und Begriffsjurisprudenz. In: Heinz Barta, Michael Ganner and Caroline Voithofer (eds.), *Zu Eugen Ehrlichs 150. Geburtstag und 90. Todestag*. Innsbruck: Innsbruck University Press, pp. 89-100.

Dobler, Philipp (2013), Die Kontroverse zwischen Eugen Ehrlich und Hans Kelsen. In: Heinz Barta, Michael Ganner and Caroline Voithofer (eds.), *Zu*

Eugen Ehrlichs 150. Geburtstag und 90. Todestag. Innsbruck: Innsbruck University Press, pp. 177-190.

Dux, Günter (1978), *Rechtssoziologie: eine Einführung*. Stuttgart: Kohlhammer.

Ehrlich, Eugen (1903/1967), Freie Rechtsfindung und freie Rechtswissenschaft. Reprinted in: Eugen Ehrlich, *Recht und Leben*, edited by Manfred Rehbinder. Berlin: Duncker & Humblot, pp. 170-202.

Ehrlich, Eugen (1911/1967), Ein Institut für lebendes Recht. Reprinted in: Eugen Ehrlich, *Recht und Leben*, edited by Manfred Rehbinder. Berlin: Duncker & Humblot, pp. 28-42.

Ehrlich, Eugen (1912/1967a), Das lebende Recht der Völker der Bukowina. Reprinted in: Eugen Ehrlich, *Recht und Leben*, edited by Manfred Rehbinder. Berlin: Duncker & Humblot, pp. 43-60.

Ehrlich, Eugen (1912/1967b), Gutachten über die Frage: Was kann geschehen, um bei der Ausbildung (vor oder nach Abschluß des Universitätsstudiums) das Verständnis des Juristen für psychologische, wirtschaftliche und soziologische Fragen in erhöhtem Maße zu fördern? Reprinted in: Eugen Ehrlich, *Recht und Leben*, edited by Manfred Rehbinder. Berlin: Duncker & Humblot, pp. 61-79.

Ehrlich, Eugen (1912/1992), Der Staat, die Gesellschaft und ihre Ordnung. *Zeitschrift für Rechtssoziologie* 13:3-15.

Ehrlich, Eugen (1913/1967), *Grundlegung der Soziologie des Rechts*, 3rd edition. Berlin: Duncker & Humblot.

Ehrlich, Eugen (1915/1916), Montesquieu and Sociological Jurisprudence. *Harvard Law Review* 29:582-600.

Ehrlich, Eugen (1916/2007), Die Aufgaben der Sozialpolitik im österreichischen Osten (Juden- und Bauernfrage), 4th edition. Reprinted in: Eugen Ehrlich, *Politische Schriften*, edited by Manfred Rehbinder. Berlin: Duncker & Humblot, pp. 191-200.

Ehrlich, Eugen (1918), *Die juristische Logik*. Tübingen: Mohr.

Ehrlich, Eugen (1920/21/2007), Über das 'lebende Recht'. Reprinted in: Eugen Ehrlich, *Politische Schriften*, edited by Manfred Rehbinder. Berlin: Duncker & Humblot, pp. 191-200.

Ehrlich, Eugen (1922/1992), Testament. Printed in: *Zeitschrift für Rechtssoziologie* 13:1-2.

Ehrlich, Eugen (1922), The Sociology of Law. *Harvard Law Review* 36:130-145.

Ehrlich, Eugen (1936/2002), *Fundamental Principles of the Sociology of Law*, translated by Walter L. Moll. New Brunswick/London: Transaction.

Eppinger, Monica (2009), Governing in the Vernacular: Eugen Ehrlich and Late Habsburg Ethnography. In: Marc Herthog (ed.), *Living Law. Reconsidering Eugen Ehrlich.* Oxford: Hart, pp. 21-47.

Fuchs, Walter (2013), Eugen Ehrlich und der Rechtspluralismus. In: Heinz Barta, Michael Ganner and Caroline Voithofer (eds.), *Zu Eugen Ehrlichs 150. Geburtstag und 90. Todestag.* Innsbruck: Innsbruck University Press, pp. 115-134.

Geiger, Theodor (1947/1987), *Vorstudien zu einer Soziologie des Rechts*, 4th edition, edited by Manfred Rehbinder. Berlin: Duncker & Humblot.

Girtler, Roland (1976), *Rechtssoziologie – Thesen und Möglichkeiten*. Munich: Fink.

Gordimer, Nadine (2012), Die Lady mit dem Löwenherzen, interview, *Neue Zürcher Zeitung*, 20 September 2012, p. 23.

Hagen, Johann Josef (2013), Eugen Ehrlich, der Begründer der Rechtssoziologie. In: Heinz Barta, Michael Ganner and Caroline Voithofer (eds.), *Zu Eugen Ehrlichs 150. Geburtstag und 90. Todestag*. Innsbruck: Innsbruck University Press, pp. 45-58.

Hesse, Hans Albrecht (2004), *Einführung in die Rechtssoziologie*. Wiesbaden: VS-Verlag für Sozialwissenschaften.

Hirsch, Ernst E. (1984), *Rechtssoziologie für Juristen*. Berlin: Duncker und Humblot.

Hirsch, Ernst E., and Rehbinder, Manfred (eds.) (1967/1971), *Studien und Materialien zur Rechtssoziologie*. Kölner Zeitschrift für Soziologie und Sozialpsychologie, Sonderheft Nr. 11, 2nd edition. Opladen: Westdeutscher Verlag.

Kelsen, Hans (1915/2003), Eine Grundlegung der Rechtssoziologie. Reprinted in: Klaus Lüderssen (ed.), *Rechtssoziologie und Rechtswissenschaft*. Baden-Baden: Nomos, pp. 3-54.

Kißler, Leo (1984a), *Recht und Gesellschaft*. Opladen: Leske und Budrich.

Kißler, Leo (1984b), *Rechtssoziologie für die Rechtspraxis*. Neuwied/Darmstadt: Luchterhand.

Langer, Thomas (2004), *Die Verbildlichung der juristischen Ausbildungsliteratur*. Berlin: Tenea.

Lüderssen, Klaus (2003), Einführung. In: Klaus Lüderssen (ed.), *Rechtssoziologie und Rechtswissenschaft*. Baden-Baden: Nomos, pp. V–XXI.

Lüderssen, Klaus (ed., 2003), *Rechtssoziologie und Rechtswissenschaft*. Baden-Baden: Nomos.

Luhmann, Niklas (1993), *Das Recht der Gesellschaft*. Frankfurt on Main: Suhrkamp.

Machura, Stefan (2012), The German Sociology of Law: A Case of Path Dependency. *International Journal of Law in Context* 8:506-523.

Machura, Stefan, and Ulbrich, Stefan (2001), Globalizing the Hollywood Courtroom Drama. *Journal of Law and Society* 28: 117-132.

Miriburg, Georg (2013), Alles was Recht ist – Überlegungen zu den Rechtsbegriffen bei Eugen Ehrlich und Max Weber. In: Heinz Barta, Michael Ganner and Caroline Voithofer (eds.), *Zu Eugen Ehrlichs 150. Geburtstag und 90. Todestag*. Innsbruck: Innsbruck University Press, pp. 207-217.

Porsche-Ludwig, Markus (2011), *Eugen Ehrlich interkulturell gelesen*. Nordhausen: Traugott Bautz.

Raiser, Thomas (1986), Rechtssoziologie und Rechtsdogmatik. In: Klaus F. Röhl (ed.), *Ergänzbares Lexikon des Rechts*, Vol. 1, group 3 'Rechtssoziologie' (no. 210), loose-leaf edition. Neuwied: Luchterhand.

Raiser, Thomas (1995), *Das lebende Recht*, 2nd edition. Baden-Baden: Nomos.

Raiser, Thomas (2007), *Grundlagen der Rechtssoziologie*. Tübingen: Mohr Siebeck (6th edition, Tübingen: Mohr-Siebeck 2013).

Rehbinder, Manfred (1967), Einleitung. In: Eugen Ehrlich, *Recht und Leben*, edited by Manfred Rehbinder. Berlin: Duncker & Humblot, pp. 7-9.

Rehbinder, Manfred (1986), *Die Begründung der Rechtssoziologie durch Eugen Ehrlich*, 2nd edition. Berlin: Duncker and Humblot.

Rehbinder, Manfred (1995), Rechtspluralismus und Rechtseinheit. In: Manfred Rehbinder, *Abhandlungen zur Rechtssoziologie*. Berlin: Duncker & Humblot, pp. 234-251.

Rehbinder, Manfred (2003a), Aus den letzten Jahren im Leben und Schaffen von Eugen Ehrlich. In: Dieter Dölling (ed.), *Jus Humanum. Grundlagen des Rechts und Strafrecht. Festschrift für Ernst-Joachim Lampe*. Berlin: Duncker & Humblot, pp. 199-210.

Rehbinder, Manfred (2003b), *Rechtssoziologie*, 5th edition. Munich: Beck (7th edition 2009).

Rehbinder, Manfred (2005a), Der Pluralismus des Rechts im Zeitalter der Globalisierung. Zum Rechtsbegriff in der Rechtssoziologie. *Problemi Filosofiyi Prawa* 3, No. 1-2:227-232.

Rehbinder, Manfred (2005b), Eugen Ehrlich als Rechtslehrer. *Problemi Filosofiyi Prawa* 3, No. 1-2:140-146.

Rehbinder, Manfred (2005c), Eugen Ehrlichs Seminar für Lebendes Recht: eine Einrichtung für die Weiterbildung von Rechtspraktikern. *Problemi Filosofiyi Prawa* 3, No. 1-2:135-139.

Rehbinder, Manfred (2007a), Die Politischen Schriften des Rechtssoziologen Eugen Ehrlich auf dem Hintergrund seines bewegten Lebens. *Anuarul Institutului de Istorie "G. Bariţiu" din Cluj-Napoca* 46:269-281.

Rehbinder, Manfred (2007b), Einleitung des Herausgebers. In: Eugen Ehrlich, *Politische Schriften*, edited by Manfred Rehbinder. Berlin: Duncker & Humblot 2007, pp. 7-16.

Rehbinder, Manfred (2008), Die Rechts- und Staatswissenschaftliche Fakultät der Franz-Josephs-Universität in Czernowitz, ihr Beitrag zur Erforschung des Rechts in einer multikulturellen Gesellschaft. *Anuarul Institutului de Istorie "G. Bariţiu" din Cluj-Napoc* 47:199-218.

Rehbinder, Manfred (2013), Valtazar Bogišić in der Sicht des Rechtssoziologen Eugen Ehrlich. In: Heinz Barta, Michael Ganner and Caroline Voithofer (eds.). *Zu Eugen Ehrlichs 150. Geburtstag und 90. Todestag*. Innsbruck: Innsbruck University Press, pp. 37-43.

Röhl, Klaus F. (ed., loose-leaf edition), *Ergänzbares Lexikon des Rechts. Rechtssoziologie*. Neuwied: Luchterhand.

Röhl, Klaus F. (1987), *Rechtssoziologie*. Köln: Heyman. Also available online: http://www.ruhr-uni-bochum.de/rsozinfo/, last accessed 21 November 2012.

Röhl, Klaus F. (1991a), Recht (als soziologischer Begriff). In: Gerd Reinhold et. al. (eds.), *Soziologie-Lexikon*. Munich: Oldenbourg, pp. 469-472.

Röhl, Klaus F. (1991b), Rechtssoziologie. In: Gerd Reinhold et. al. (eds.), *Soziologie-Lexikon*. Munich: Oldenbourg, pp. 472-475.

Röhl, Klaus F. (2012), Entwicklungshilfe durch Recht und die Konvergenzthese. Manuscript printed in: Michael Bäuerle, Philipp Dann und Astrid Wallrabenstein (eds.), *Demokratie-Perspektiven. Festschrift for Brun-Otto Bryde*. Tübingen: Mohr Siebeck 2013, pp. 675-710.

Röhl, Klaus F., and Machura, Stefan (2013), 100 Jahre Rechtssoziologie: Eugen Ehrlichs Rechtspluralismus heute. *Juristenzeitung* 68: 1117-1128.

Röhl, Klaus F., and Röhl, Hans Christian (2008), *Allgemeine Rechtslehre*, 3rd edition. Köln: Heymann.

Rottleuthner, Hubert (1981), *Rechtstheorie und Rechtssoziologie*. Freiburg/Munich: Alber.

Rottleuthner, Hubert (1984), Rechtstheoretische Probleme der Soziologie des Rechts. Die Kontroverse zwischen Hans Kelsen und Eugen Ehrlich (1915/1917). In: Werner Krawietz and Helmut Schelsky (eds.), *Rechtssystem und gesellschaftliche Basis bei Hans Kelsen*, Rechtstheorie Beiheft 5. Berlin: Duncker and Humblot, pp. 521-551.

Rottleuthner, Hubert (1986), Drei Rechtssoziologien: Eugen Ehrlich, Hugo Sinzheimer, Max Weber, manuscript. Printed in: Erk Volkmar Heyen, Hrsg., *Historische Soziologie der Rechtswissenschaft*, Ius Commune Sonderheft 26. Frankfurt at the Main: Klostermann, pp. 227-252.

Rottleuthner, Hubert (1987), *Einführung in die Rechtssoziologie*. Darmstadt: Wissenschaftliche Buchgesellschaft.

Rottleuthner, Hubert (2005), *Foundations of Law*. Dordrecht: Springer.

Rottleuthner, Hubert (2014), Das lebende Recht bei Eugen Ehrlich und Ernst Hirsch. *Zeitschrift für Rechtssoziologie* 33:191-206.

Ryffel, Hans (1974), *Rechtssoziologie. Eine systematische Orientierung*. Neuwied/Berlin: Luchterhand.

Schelsky, Helmut (1975), *Die Arbeit tun die anderen. Klassenkampf und Priesterherrschaft der Intellektuellen*, 2nd edition. Opladen: Westdeutscher Verlag.

Struck, Gerhard (2011), *Rechtssoziologie*, Baden-Baden: Nomos.

Teubner, Gunther (1996), Global Bukowina: Legal Pluralism in the World Society. In: Gunther Teubner (ed.), *Global Law Without a State*. Dartmouth: Aldershot, pp. 3-28. Available at SSRN: http://ssrn.com/abstract=896478, accessed 24 November 2012.

Treiber, Hubert (2011), Insights into Weber's Sociology of Law. In: Knut Papendorf, Stefan Machura and Kristian Andenæs (eds.), *Understanding Law in Society*. Zurich/Berlin, pp. 21-79.

Vogl, Stefan (2003), *Soziale Gesetzgebungspolitik, freie Rechtsfindung und soziologische Rechtswissenschaft bei Eugen Ehrlich*. Baden-Baden: Nomos.

Weber, Max (1895/1993), "Römisches" und "deutsches" Recht. Reprinted in: Max Weber, *Gesamtausgabe*, Vol. I/4, edited by Horst Baier et al. Tübingen: Mohr, pp. 526-534.

Weber, Max (1913/1988), Über einige Kategorien der verstehenden Soziologie. In: Max Weber, *Gesammelte Aufsätze zur Wissenschaftslehre*, edited by Johannes Winckelmann. Tübingen: Mohr, pp. 427-474.

Weber, Max (1914/1973), Der Sinn der "Wertfreiheit" der Sozialwissenschaften. In: Max Weber, *Soziologie. Universalgeschichtliche Analysen. Politik*, edited by Michael Baumgarten. Stuttgart: Kröner, pp. 263-310.

Weber, Max (1917/1968), Parliament and Government in a Reconstructed Germany. In: Max Weber, *Economy and Society; an Outline of Interpretive Sociology*, translated by Ephraim Fischoff et al., edited by Guenther Roth and Claus Wittich. New York: Bedminster Press, pp. 1381-1469.

Weber, Max (1922/1968), *Economy and Society; an Outline of Interpretive Sociology*, translated by Ephraim Fischoff et al., edited by Guenther Roth and Claus Wittich. New York: Bedminster Press.

Ziegert, K. Alex (1998), A Note on Eugen Ehrlich and the Production of Legal Knowledge. *Sydney Law Review* 20:108-125.

Zippelius, Reinhard (1980), *Gesellschaft und Recht: Grundbegriffe der Rechts- und Staatssoziologie*. Munich: Beck.

Zippelius, Reinhard (2012), *Grundbegriffe der Rechts- und Staatssoziologie*. 3rd edition, Tübingen: Mohr Siebeck.

'Living Law' as a Political and Analytical Concept

Franz and Keebet VON BENDA-BECKMANN

Introduction

When Ehrlich developed his ideas about law and legal sociology at the turn of the 20th century, he was one of the first to warn that what can be considered 'law' is not necessarily what is defined as law by legislators and state court judges or law professors; and that the significance of any law cannot be deduced from its normative content (Ehrlich 1989/1913; 1911; 2002). As one of the most important forerunners of a non-dogmatic, sociological approach to law, he figures in all major introductions to the sociology of law, besides Max Weber and the American legal realists, and for many German-reading scholars, also besides Theodor Geiger.[1] Similarly, Ehrlich is a key reference in legal anthropology and for studies problematizing legal pluralism (see e.g. Rouland 1994, Griffiths 1986). While reference to Ehrlich as a precursor of the sociology of law has always been frequent, for a long time his work was not discussed in detail. During the past fifteen years there has been a remarkable renaissance of his work in academic discussions that inquire to what extent Ehrlich might be important for current debates. This interest was triggered in 1997 by Teubner's article on the *Global Bukovina*, in which he translated Ehrlich's ideas into the transnational field of global law. The new English language edition of 2002 (after the edition of 1936) with the long introduction by Klaus Ziegert also stimulated such discussion. In 2006, Marc Hertogh and Marc Galanter organized a workshop in Oñati that was entirely devoted to Ehrlich's work (Hertogh 2009), as is the present workshop here in Oslo. However, and perhaps even more interestingly, the term 'living law' as a legal concept has also become incorporated into official legal systems, especially the purpose of being applied in courts, for instance in Indonesia, Japan and, recently, in South Africa. This has generated new discussions of both an analytic-doctrinal and legal-political character (Bennett and Bleazard 2009, Himonga 2005, Hellum et al. 2011).

1 See Rehbinder 1967, Ziegert 2002, Cotterrell 2006, Hertogh 2009, Nelken 1984, 2009; Banakar 2003.

The acknowledgement of Ehrlich as one of the few thinkers who did not make his definition of law dependent on the state has always been part of our academic writing. We also started out from the idea that other social formations – associations, *Verbände*, the relation- and interaction networks called semi-autonomous social fields by Moore (1973) – could create and shape law; and that indeed documents were important sources of law in which law was, in our terminology, 'concretized' (F. von Benda-Beckmann 1979; K. von Benda-Beckmann 1984). But we never made an attempt to use 'living law' as an analytical concept. Our interest concerned the significance the term acquired in academic treatises, or as a normative category in legal texts, in judicial decision-making and in legal politics in countries like Indonesia.

The term 'living law' is used in many different ways. It is used as a descriptive and analytical device to identify as law specific normative rules, principles and decisions, that is, those actually emerging and being followed in social life. But it is also used as a normative category through which these rules, principles and procedures are elevated to a level where it is, or should be, regarded as valid and applicable law in the realm of the official state legal order. The 'living' character of law at times seems to be the main justification for applying certain rules in decision-making processes, if not the reason for calling it law. This multitude of meanings poses a problem if one wants to consider whether Ehrlich's concept 'living law' might serve as an analytical tool. In this contribution we will therefore first dwell briefly on the different meanings of 'living law' in theoretical writings. We then move on to instances in which the concept has become part of doctrinal and pragmatic law application. In the last part of our talk we shall explain why we think that 'living law' is not less, but also not more than an inspiring metaphor that contains a useful warning: that it is important to study whether, why, and how the term is used in processes of legislation and court decision-making; and that it serves as a mirror that challenges us to revisit our own conceptual preoccupations and the assumptions on which they rest. However, as we will explain, the term is too imprecise to serve as a powerful descriptive and analytical device.

Living law in legal theory and social scientific approaches to law

To understand Ehrlich's project it is as well to contemplate briefly what he was arguing against. In the last chapter of his book *Fundamental Principles of the Sociology of Law*, called *Methods of the Sociology of Law* (Ehrlich 2002, 486-506) he criticizes the prevailing school of legal sciences for making what were in his eyes the following erroneous assumptions:

1. The totality of law is to be found in legal propositions
2. All legal propositions are to be found in the statutes
3. All that is necessary to know the law of the present time is to:
   (a) Gather material from the statutes
   (b) Ascertain the content by one's own interpretation
   (c) Utilize this interpretation for the purposes of juristic literature and judicial decision. What fields are studied and what principles interpreted depends on the individual interest of the analyst.
4. Occasionally legal propositions may arise independently of statute – an example would be 'usage' in commercial law.
5. Legal propositions of the present time are rooted in the past. Ehrlich argues that "This is an error in principle ... We arrive at an understanding of the past through the present, and not vice versa.[2]

If one confines the analysis of law to these areas, Ehrlich argued, it is impossible to capture the totality of law. He therefore calls for a comprehensive approach drawing on statistics, political geography and "sociology with a geographical mind", as well as history and psychology.

Manfred Rehbinder, whom Keebet von Benda-Beckmann had the privilege to work with in her very first academic appointment in 1972/73 as his assistant at the law faculty in Zürich, was the first sociologist of law who made a comprehensive study of Ehrlich. In a passage devoted to the term

[2] Ehrlich 2002, 488-489. "History of law and ethnological legal science will not be of value for an understanding of the existing law, but only for the study of the development of law" (489). But on p. 496 he calls for the technique developed in legal history of studying legal documents (contracts etc.) and deriving the living law from it. This is done by looking for "...content that is of general importance, typical, and ever recurring, to treat juristically and to evaluate them from every angle according to their importance from the point of view of society, economics, and legislative policy." (496). On p. 502 he clarifies "...the historical connection ... [lies] in the present, out of which the legal proposition grows." And (504); "...the path to the understanding of the innermost nature of the present lies through the understanding of the past". This seems a contradiction of what he argued previously.

living law, Rehbinder (1967, 29-30) points out that Ehrlich distinguishes three categories of law: first, the law of an association that can be directly derived from the facts; second, lawyers' legal norms that emerge in a complex social process from such concrete legal norms. These lawyers' legal norms have a looser relation with the facts than the concrete legal norms. The third category is the law that refers to the state as an overarching umbrella association. These three categories are closely interrelated but they are not identical, and can exist side by side. Ehrlich's concept of living law, however, is a *scientific* concept, and Rehbinder insists that this is definitely *not* the same as the law of associations, the rules that emerge from the association itself. Rather, in Rehbinder's view, living law according to Ehrlich is social law at a higher level of abstraction, namely at a level that has been generated in reaction to lawyers' law and the law of the state. At this level law is a 'lived order', and the legal norm a norm of social behaviour. Ehrlich (2002, 498) therefore argues that the "standard against which a sociological school of jurisprudence must test not only legal propositions, but also the legal documents, is actual life." But in a circular argumentative loop he reminds us that "[o]nly what enters into life becomes a living norm, the rest is only teaching, norm for decision-making, dogma or theory." However, "It is not true ... that the investigation of the living law is concerned only with "customary law" or with "business usage." ... "But only concrete usages .... yield the rules according to which men regulate their conduct." (Ehrlich 2002, 501)

Ehrlich wanted to understand how an orderly economic and social life could exist when the law of the Austrian empire was so clearly irrelevant in so many domains. He noted that in the realm of commercial law legal science was not totally useless, for it was "the only branch of the juristic science which is based not merely incidentally, but throughout, on actual usage." (Ehrlich 2002, 492)

Ehrlich (2002, 502) saw two ways in which the living law was socially significant:

1. Living law has and must have an influence upon the norms for court decisions and upon the content of statutes.
2. The concept also has in independent value: it "constitutes the foundation of the legal order of human society."

As Rehbinder (1967, 23-24) points out, Ehrlich not only suggests that law primarily emerges in society itself, rather than in legislation, legal theory, or court cases. He also proposes a method to know this law. Law is imagined; it exists in people's minds. Law is therefore situated in the tangible, observable reality that is the basis of law, and from which legal notions emerge. The methodological implication is that the task in what he calls "the laboratory of law" is to look for such facts that can be observed. Law, as the organization of human associations, is a rule that assigns individuals their position and tasks within that association. The facts that have to be found are those to which the human mind attaches such rules. There are four basic categories of such facts: practice (*Übung*), authority, property, and declaratory acts (*Willenserklärung*). Among the last category are contracts, constitutions, and wills. Thus, one can learn about the living law by observing concrete practice and by studying legal documents. But legal documents are 'heterogeneous'. They also contain elements that are historical, simply copied from other documents. They may also contain numerous clauses relating to what might happen if things go wrong, including penalties that are never imposed (Ehrlich 2002, 497). These elementsdo not yield insight into the way people organise their lives and therefore cannot be used as a basis for eliciting propositions of living law. These can only be drawn from the clauses that are actually put to practice. This so far is Rehbinder's interpretation of Ehrlich.

As we mentioned above, in the course of time the term living law has acquired many different meanings. There are a number of reasons for this. The first is that Ehrlich's explanation of the term was not entirely clear, and authors who tried to find the "correct" interpretation of his work could not agree. A second reason has recently been discussed by Nelken (2009), who shows that authors such as Ziegert (2002) und Teubner (1997), who are currently using the concept, deliberately adjust the term to serve their academic interests and analytical purposes. Though each of them attempts to understand Ehrlich's work, they are less interested in trying to represent the authentic thoughts of Ehrlich than in appropriating his ideas for their own scientific project. This started, as Nelken argues, with Roscoe Pound. Ziegert has tried to demonstrate the close similarity of Pound's notion of law in action and Ehrlich's living law, though Nelken (1984) regards this as a misinterpretation of Ehrlich's work by Ziegert. Teubner, the best-known current interpreter of Ehrlich's work, does not even claim to give a correct interpretation of Ehrlich's ideas in his own work on the *lex mercatoria*, but finds living law a useful addition to systems theory and his 'autopoietic project', as Nelken(2009) calls it. But in his eyes others, such as Ellickson, Michaels, and Mathiesen have also appropriated the concept.

A second problem is that Ehrlich has not been the only scholar to use the term 'living law', a fact that is less well known. There are other genealogies of the term and it is not at all clear whether and, if so, how they relate to each other. The Dutch legal scholar Cornelis Van Vollenhoven, whom we shall consider shortly, coined the term 'living law' (Dutch: *levend recht*) even before Ehrlich in connection with the adat laws of Indonesian legal communities. He too was of the opinion that much of the life of the people within legal communities was regulated by law other than that of the state. Like Ehrlich, he used the term 'law' to capture rules, principles and procedures generated in associations, *rechtsgemeenschappen* in his terminology, for the purpose of studying the social significance of such law. Both explicitly rejected the concept of 'customary law' (*Gewohnheitsrecht)* because of the connotation this had in prevailing legal doctrines.[3] And like Ehrlich, Van Vollenhoven also pursued a legal political goal of making these insights usable for legal decision-makers, particularly judges. But he did not aim at a universal concept of law, or a social science of law on the basis of the notion of living law. To understand the difference between the two scholars it is important to note that they developed their ideas in totally different political contexts. Ehrlich discussed the self-regulation of relatively powerful businessmen on the margins of an empire that had difficulty in imposing its law on them. By contrast, Van Vollenhoven's main concern was with colonized communities that were disenfranchised by the colonial state. This was possible because what Van Vollenhoven saw as their living adat law was regarded in the prevailing legal interpretation as mere custom, which the state could and did set aside at will.[4] Van Vollenhoven was not particu-

[3] Ehrlich (2002, 501): 'If one does any thinking at all when one uses these words – which is not always the case – one will realize that they do not refer to the concrete but to what has been universalized. But only the concrete usages... yield the rules according to which men regulate their conduct.

[4] Most adat laws were living law according to Van Vollenhoven, but he recognized the possibility of obsolete, 'dead' adat law rules and principles. The 'living' characteristic was not a precondition of calling adat law 'law'.

larly concerned with the possible disenfranchisement of certain categories of adat citizens under adat law, an issue that would arise only much later.

We can only speculate why it was that two scholars came up with this concept around the same time. We have no indication that the two knew each other, or of each other. One explanation might be that something like a notion of living law was in the air; that some legal scholars were beginning to drift away from the strict legal doctrines that had preoccupied legal science in the 19th century. The interest of the historical school of Von Savigny and Beseler, with their glorification of people's or folk law (*Volksrecht*) on the one hand, and on the other, the general and increasing interest in Europe in changing social relations, in problems of class, in the role of the state and its institutions were powerful forces challenging established legal science.[5] Legal scholars responded to these challenges and became more interested in how social life was organized. Many also became interested in ethical questions relating to law, and how it might play a role in improving the life of the underprivileged. But compassion for the underprivileged was not the only motive. In different ways many intellectuals were grappling with the central issue of what the law of the state could achieve, and where the law of the state met its limits and collided with internal regulatory systems of associations beyond its reach. This question was all the more pressing in the colonial and colonial-like contexts in which Ehrlich and Van Vollenhoven worked. What we are suggesting is that it was perhaps not entirely by chance that these scholars came up with the notion of living law, though their conceptions of it did not entirely coincide.

A third problem with the term 'living law' is that most authors that have taken up the term today gloss over Ehrlich's conceptual distinctions and use the term more loosely to refer to the norms according to which people live. For example Hellum, Ali and Griffiths (2011, 4) discuss the "transnational moral, social or economic practices, norms, and values that transgress the territorial and legal boundaries of the nation state", and discuss the "robust living law dimensions" in Islamic law through the secondary sources including '*urf*' (Hellum et al. 2011, 9) as practices in Islamic councils, and the role of internet *fatwa*.[6] The meaning of the term as they use it comes

5 Such science, as Julius von Kirchmann (1848) wrote as early as 1848, was without any value.

6 On the 'living *fiqh*' in Indonesia, see Bowen 2003, 91, F. and K. von Benda-Beckmann 2009, 186.

much closer to what Van Vollenhoven called living adat law, and to what Ehrlich called the internal norms governing associations.[7] In their use of it these studies demonstrate considerable interest in the nature of these associations or social fields, and in the level of debate and contestation that goes on within these fields, especially under conditions of globalisation and migration. And here we have a fourth reason why the term is problematic. Studies suggest that it is both theoretically and empirically highly problematic to identify the relevant social units, whether one calls them fields, associations, or networks, or to identify the sets of norms that organise the networks. Keebet has argued elsewhere that norms relating to social care may differ considerably within transnational social fields and networks of actors, depending on where actors are positioned, and on the place they take in other, overlapping social fields within the country of origin or one of the countries of migration. If such fields are characterised by persisting fundamental differences in the content of relevant norms, how does that affect an analysis of living law? In short, such studies open up a wide range of important empirical and theoretical issues that Ehrlich and Van Vollenhoven did not address, and perhaps did not even need to address in their time.

Living law in jurisprudence and court decisions

The term 'living law' has not remained a purely theoretical concept. It has occasionally found its way into normative jurisprudence, legal policy discussions and court judgments, where it has obtained surprising new meanings. We ourselves (2009) have described how Van Vollenhoven's notion of *levend recht* has been appropriated and transformed into a doctrinal legal concept in legislation and court decisions in Indonesia. Vogl (2009) has shown how prominent Japanese legal scholars have adapted the notion to help Japanese judges deal with the received German law. The most recent, interesting and vibrant development in this respect can be observed in the South African legal world. There are some similarities but also considerable differences in how living law is used and what living law means in these contexts.

[7] But one wonders if they use the concept consistently. When they comment that there is no cross-fertilization between institutions and that it is, moreover, "not clear whether Muslim communities internalize the *fatwas* from the European Council for *Fatwa* and Research and from the internet." If this is not the case, why call it living law at all?

In the Japanese case described by Vogl, Ehrlich's notion of living law has been instrumentalised, most prominently by the famous legal scholar Suehiro, to help Japanese judges to 'ease the judges' dilemma' (Vogl 2009, 195) when dealing with the problem of how to adapt the substantive provisions of received German law to Japanese conditions. Vogl shows how Suehiro radicalized Ehrlich's theory. He confined it to 'living law in the courtroom' (Vogl 2009, 107) and '[dogmatized] Ehrlich's sociological(ly intended) theory to liberate the judiciary from statutory law' (Vogl 2009, 108). However, as far as we know, there is no evidence that judges ever actually used the notion of living law in the rationalization and justification of their judgments. This has been the case in Indonesia and South Africa where the notion of living law has been used in court decisions.

In Indonesia, the notion of living law (Dutch: *levend recht,* Ind. *hukum hidup*) became common in the circle of the pupils of Van Vollenhoven, many of whom were Indonesian legal scholars. The notion moved with them to Indonesia, especially after the establishment in 1924 of the Law College (*Rechtshogeschool*) in Batavia, the capital of the Dutch East Indies, now Jakarta.[8] Living law – for most living adat law, but sometimes used in a wider sense – remained an important concept for lawyers and anthropologists until the 1970s (see F. and K. von Benda-Beckmann 2009, 183). After independence, Indonesia's legal establishment tried to strike a balance in the state-religion-adat triangle that characterizes legal pluralism in Indonesia. In many regions of Indonesia the main tensions were between adat and Islam, the most hotly disputed issue being which law was valid for problems relating to inheritance. In this context, living law was used as a device to flexibly navigate between the demands of adat, religion, the existing state law and demands for a new Indonesian national law. These developments occurred during the period in which the parliamentary constitution of 1950 was replaced by a strong executive constitution, and the concern with 'rule of law' gave way to the 'law of revolution' (Lev 1965, 289). As Lev (1972, 79) notes, 'living law' was used during the revolution to allow judges to avoid the rigidities of colonial concepts of adat law. The concept of "the living law of society" appeared for the first time in a draft bill in 1948 to justify a continuing role for adat authorities outside the new

[8] Wignjodipuro 1973, 2. Ihromi (1981, 157), a well known anthropologist and lawyer, also identifies adat law with the law that lives in society.

civil courts (Bowen 2003, 53). The living law formula was then used in Emergency Law 1 of 1951, which "abolished or anticipated the abolition of adat courts everywhere in Indonesia, except religious justice where, according to the living law, such justice forms an independent part of adat justice." The first systematic post-independence regulation of the competence of religious courts in Indonesia, Government Regulation No. 45 of 1957, stated that Islamic courts would be competent in the issues mentioned, that is, mainly family law and inheritance, to the extent "that according to the living law these issues are to be resolved according to the law of Islam" (Lev 1972, 116; F. von Benda-Beckmann 1979, 126). In practice, living law was mainly interpreted by judges in the civil law court system, including the Supreme Court of Indonesia, and in their interpretation adat law was the living law.[9] As Lev (1972, 116) said "one has to read 'living law' as being equal to adat law plus, in reality, the discretionary judgment of civil law judges about what social rules remain in effect." In terms of substantive law, on the other hand, the notion of living law was used to change elements in adat law that were deemed to be old fashioned and unjust. For example, the curtailed inheritance rights – or absence of any rights – for daughters or widow to the property of their deceased father or husband. The yardstick for 'appropriateness' and 'justice' was derived from the spirit of modernity and equality, and in the 1950s and 60s the Supreme Court took on the task of reconstructing local adat laws to fit post-revolutionary national sensibilities.[10] In particular, the court's President, Wirjono Prodjodikoro, wanted to establish a widow's right to inherit her husband's property in these societies (Lev 1962, 215). In January 1959 the Supreme Court, in a case relating to inheritance among Christian Karo Batak, ruled that "according to the knowledge of the Supreme Court itself ... Batak adat law at the present time provides that both widows and children should inherit

---

9 The Supreme Court stated: "the Supreme Court regards it as clear that in all of Indonesia with respect to inheritance it is essentially the adat law which applies, which in areas in which Islamic law is strong contains more or fewer elements of Islamic law" (Lev 1972, 68).

10 Simbolon 1998; Bowen 2003, 53. In his research on Supreme Court inheritance decisions, Lev analysed the legal interventions of the Supreme Court on adat law in the 1950s, especially in cases where the question of whether widows or daughters could inherit under adat laws with patrilineal and bilateral systems was at stake. See Lev 1962. See also Bowen (2003, 55); Benda-Beckmann, F von 1979, 340, quoting the judgement from Subekti, R and Tamara (1965, 198). See also Hadikusuma 1993.

community property" (Lev 1962, 221). The Supreme Court (Decision No. 179 K/Sip/1961) recognized that women (daughters) and men (sons) had equal inheritance rights. In his considerations, the Supreme Court stated that Batak adat does not recognise women's inheritance rights, but "... that on the basis of general feelings of humanity and justice, and of absolutely equal rights between men and women, it should be considered the living law throughout Indonesia that daughters and sons are equally entitled to the parental inheritance".[11] Bilateral inheritance was declared to be "living law throughout Indonesia" (Subekti and Tamara 1965, 85). Thus, though living law was usually equated with adat, living law could also be used to challenge adat. It could also be applied to Islamic law in order to soften demands for a full validation of the *Sharia* as official law. In the debates surrounding the 1989 Law on the Jurisdiction of Religious Courts, a drafting committee of Supreme Court justices and people from the Ministry of Religious Affairs interviewed 166 religious authorities (*ulama*) on the 'living *fiqh*', a concept that extended the Supreme Court's living adat law idea into the realm of the *fiqh* .[12]

The ideas about living law expressed in these judgments, and political legal rhetoric had moved a long way from the law as used and developed in Indonesian *rechtsgemeenschappen* or for that matter, Ehrlich's 'inner order of social associations'. The law declared by the judges as 'living' was not the law that was widely shared or appreciated by the majority of the population. Some people, among them judges in the lower courts, felt that the Supreme Court had gone too far in deviating from adat law, and criticized that it was disregarding social realities in certain areas, and had gone "beyond the people's true sense of justice" (Lev 1962, 222). Commenting on the Karo Batak inheritance case mentioned earlier, a book on Karo Batak adat law published in 1979 stated that the court's decision was unfortunate and, had it been followed, would have caused extensive social disruption (Bowen 2003, 54). In 1981 Ihromi, a Toba Batak professor in law and anthropology at Universitas Indonesia, who was strongly committed to gender

---

11 Case Reg. No. 179K/Sip./1971; Slaats and Portier 1986; Bowen 2003.

12 Bowen 2003, 190. The result of these consultations was made into a 'compilation' of Islamic law. The compilation was introduced as Presidential Instruction (*Instruksi Presiden*) no 1-1991. About the compilation of Islamic law, it was said that 'in its essence the Compilation is the living law [in English] that has been voluntarily applied for centuries ... ' (Bowen 2003, 192).

equality, dryly characterised the 1961 judgment as "rather brave and not really based on empirical regularities" (Ihromi 1981, 174).[13]

In post-revolutionary Indonesia living law was thus used in a kind of *Freie Rechtslehre* by the legal elite and judges of the highest court, while the majority of the population, and lower court judges adhering to an understanding of living law that came closer to Van Vollenhoven's, did not agree with these interpretations. Living law in Indonesia had thus become the opposite of what Ehrlich had meant by the term, and what Van Vollenhoven understood as *levend recht*. After the 1970s, the term gradually fell out of use. But after the fall of the autocratic regime of Suharto in 1998, adat law arose like a phoenix from the ashes to serve as a powerful weapon against state law, especially in the area of land law, where it is used to challenge forced expropriations carried out by the Suharto regime (F. and K. von Benda-Beckmann 2006; 2013). Along with this revitalised adat law, notions of living law also reappeared. However, this living law is no longer a construction of progressive judges, as in the post-revolutionary period, but goes back to 'the law of the people', to living law in the earlier sense.[14] Indonesia's living law seems to have gone full circle, and now faces the same allegations of romanticism and conservatism as in Van Vollenhoven's time. And, as was the case a century ago, critics conveniently tend to forget that reliance on this living law serves to redress serious underlying social problems of land expropriation.

South Africa

It is interesting to compare these developments with the role that the notion

[13] On the Batak adat see Sitorus 2000. Sitorus did research in the 1990s. Old adat experts insisted on the adat rule that daughters could not inherit, while young adat leaders said that daughters could inherit. In practice, there was variation, but cases in which daughters received some portion were found. There were also cases where it was said that daughters had no rights, but where they nonetheless received part of the inheritance (Sitorus 2000). See also Irianto 2003.

[14] This is nicely illustrated in a cartoon series published by an Indonesian Human Rights organisation, HuMa (Huma 2002). After having traced the history of European thought on folk or people's law (Kant, Austin, von Jhering, Binder, Marx, von Savigny) the cartoon goes on to quote Supomo, adat law scholar and Minister of Justice 'Adat law is a kind of law that lives, because it expresses the true legal feelings of society… adat law is in a constant process of emergence and growth like life itself'. See F. and K. von Benda-Beckmann 2009, 189, 193 for the cartoons.

of 'living customary' or 'indigenous law' plays in South African legal scholarship and in judgments of the Constitution Courts.

Most of the discussion in the literature on 'living law' and court decisions go back to an article written by Sanders in 1987 with the title 'how customary is customary law?' Sanders (1987, 405) refers only in passing to Ehrlich, noting that he "distinguishes between rules for decision (book law or positive law) and rules of conduct (living law)." While one may object that this is not a correct representation of Ehrlich's work, this is not really relevant to the rest of the paper, which deals with the important issue of what he calls the "multiple life of African customary law" (ibid.). He observes that there are three different manifestations of 'customary law'. One is 'official customary law', that is, customary law as interpreted and transformed by colonial state law and courts. This is, by the way, what the Dutch adat law scholars had called *adat juristenrecht*, as distinguished from *adat volksrecht*. Second, there is 'academic customary law', basically jurisprudential or social science approaches to non-state law. Thirdly and most importantly, there is what he calls, using Allott's (1985, 24) notion, 'autonomic customary law' (Sanders 1987, 409) that comes close to Van Vollenhoven's '*volksrecht*'. Seeking a way out of the jungle of connotations of the many terms referring to non-state, unofficial law, such as customary law, folk law, people's law, or popular law, Allott suggested referring to the field of study as 'autogenous regulation' or 'autonomics, which may be taken to mean a 'spontaneous and self-regulating system'.[15]

Since Sanders wrote this paper, living customary law has been distinguished from codified (and obsolete) customary law, and judges and academics grapple with the problem of identifying or establishing living customary law.[16] In Himonga's words (2005, 168, referring back to Chanock 1985) "official customary law denotes the customary law that is recorded in textbooks, and in court precedents, and codified in legislation, while liv-

15 Allott 1985, 24. He referred here to his earlier (1980) distinction between 'catanomic' and 'paranomic' norm-making. Catanomic was used to denote people's norm making in accordance with the official law, paranomic as apparently in contradiction or defiance of the existing legal system (Allot 1985, 24).

16 Alexkor Ltd. and another versus The Richtersveld Community and others 2004 (5) SA 460 (CC), and Bhe versus Magistrate, Khayelitsha and others (Commission for Gender Equality as amicus curiae 2005 (1) SA 580, 2005 (1) BCLR 1 (CC). On Bhe, see Himonga 2005. On the notion of 'living customary law' in South African jurisprudence, see Bennett 2004, 2006, 2009; Bennett and Bleazard 2009.

ing (unofficial) customary law means the customary practices or norms observed by the people living under customary law in their day-to-day lives". The difference between 'official customary law' and 'living customary law' is generally recognized by South African courts and the legal literature. The question is how courts should go about ascertaining these versions, and how they should apply, develop or change them, if either or both contradict the constitution by which the court is bound. In the much discussed *Bhe* case, the court invalidated the 'official customary law' of intestate inheritance with its provision for male primogeniture, which was embodied in the Black Administrations Act of 1927 (see Himonga 2005), an example of customary law selectively incorporated into state law. Commentators complained that the court limited itself to developing the official customary law, while refusing to also develop the living customary law – despite the fact that the court acknowledged the existence of both kinds of customary law. Himonga criticizes the decision on the grounds that the court had not dealt with the situation of women under living customary law or tested the constitutionality of this form of law (Himonga 2005, 170). The court thus only tinkered with the judicially constructed customary law, and did not address the reality of women's experiences. The decision is therefore seen to have only limited relevance for people living under the judicially constructed customary law, as opposed to those living under living customary law (ibid., 171) The minority opinion in the case had noted that there might be differences between the two forms of customary law, and that living customary law may already have adjusted to the rights of women under the constitution (ibid., 173). The court, Himonga argues, should therefore have taken its constitutional task of developing customary law seriously and gone on to develop living customary law.[17]

The confusion seems to be total. We can conclude that the notion of living customary law in South Africa, despite references to Ehrlich, and the absence of references to Van Vollenhoven, is much closer to the Dutch notion of living law or living adat law, adat *volksrecht*, than to Ehrlich's living law. Yet what Himonga and others are calling for is remarkably similar to the revolutionary courts of post-Independence Indonesia, rather than to Van Vollenhoven's ideas.

[17] Himonga 2005, 175. In 2011, we had the pleasure of participating in a workshop organized by Prof. Chuma Himonga, professor for customary law, of the University of Cape Town in which she explained her conceptual and political struggles with the term.

The value of metaphors

By way of conclusion we want to raise for discussion some difficult questions that emerge from our analysis. Living law is an appealing metaphor. It points to the autonomic character of people's laws, to the co-existence of legal orders, to the merits of an 'underall perspective' on law and legal development, and cautions against the blinkers of a state-focused understanding of law. But we think – and raise this as a matter for discussion – that the concept is only of limited descriptive and analytical value. The examples that we have discussed also suggest that the transformation of a descriptive and analytical term into a normative category may create more problems than it solves.

The most important deficiency of Ehrlich's term 'living law' is that it does not define three core component concepts: law, the relevant associations of communities, and 'living'. It simply presupposes an understanding of what is 'legal'. Cotterell has formulated this criticism succinctly: "Ultimately, the basis for Ehrlich's sociological identification of law seems to be that: (i) law consists of those norms that regulate matters that are seen as of general social significance; and (ii) law is rooted in certain specific types of action and relationships that tend to historically assume economic importance and attract state supervision" (Cotterrell 2009, 90). He finds this "a weak basis for specifying the distinctiveness of law ...".[18]

Defining the relevant association or community raises equally thorny issues. It may have been possible at the time when Ehrlich and Van Vollenhoven developed their ideas, because the communities and associations they were studying were relatively identifiable, though one might question whether they had enough awareness of the complex transnational networks in which people were operating at the time. Today, in a globalized world linked by the internet, migration, and chains of disaggregated production, it is immeasurably more difficult to define the boundaries of associations and communities. It is no accident that social scientists have adopted the terms 'network' and 'social field' as central concepts for analysing social relations, because this term does not have the connotation of locally bounded

[18] Cotterrell 2009, 91. As early as 1984, Cotterrell (1984, 37) stated "It is a concept solely devised for polemic purposes, by a lawyer concerned to organize the data of social life in a way that would directly challenge lawyers" conceptions and categories. Paradoxically, to achieve this, the data had to be organised in terms of those conceptions and categories.

units. These terms are well suited to being used to include infra-state, state and transnational social fields. But we have seen that such fields are by no means homogenous, and may contain different and at times conflicting norms. A more differentiated conceptual apparatus would be necessary to capture the variation and relative indeterminacy within such communities and associations.

Another, related problem is that, without further conceptual differentiation, the internal norms of associations tend to conjure up an image of unity and consensus, and gloss over the dissent and frustrated ambition that is also present, as Webber (2009) has argued. The law that dominates social life may be awful, at least for part of the population of the association or community – whether it is state, religious, ethnic or international law. To be fair, Ehrlich was quite aware of the fact that living law too could be oppressive. The criticism that they romanticized 'living law', often levelled at proponents of living law, was certainly misplaced in the case of Ehrlich.

In addition to these problems, the question arises what 'living' in the term 'living law' means. If Ehrlich tells us that 'it dominates social life' we are not much the wiser. Is law 'living' only if it is followed or applied in social life? And how would one establish whether that is the case? By the fact that it appears in documents or is referred to in disputes, as Ehrlich suggests? The deeper issue here is that within associations and communities there may be dissent, differences of opinion, and minority views. There is a danger in identifying living law with customary law, as is often done. Can we really, for descriptive or political purposes, say that 'customary law' only deserves the label 'law' if its subjects live in conformity with it, as the legalistic understanding of 'customary law' demands? To be sure, discussions in South Africa have emphasized the fluidity and adaptability of 'living' customary law, the 'autonomic' as Sanders called it, which enabled it to escape the strictly legal construction of 'customary law' which needed 'customariness' as one of the conditions for being recognized as law at all. But what about customary law, and rights based on customary law, that have been perverted or largely destroyed, abrogated through state law or by sheer violence, with the consequence that it can no longer govern social life, that people can no longer live according to its principles and rules because state agents or landowners have made it impossible to do so? What about the law that, for these reasons, did not govern social life, although it continued to live on in memory? Is the 'revitalisation' of such law, and of claims based on it under new circumstances, just another invention of tradition, or an opportunistic and inauthentic strategic move? Could it be that we should regard it as law that –so to speak – went into hiding but which remained the people's law, albeit in memory and tradition only, and was always a reason for not accepting the legitimacy of the law violently imposed by the colonizers (see F. von Benda-Beckmann 1997)?

A brief illustration from our research in Indonesia after the fall of the Suharto regime in 1998 might clarify what we mean. In 1999, in order to stem the tide of protests against the previous arbitrary state resource policies and land expropriations, the central government drafted a new regulation to resolve the problems of the village commons (*ulayat* land) of *adat* law communities by conceding limited recognition of *ulayat* rights based on adat law. Though this might at first sight be interpreted as a strengthening of adat-based titles to communal land, the regulation met with strong protest in West Sumatra. Kamal called it a set of 'injections to kill the *adat* law communities'.[19] Why? Kamal identified three injections. The first was the definition of *ulayat* land as 'land that has been handed down through the generations since ancient times, and where the relations between the *adat* law community and its territory (*wilayah*) have not been severed'. This was regarded as a great restriction of adat rights, given that much (former) *ulayat* land had been deprived of its status through statutory law or other uses of state power. The second injection was that such land was recognised only "as far as *ulayat* still exists in reality". The third and perhaps most fatal injection was the stipulation that *ulayat* rights cannot be exercised over land a) which has been declared by the regional government to belong to private individuals or legal entities holding rights under the Basic Agrarian Law; and b) which has been freed or otherwise obtained by governmental agencies, legal entities or individuals in accordance with governmental regulations. This, Kamal concluded, would validate with a stroke of the pen all expropriations and other actions regarding village commons taken by the government in the past.

All these issues come back with force once living law is transformed from a descriptive analytical device into a normative construct. At the level of jurisprudence and normatively oriented legal theory, Teubner and Ehrlich

---

19 Kamal 1999, 199. A comment in a local newspaper (*Singgalang*, 5 July 1999) spoke of a Minangkabau *harakiri*.

are in same position in arguing against a dominant strand of lawyers' ideas about law (Teubner 1997, 8). Both want to convert something that, from an analytical social science perspective, can be called law, into law that is such and is generally recognized as such in the world of official law.[20] This already creates confusion, as Teubner's work shows. He overlooks the fact that differences between a social science and a normative perspective only constitute a paradox if one assumes that there should not be a difference (Teubner 1997, 17). But criticizing lawyers for not accepting social science arguments, and not accepting as law what sociologists call 'law', including *lex mercatoria*, misses the point. They are not, as Teubner (1997, 21) claims 'wrong'; they are doing a different job.[21] That both act in the name of 'theory' should not lead us to forget the difference.

The problems are even more pressing if like Himonga, one wishes to make the term 'living law' useful for political engagement. This is particularly so in relation to gender issues, but it probably applies to social justice in general. It is an illusion to believe that mere recognition would solve the underlying social problems that recognition is called for. To be fair, Himonga and her South African colleagues are clearly aware of this. The examples from South Africa and Indonesia that we have just discussed give an inkling of the kind of problems that arise when political engagement aims at bringing about substantive change in the law as it is recognized in

[20] Teubner's arguments (1997, 10) are similar to Ehrlich's, see Nelken 2009. We agree with Teubner's conclusion regarding "the tremendous resistance that Ehrlich's global Bukowina has to face in a legal world still dominated by the nation-state". We would also agree that lex mercatoria breaks a double taboo (Teubner 1997, 10, 11) but this is simply always the case where analytical sociological or anthropological conceptions of law come up against ideological and dogmatic conceptions. When Teubner discusses the lex mercatoria and proposes to elevate this to 'law', he is in some respect engaged in a similar enterprise as Ehrlich; see Nelken 2009.

[21] When Teubner (1997, 3) for instance writes that "Ehrlich's theory turned out to be wrong for the national law of Austria" what does he mean? That the official judicial system of Austria did not accept Ehrlich's conceptualization of law implicit in the term living law? or that Austrian courts did not apply the (non-state, non-lawyer) living law, and that Austrian jurisprudence did not adopt a sociology of law as envisaged by Ehrlich? Of course, this all is true, but that does not affect Ehrlich's 'theory'. If it fits certain forms of global or transnational law in the global context as well as it did the living law in the Bukowina in the Austrian context, this can only mean that Ehrlich provided a useful way of looking at a wider body of law than his more dogmatically inclined lawyer-colleagues did, but this also applies to Teubner arguing against those who do not want to recognize the legal character of the *lex mercatoria*.

state law. Note in the first place that the intervention that was pursued by Van Vollenhoven and his students was intervention into the dominant and very living state law in order to force the colonial state to refrain from its oppressive meddling with the local population and expropriation of their land. The kinds of intervention envisaged by the Supreme Court of Indonesia and the courts in South Africa were, by contrast, meant to change the non-state law of certain populations, in order to improve the legal position of certain categories – women – within the living law. This is an entirely different enterprise and one that, we fear, bears remarkable structural similarity to colonial interventions in property law. The ultimate social aim was different: capitalist economic growth in the case of the colonial Dutch Indies, gender equality in the case of revolutionary Indonesia and South Africa. However, in all cases, the law or the courts of the state were the instruments used in attempts to change undesirable elements of the living law of communities.

From a social science perspective it is by no means self-evident that such political instrumentalization of the concept of living law or living customary law would be the most promising way to reach one's objectives; to attain, for instance, gender equality in any kind of law and in social practices. One would need more conceptual sophistication and theoretical analysis to predict whether courts or legislation would be the most appropriate means to bring about the desired social change, or whether the change in conduct and rules of conduct should be stimulated by other, largely non-legal means. Such a theoretical framework would at the very least have to be able to identify the conditions under which the living law of an association or community might be receptive to change initiated by courts, constables, and constitutions.

In short, the concept of living law is too weak to serve as a core concept for a social theory of the social working of law under conditions of legal pluralism. Such a theory would also have to deal with the question of what happens if an analytical concept becomes a normative concept. Discussions about living law as a core had the merit of pointing out some of the problems, but the term has done little to solve these theoretical and empirical problems.

References

Allott, Anthony N. (1980), *The Limits of Law*. London: Butterworths.

Allott, Antony N., and Woodman, Gordon R. (eds., 1985), *People's Law and the State Law: The Bellagio Papers*. Dordrecht, Berlin: Foris Publications, Walter de Gruyter.

Banakar, Reza 2003 *Merging Law and Sociology: Beyond the Dichotomies in Sociolegal Research*. Glienicke and Madison: Galda and Wilch.

Benda-Beckmann, Franz von (1979), *Property in Social Continuity: Continuity and Change in the Maintenance of Property Relationships through Time in Minangkabau, West Sumatra*. Verhandlingen van het Koninklijk Instituut voor Taal-, Land- en Volkenkunde, Vol. 86. The Hague: Martinus Nijhoff.

Benda-Beckmann, Franz von, and Benda-Beckmann, Keebet von (2006), Changing One Is Changing All: Dynamics in the Adat-Islam-state Triangle. In: Dynamics of Plural Legal Orders. *Journal of Legal Pluralism and Unofficial Law* No 53-54/2006, edited by Franz von Benda-Beckmann and Keebet von Benda-Beckmann. Berlin: Lit. pp. 239-270

Benda-Beckmann, Franz von, and Benda-Beckmann, Keebet von (2009), The Social Life of Living Law in Indonesia. In: Marc Hertogh (ed.), *Living Law: Reconsidering Eugen Ehrlich*. Oxford and Portland Oregon: Hart, pp. 177-97.

Benda-Beckmann, Franz von and Benda-Beckmann, Keebet von (2013). *Political and Legal Transformations of an Indonesian Polity. The Nagari from Colonization to Decentralisation.* Cambridge, Cambridge University Press.

Benda-Beckmann, Keebet von (1984), *The Broken Stairways to Consensus: Village Justice and State Courts in Minangkabau*, Verhandelingen van het Koninklijk Instituut voor Taal-, Land- en Volkenkunde, Vol. 106. Dordrecht, Leiden, Cinnaminson: Foris Publications, KITLV Press.

Bennett, Tom W. (2004), *Customary Law in South Africa*. Juta & Co.

Bennett, Tom W. (2006), The Contribution of Legal Theory and Judicial Practice to the Future Development of Customary Law. In: Graham Glover (ed.), *Essays in Honour of A. J. Kerr.* Durban: Lexis Nexis Butterworths, pp. 181-199.

Bennett, Tom W. (2009), Re-introducing African Customary Law to the South African Legal System. *American Journal of Comparative Law* 57:1-32.

Bennet, Tom W., and J. Bleazard (2009), The Re-invention of Customary Law: South African Courts as Constitutional Law-makers. *Recht in Afrika* 12:1-20.

Bowen, John (2003), *Islam, Law and Equality in Indonesia*. Cambridge: Cambridge University Press.

Chanock, Martin (1985), *Law, Custom and Social Order: the Colonial Experience in Malawi and Zambia*. Cambridge: Cambridge University Press.

Cotterrell, Roger (1984), *The Sociology of Law: An Introduction*. 1st edition, London: Butterworths.

Cotterrell, Roger (2006), "From "Living Law? to the "Death of the Social?: Sociology in Legal Theory? in Michael D. A. Freeman (ed.), *Law and Sociology.* Oxford: Oxford University Press, pp. 16-31.

Cotterrell, Roger (2009), Ehrlich at the Edge of Empire: Centres and Peripheries in Legal Studies In: Marc Hertogh (ed.) Living law: Reconsidering Eugen Ehrlich. Oxford: Hart, pp. 75-94

Ehrlich, Eugen (1911), Die Erforschung des lebenden Rechts. *Schmollers Jahrbuch für Gesetzgebung, Verwaltung und Volkswirtschaft im Deutschen Reich* 35:129-147.

Ehrlich, Eugen (1913/1989), *Grundlegung der Soziologie des Rechts.* 4th edition, Berlin: Duncker & Humblot.

Ehrlich, Eugen (2002), *Fundamental Principles of the Sociology of Law.* New Brunswick and London: Transaction Publishers.

Griffiths, John (1986), What Is Legal Pluralism? *Journal of Legal Pluralism* 24:1-55.

Hadikusuma, Hilman (1993), *Hukum adat dalam yurisprudensi: Hukum kekeluargaan, perkawinan, pewarisan.* Bandung: PT Citra Aditya Bakti.

Hellum, Anne, Sardar Ali, Shaheen and Griffths, Anne (2011), Introduction: Transnational Law in the Making. In: Anne Hellum, Shaheen Sardar Ali, and Anne Griffths (eds.), *From Transnational Relations to Transnational Law: Northern European Laws at the Crossroads.* Farnham: Ashgate, pp. 1-26.

Hertogh, Marc (ed., 2009), *Living Law. Reconsidering Eugen Ehrlich.* Oxford and Portland Oregon: Hart.

Himonga, Chuma (2005), African Customary Law in South Africa – Many Faces of Bhe v. Magistrate Khayelitisha. *Recht in Afrika* 2005, No. 2:163-183.

HuMa (2002), *Hukum adat, hukum kami. Seri komik adat dan masyarakat,* No. 1 and 2. Jakarta: HuMa.

Ihromi, Tapi Omas (1981), *Adat perkawinan Toraja Sa' dan dan tempatnya dalam hukum positip masa kini.* Yogyakarta: Gadjah Mada University Press.

Irianto, Sulistyowati (2003), *Perempuan di antara bebagai strategi pilihan hukum.* Jakarta: Yayasan Obor.

Kamal, Miko (1999), Injeksi mematikan untuk masyarakat adat: Catatan kritis atas PERMENAG No. 5/1999. Paper presented at a Workshop on Tanah Ulayat held in Padang in 1999.

Kirchmann, Julius von (1956 [1848]), *Die Wertlosigkeit der Jurisprudenz als Wissenschaft.* Ein Vortrag gehalten in der Juristischen Gesellschaft zu Berlin. Darmstadt: Wissenschaftliche Buchgesellschaft.

Lev, Daniel S. (1962), The Supreme Court and Adat Inheritance Law in Indonesia. *The American Journal of Comparative Law* 11:205-224.

Lev, Daniel S. (1965), The Lady and the Banyan Tree: Civil-Law Change in Indonesia. *The American Journal of Comparative Law* 14:282-307.

Lev, Daniel S. (1972), *Islamic Courts in Indonesia: a Study in the Political Bases on Legal Institutions*. Berkeley, Los Angeles: University of California Press.

Moore, Sally Falk (1973), Law and Social Change: the Semi-autonomous Social Field as an Appropriate Subject of Study. *Law & Society Review* 7:719-746.

Nelken, David (1984), Law in Action or Living Law? Back to the Beginning in Sociology of Law. *Legal Studies* 4:157-174.

Nelken, David (2009), Corruption as Governance? Law, Transparency and Appointment Procedures in Italian Universities. In: Franz von Benda-Beckmann, Keebet von Benda-Beckmann, and Julia Eckert (eds.), *Rules of Law and Laws of Ruling. On the Governance of Law*. Farnham and Burlington: Ashgate, pp. 257-277.

Rehbinder, Manfred (1967), *Die Begründung der Rechtssoziologie durch Eugen Ehrlich*. Berlin: Duncker & Humblot.

Rouland, Norbert (1994), *Legal Anthropology*. London: Athlone Press.

Sanders, A. J. G. M. (1987), How Customary is African Customary Law? *The Comparative and International Law Journal of South Africa* 20:405-410.

Simbolon, Indira J. (1998), Peasant Women and Access to Land: Customary Law, State Law and Gender-based Ideology – the Case of Toba-Batak – North Sumatra. PhD Thesis, Wageningen University.

Sitorus, Felix M. T. (2000), Hak waris janda dan anak perempuan Batak Toba. In: E. K. M. Masinambow (ed.), *Hukum dan kemanjemukan budaya*. Jakarta: Yayasan Obor, pp. 287-304.

Slaats, Herman M. C., and Maretta K. Portier (1986), Legal Plurality and the Transformation of Normative Concepts in the Process of Litigation in Karo Batak Society. In: Keebet von Benda-Beckmann, and Fons Strijbosch (eds.), *Anthropology of Law in the Netherlands*. Dordrecht, Berlin: Foris,Walter de Gruyter, pp. 217-239.

Subetki, R., and Tamara, J. (1965), *Kumpulan putusan mahkamah agung mengenai hukum adat*. Jakarta: Gunung Agung.

Teubner, Gunther (ed., 1997), *Global Law Without a State. Studies in Modern Law and Policy*. Aldershot, Brookfield USA, Singapore and Sydney: Dartmouth.

Van Vollenhoven, Cornelis van (1909). *Miskenningen van het adatrecht*. Leiden: Brill.

Vogl, Stefan (2009), Eugen Ehrlich's Linking of Sociology and Jurisprudence and the Reception of his Work in Japan. In: Marc Hertogh (ed.), *Living Law: Reconsidering Eugen Ehrlich*. Oxford: Hart, pp. 95-123.

Webber, Jeremy (2009), Naturalism and Agency in the Living Law. In Marc Hertogh (ed.), *Living Law: Reconsidering Eugen Ehrlich*. Oxford: Hart, pp. 201-221.

Wignjodipuro, Surojo (1973), *Pengantar dan azas-azas hukum adat*. Bandung: Alumni.

Ziegert, K. A. (2002), Introduction to the Transaction Edition. In: Eugen Ehrlich

(ed.), *Fundamental Principles of the Sociology of Law*. New Brunswick and London: Transaction Publishers, pp. xix–l.
Ziegert, Klaus A. (2009), World Society, Nation State and Living Law in the Twenty-first Century. In: Marc Hertogh (ed.), *Living Law: Reconsidering Eugen Ehrlich*. Oxford: Hart. 2009, pp. 223-236.

Ehrlich in Scandinavia

Legal Pluralist Perspectives in Scandinavian and African Women's Law*

Anne HELLUM

Living law and legal pluralities in feminist jurisprudence: Scandinavian and African women's law in the throes of change

Theories of living law and legal pluralism have in recent years become an ingredient in the diverse body of "post-Westphalian" legal scholarship which moves beyond considering states as the sole actors in international and national law. An example of this trend is the growing body of feminist legal studies dealing with the intricacies of enhancing women's access to law and justice in a rapidly changing world where law to a large extent is constituted in a process of interacting international, national and local norms. To better understand how claims for women's rights are made and responded to at different levels of law and within different social, cultural, economic and political contexts many feminist legal scholars are today turning their attention to the legal pluralities that operate in women's lives.[1]

This article describes how scholars of Scandinavian and African women's law, seeking an empirical understanding of women's interaction with the law in contemporary western welfare states and contemporary post-colonial states in Southern Africa, in the 1990s turned to theories of living law and legal pluralism. How a wide range of theories, ranging from Eugen Ehrlich's early 19th century theory of living law to post-colonial anthropological theory on legal pluralism, were employed for various purposes is the overall theme. Both in Scandinavia and in Southern and Eastern Africa women's law has been defined as a socio-legal discipline that set out to describe, understand and change the position of women in law and so-

* I would like to thank Ingunn Ikdahl, Monika Lindbekk, Hanne Petersen and Bill Derman for comments on this article.

1 Petersen (1991); Mehdi and Shaheed (1997); Griffiths (1997); Bentzon et al. (1998); Hellum (1999); Hellum et al. (2007); Mehdi et al. (2008); Ikdahl (2010); Hellum et al. (2011); Taj (2013); Derman et al. (2013); Stewart (2013); Sieder and John McNeish (2013); Mir-Hosseini et al. (2013).

ciety (Dahl 1987; Tsanga and Stewart 2011). To illustrate some lines of development within women's law, I have used as the basis for this article the women's law research carried out between 1975 and 2000 by scholars at the Faculty of Law in Oslo, the Faculty of Law in Copenhagen and the Faculty of Law in the University of Zimbabwe. I have selected texts written during this period by scholars who, in order to describe, understand and change the position of women in law and society, turned their attention to the legal pluralities operating in women's lives. Within this branch of research key authors were Hanne Petersen and Agnete Weis Bentzon from the University of Copenhagen, Mary Maboreke, Julie Stewart and Welshman Ncube from the University of Zimbabwe and Anne Hellum from the University of Oslo.

The overall aim is to show how legal scholarship analyzing women as actors in the process of law evolved within an analytical framework which combined the methodological principle of taking women's lived experiences as the starting point with theories that see law as a multi-sited process of interacting norms and practices. A related aim is to show how scholars within this stream of research used different theories of living law and legal pluralism for different purposes. To this end the article focuses on three aspects of the relationship between women's law, legal pluralities and living law. Firstly, it addresses how women's law scholars, in a situation where the prevailing state-centered notion of law blocked engagement with the complex normative situation which was part of women's everyday life, used Eugen Ehrlich's (1963) theory on living law as a historical link to a holistic legal tradition. Secondly, it describes how, in order to understand the way women's rights claims were shaped and responded to in a post-war and post-colonial context, women's law scholars turned to theories that explored law's semi-autonomy in terms of interacting international, national and local norms. Thirdly, it demonstrates how, seeking to change normative structures that negatively affected women's access to justice and equality, women's law scholars considered the options and limits of using living law and legal pluralism as an analytical, legal and political tool[2].

[2] For a critique of the analytical, legal and political use of living law and legal pluralism in legal research on African customary law and Islam, see Franz and Keebet von-Benda Beckmann's chapter in this book.

Women's law: gender-neutral law and gendered realities

Women's law was introduced as a legal discipline by students and teachers at the Faculty of Law at the University of Oslo in 1975. The aim was to describe, understand and improve the position of women in law and society (Dahl 1987). This new legal discipline met with considerable resistance from mainstream legal science because of its close relationship to the social sciences and to the women's rights movement. An overarching research theme was the relationship between increasingly gender-neutral state law and the asymmetric gender relationships that persisted in social life.

Taking as the starting point women's lived realities, there was series of research projects that explored the relationship between gender-neutral state law and women's and men's different living conditions, life values and life cycles. By this means a feminist jurisprudence was developed: it uncovered how law was moulded by male life experiences and values, and aimed to change it, by writing women's life experiences and life values into such legal principles as justice and freedom (Dahl 1987). This interdisciplinary approach stood on the shoulders of a long-standing Norwegian tradition of "problem-oriented empiricism" and "action research", which had a strong influence on legal science, sociology of law and women's studies in the 1970s (Mathiesen 2001; Widerberg 2000; Kalleberg 2013).

Through its analysis of the relationship between gender-neutral law and gendered realities women's law pushed the boundaries of legal science. To make women's life experiences relevant in legal discourse Tove Stang Dahl (1987, 55) outlined three fundamental sources requiring different methodological approaches: "(1) empirical data about the living facts of women in society and the operation of legal rules; (2) sources of law and legal doctrine; and (3) certain women-centered policy considerations."

As regards her empirical starting point Tove Stang Dahl (1987, 56) stated: "It is nothing new that a legal discipline should formulate a program linking it to empirical data or to policy considerations, in addition to maintaining its anchor in the more narrow legal doctrine." To support her claim she referred to the reflections of the Norwegian law professor Fredrik Stang from the 1930ies regarding the relationship between law and social science: "...never have there been more favorable conditions for a sociologically and economically focused legal science, and never before could it have had a greater usefulness" (Stang 1933, 139). Fredrik Stang, who was a proponent of a comparative and interdisciplinary legal science, founded the Institute for Comparative Cultural Studies in Oslo in 1923 (Skirbekk 1991). His legal scholarship, which encompassed comparative and empirical studies in commercial law and property law, made use of empirical insights into living conditions in the area of study.[3] In his academic writings he made extensive references to contemporary anthropology, and the emerging discipline of anthropology of law (Skirbekk 1991). Fredrik Stang's empirical approach had much in common with Eugen Ehrlich's theory about living law, which emphasized that the main objective of legal science should be the investigation of "living law" seen as "the law that dominates in life itself, even though it has not been posited in legal propositions" (Ehrlich 1963, 493-494). Like Eugen Ehrlich, Fredrik Stang (1934, 168) rejected the common assumption in European law that customary law arose from state law.[4]

Through inclusion of sources that took account of the female life situation, for example agreementes between spouses about time and money the discipline of women's law pushed at the boundaries between the private and the public, and between law and social science (Dahl 1987; Fastvold and Hellum 1988). How different groups of married women negotiated access to time and money within the family was described and analyzed in a study called "Money and Work in Marriage" which I conducted with Marianne Fastvold. A key source was unwritten agreements between the spouses which emerged from qualitative interview methods. Looking at the situation of women farmers in Eastern Norway, Tove Bolstad, who herself was a farmer, analyzed the way in which women's time and work was appropriated by her marital family on the basis of "kår contracts"[5] to satisfy their caring needs (Bolstad 1995). Studies of agreements between spouses

---

3 See Fredrik Stang *Innledning til formueretten* (Introduction to commercial law) from 1934, p. 168 where he concludes:' 'Og vil en videnskabelig forfatter gi de siste grunner for de avgjørelser han anviser, må han la sitt kjennskap til de reale livsforhold flyte inn i fremstillingen".

4 See Papendorf's chapter in this book emphasizing the commonalities between Stang's analysis of trade usage and Eugen Ehrlich's approach to living law, particularly his rejection of the widespread legal assumption that customary law only arises from juristic law or state law. Only in his book on Trade Usages did Fredrik Stang refer to some of Eugen Ehrlich's works.

5 Contracts between the male farmer and his parents about their right to housing, food and care.

and "kår contracts" were used to question family law theory, that portrayed the family as a harmonious unit, with women's lived realties. These concepts challenged the separation of the public and the private sphere, and the separation between law and society which was upheld by the state-centred notion of law at that time embedded in both legal science and sociology of law.[6]

From lived realities to legal polycentricity, legal pluralities and living law

A turning point in the conception of law in Scandinavian legal science was the theory on legal polycentricity of the Danish legal scholar Henrik Zahle from the University of Copenhagen (Zahle 1986). His theoretical proposition, which also drew inspiration from women's law theory, was that legal norms were generated in a multiplicity of fora, explicitly challenging the established theory of law based on a statist, monistic and hierarchic perception of law. A number of new studies in women's law contributed to a polycentric legal theory through examiniation of of the rule-generating processes taking place in other legal forums than the higher state- courts. The first doctoral thesis in women's law in Scandinavia, Kirsten Ketscher from the University of Copenhagen's "Public Childcare" was based on an empirical study of administrative practice (Ketscher 1989).

This broad perspective on law opened the way for further exploration of norm-generating processes taking place outside the courts and administrative agencies. Agnete Weis Bentzon, who had retired from her position as professor of sociology of law at Roskilde University, became professor emeritus at the Faculty of Law at the University of Copenhagen in 1987. On the basis of her rich fieldwork experiences in Greenland she was a strong proponent for a legal science based on empirical investigations of the norms evolving on the ground.[7] Through retroactive analysis of the Greenlandic

6 Thomas Mathiesen's textbook of sociology of law, *Retten i samfunnet* (Law in Society, 1984 and 1992 editions), addressed the social, economic and political landscape in which it operates. It focused on how social realities and conflicts were made into legal rules. Law, in this textbook, was defined as the rules that were developed and applied in state legal institutions. In later editions of the textbook *Retten i samfunnet* (1997, 2001, 2005 and 2011) there is a broader definition of law, including theory on legal pluralism.

7 See Hanne Petersen's article in this volume which addresses her main works in this respect, Bentzon 1968.

expedition's studies of the living customs of the Inuit, which were used as basis for law reform in connection with home rule (see Hanne Petersen and Knut Papendorf's chapters in this book), she emphasized the general relevance of a wide range of theories on living law and legal pluralism (Bentzon 1991, 1992, 1994, 1996).[8]

Hanne Petersen's doctoral thesis "Informal Law and Gendered Practices in Women's Workplaces" (Petersen 1991, 1996) took up this challenge. In her doctoral work she described the informal rules operating in four female workplaces in Copenhagen. Her work, which followed on from of women's law research focusing on the relationship between women's caring work and the law, was premised on the assumption that formal legal regulations were inadequate to secure a person's needs, or resolve conflicts where the worker was a woman with caring obligations in the family. With reference to the law's western and patriarchal nature Petersen turned to anthropological theory that recognized the law-making capacity of non-state actors in all modern nation states. Like the legal anthropologist Sally Falk Moore, Petersen saw women's workplaces as semi-autonomous social fields which, while regulated by state-law, also had the capacity to generate and enforce rules internally (Moore 1973). The different local and particular arrangements that were negotiated by the female workers, Petersen argued, were informed by a general norm she termed the norm of consideration:

> "The workplace has an (actual) obligation to secure that employees can make their working life and family life function under (the greatest possible) consideration of the actual conditions, needs and interests, which govern family life and the workplace respectively." (Petersen 1996, 47)

Rather than seeing women as objects of state law Petersen showed how, through interaction with fellow workers and their employers, women constantly negotiated arrangements that enabled them to reconcile their family obligations with their work obligations. The norm of consideration was seen as the outcome of this multitude of local and particular arrangements. In her conception of law Hanne Petersen (1996, 76) turned to newer the-

8 Agnete Weis Bentzon was a member of the Commission on Folk Law and Legal Pluralism and she regularly participated and presented papers at conferences arranged by the Commission. Her participation in this network influenced her theoretical understanding of the work of the Greenlandic expedition.

ory on the polycentricity of law and anthropology of law not linking law to "one exclusive authority to whom or which all other norm-initiating entities are subjugated." She made extensive reference to John Griffiths, who in his article on legal pluralism said: "The legal order of all societies is not an exclusive, systematic, unified, hierarchical ordering of normative propositions depending onthe state, but has its sources in the self-regulatory activities of all the multifarious social fields represented in society." (Petersen 1996, 76)

Linking a legal insider perspective on law provided by legal polycentricity with a sociological outsider perspective provided by legal pluralism Petersen (1996, 78) wrote:

> "The theoretical approaches to law, which we have called legal polycentricity, seem to allow for an inclusion for multiple norms –and multiple forms – arising from multiple centers. This is an approach which is also favorable towards an inclusion of a plurality of values. Thus, it does also allow for a reflection and incorporation of practices and principles of relevance for women's lives."

As a justification for a legal approach that in its description and analysis of law focused on the norms that regulate people's everyday lives Hanne Petersen, like Tove Stang Dahl, used earlier theories that did not make a sharp distinction between social and legal norms. Hanne Petersen, who grew up in a Danish minority community in Germany and was fluent in German, had read the original German version of Eugen Ehrlich's theory of living law.[9] Referring to Ehrlich's definition of living law as "the law that dominates in life itself, even though it has not been posited in legal propositions" Petersen (1991, 67) argued that law was not confined to the norms that were applied and enforced through the state legal institutions. Eugen Ehrlich's approach to customary law, particularly the distinction between "norms of conduct" and "norms of decision", is referred to in her thesis but not used in the analysis of the practices observed at the women's work places. In her discussion of the thesis, Agnete Weis Bentzon (1992) commented that different theories of living law and legal pluralism could have been used as a legal tool to ascertain whether the practices observed constituted customary law.

From a feminist legal perspective Hanne Petersen's thesis contributed to an understanding of law as a gendered process. By using the law's semi-autonomy as an analytical tool she was able to show how women workers

9 Petersen 1991, 66 makes reference to Ehrlich 1913, 29.

were actors of legal change rather than passive objects of the existing state law which was moulded by men's living conditions and values. Petersen's study gave rise to debate as to whether women's interests were better protected by living law, or whether reform of the formal law was needed. In this debate Hanne Petersen was of the view that the living law was law while Agnete Weis Bentzon suggested that the question whether the norm of consideration constituted customary law should be further explored.

Post-colonial encounters: Norwegian women's law meets African customary laws

Another turning point in women's law research was the encounter with post-colonial law in Southern and Eastern Africa. In 1987 scholars at the Institute of Women's Law in Oslo and at Southern and Eastern African universities embarked on a joint North-South teaching and research program in women's law.[10] The background of this collaboration was the newly independent African states' need for legal reform that took the social, political and legal context of African women as a starting point.[11]

The programme was framed by the methodological principle of taking women as the starting point in the analysis of law. While this open-ended methodological approach held great potential, the ideological content of women's law theory (Dahl 1987) was very much a reflection of how the ostensibly unified and gender-neutral legal system of the Norwegian welfare state responded to the situation of Norwegian women in the 1980s. Mary Maboreke from the University of Zimbabwe, who was one of the African lecturers on the course, gave the following summary of her experiences:

[10] The forerunner of this programme was the bilateral agreement made in 1984 between the University of Zimbabwe and the University of Oslo, which also included law. The reason for the collaboration in the field of law was that, as part of efforts to build up a new legal system, the Faculty of Law at the University of Zimbabwe wanted to draw on legal scholarship in sociology of law, human rights law, family law and women's law in Nordic social democracies. To promote the legal rights of women the University of Zimbabwe was particularly interested in cooperation in the field of women's law and family law. On the basis of Mary Maboreke's and Welshman Ncube's master's thesis in women's law and family law the University of Zimbabwe introduced women's law as an optional legal subject in 1987.

[11] The cooperation was funded by the Norwegian Agency of Development Cooperation (NORAD) on the basis of a foreign policy with strong emphasis on the right to gender equality.

"Starting out from a Norwegian women's law framework, which of course reflects the Norwegian culture, and at the same time being African, made women's law strange and difficult. I can use the considerations of woman's law as an example: equality, justice, self-realization, self-determination and integrity. I can see that these considerations fit the Norwegian context. A person is a person, and people are evaluated on an individual basis. In an African context this is completely different. I am never just Mary Maboreke, except when I am at work. When I am at home I am the mother of Tachinga, wife of Lawrence, sister of George, etc. These relationships will continue and continue. It is such relationships that give me and other African women an identity."[12]

What was needed, the African scholars in the programme emphasized, was an empirical examination of the complex realities of women's lives in multi-ethnic, multi-racial and socially differentiated societies in post-colonial Africa, where international law, state-law, customary law and local norms coexisted and interacted. To facilitate empirical research that took the lived realities and legal pluralities of different groups of women in post-colonial Southern and Eastern Africa as starting point, in 1990 the programme was moved from the University of Oslo to the University of Zimbabwe.[13]

For Mary Maboreke, Julie Stewart and me, who were in charge of this North-South cooperation, it was a challenge to set up a framework for empirical studies of the complex legal situation of different groups of women in post-colonial Africa. The legal systems in the Southern and Eastern African countries that participated in the program were, at that point in time, in the throes of rapid and uneven change. The new independent states that had fought against colonialism and apartheid were in search of new, innovative ways of "liberating" African customary law from its colonial heritage, which had turned it into an instrument of racial segregation and patriarchal rule. Whether, and to what extent, African values – particularly African customary laws – could be reconciled with women's realities on the ground, and the demands of human rights principles such as freedom and equality for women was a highly contested issue.

Mozambique adopted a popular justice system with elected judges that on a case-to-case basis was designed to build a new normative system

12 Interview with Mary Maboreke by Børing and Grannes (1991).

13 In Ikdahl (2013, 2014) this programme's contribution to the Internationalzation strategy of the Faculty of Law at the University of Oslo is described.

merging local customary norms with socialist principles and human rights (Sachs and Welch 1990; Berg and Gundersen 1991; Gundersen 1992). In Zimbabwe the inherited Rhodesian dual legal system, in which African customary laws applied to black Africans in the field of family and personal laws, while the imported Roman Dutch law applied to the white settlers, had to be undone after independence in 1980. In a post-apartheid climate, where the black African socialists were fighting for the equal distribution of resources, and power and equality under the law, customary law was seen as a static, frozen form of law that had been distorted by the colonial legal powers. Welshman Ncube (1986), in his master's thesis on women's property rights, in the light of marxist theory concluded that new laws doing away with race and gender discrimination in customary law needed to be enacted. In spite of these critisisms of customary law the Zimbabwean government by and large upheld the colonial family law and marriage law system that recognized three types of marriages; civil law marriages, registered customary marriages, and unregistered customary marriages.

Needless to say, a key concern within this research and teaching program was how to describe, understand and change the unequal gender relations embedded in the statutory and customary laws that had been developed under colonial rule. To build up a body of knowledge a number of master's and doctoral studies that would involve empirical data about women's encounters with various forms of law in different social fields were formulated. To guide and monitor these studies a group of African and Scandinavian scholars embarked on a joint research methodology project. These were Julie Stewart and Welshman Ncube from the University of Zimbabwe, who also were members of the Women and Law in Southern African Research Project (WLSA), Agnete Weis Bentzon and Torben Agersnap from the University of Copenhagen, and Anne Hellum from the University of Oslo.[14] This joint work resulted in the book *Pursuing Grounded Theory in Law: South-North Perspectives in Developing Women's Law* (Bentzon et al. 1998). The book project constituted an arena for reflection and the development of analytical tools. It was based on experiences from the action-

[14] Agnete Weis Bentzon was guest professor at the Institute of Women's Law in Oslo from 1991 to 1996 and participated in the women's law program at the University of Zimbabwe. In the 1990s Agnete Weis Bentzon wrote a number of articles in which she analysed the data from these research projects within the framework of newer anthropological theory on legal pluralism. See Hanne Petersen's article in this volume.

oriented research carried out by the Women and Law in Southern Africa Research Project, Norwegian and Danish women's law methodology, Scandinavian sociology of law, and post-colonial anthropological studies of living law and legal pluralism. With her experience gained from the Greenlandic expedition, which had sought to identify and incorporate the Inuit's living customs into the new common legal system for Danes and Inuit in Greenland, Agnete Weis Bentzon was a strong advocate of an approach which took the norms practiced by the people on the ground as the starting point.

Seeing local communities, and the women within them, as agents of social and legal change we approached African customary laws as dynamic, flexible norms that varied with time and place. This approach was based upon anthropological, sociological and legal scholarship that rejected the view that customary law emanated from sources of state law in terms of legal codifications, or case law. It was also based on women's law theory taking women'sex periences, values and practices as starting point. Our understanding of African customary law as a form of living law that was rooted in everyday life had much in common with Eugen Ehrlich's conception of "living law" as "the law that dominates in life itself, even though it has not been posited in legal propositions" (Ehrlich 1963, 493-494). Both Agnete Weis Bentzon and I had read Eugen Ehrlich's work on living law, and used it as a reference point in a long-standing European legal tradition which included elements that had not originated from state-law (Hellum 1996, Bentzon 1996). However, to understand the creation, role and function of customary law in Southern and Eastern Africa we turned to African legal history and the growing body of post-colonial anthropology of law. A key work was Martin Chanock's classic study of how customary law was created in the early phase of colonialism, and the complex struggles in which western colonizers, African tribal authorities, and African men and women invoked and manipulated notions of western and African law to create a new form of law which was neither customary nor western (Chanock 1985). Another entry point to our understanding of African customary law was through the work of Gordon Woodman on legal pluralism. His extensive analysis, focusing on Ghana, of how colonial courts in Africa had turned the living customary norms existing on the ground into a static body of state-court customary law, had relevance for the situation in Zimbabwe and other countries in Southern and Eastern Africa (Woodman 1988).

Seeking tools to study the norms which were evolving in social life, and

African women's participation in these processes, we also drew inspiration from the anthropologist J.F Holleman's reflections on the use of trouble-cases and trouble-less cases in the study of customary law land legal reform.[15] In his 1973 article Holleman, referring to Eugen Ehrlich's theory on living law, confronted what he termed a classical dilemma in the study of customary law namely: "How to prevent the law from slipping out of its social context; or in Ehrlich's terms, how to prevent the divergence between the evolved positive law and living law" (Holleman 1973, 61). As a way out of this dilemma Holleman suggested that African customary law should be studied, not only through cases from the upper strata of the formal courts, but also in problems solved in informal local forum and most importantly in trouble-less cases of everyday life:

"In order to discover current and newly emerging regularities of popularly accepted conduct as evidence of the internal growth of law through changes in social relations and economic traffic, also a fair sample of what I have called the trouble-less cases of prevalent and trouble- avoiding practices should be included in the focus of attention. With regard to marriage, family, property, for instance the validity of marital unions, rights and obligations of conjugal partners, the legitimacy of children. These may still be insufficiently developed and not widely enough accepted to be considered truly normative, but they deserve close attention as indicators of the direction and future that shape the internal growth of living law (Holleman 1973, 61)."

The inclusion of trouble-less cases in everyday life as a source of living law became a stepping stone for research, indicating how women negotiated their position in the family and in the local community. The best-known research using this analytical approach is the inheritance research carried out by The Women and Law in Southern Africa Research Project (WLSA) between 1993 and 1995. Looking at cases resolved amicably in the family, through mediation by third parties ranging from chiefs, resettlement officers and local court officers, the WLSA research carried out in Zimbabwe

15 In his early study of Shona customary law in Rhodesia Holleman was, however, strongly inspired by structuralist kinship theory, most importantly that of A. R.Radicliffe-Brown. In the preface to his 1952 monograph on Shona customary law Holleman writes: "In this connexion I wish to add a word of deep gratitude to Prof. A.R.Radcliffe-Brown, not only because I have depended heavily on his pioneer studies of kinship structure, but especially because his correspondence with me while I was in the field, has profoundly influenced my whole concept of Shona kinship law" (Holleman 1952, xii).

documented a growing preference for the appointment of the widow as an intestate heir to the deceased husband's estate (Stewart and Tsanga 2007). The research revealed that the norms which were emerging on the ground were far more nuanced and flexible than the state courts' version of customary law. The post-colonial state courts in Zimbabwe were, following colonial case law, upholding the position that widows could not inherit under African customary law.

In their advocacy for legal change the members of the WLSA team argued that the living customary law evolving on the ground should form the basis for law reform. On the basis of this research, in 1997 the ZANU PF-dominated parliament in Zimbabwe passed a new act that recognized the rights of women to inherit on an equal basis from their deceased parents' estates (Stewart and Tsanga 2007). According to Professor Julie Stewart (who was both part of the WLSA research team and a member of the Law and Development Commission):

"This research, and a comprehensive understanding of customary patterns of inheritance and their attendant obligations, was critical in negotiating the final stages of the inheritance law reform. Although women's rights were not directly invoked in this process, they were the background influence that helped drive women lawyers' determination to obtain reform. Based on research and strategic argumentation, formal recognition of women's and all children's rights to inherit from their deceased parents' estates was recognised. The key move when patriarchal and patrilineal arguments were holding sway and likely to derail the reform process, was the capacity of one of the WLSA researchers to ask the then-President of the Council of Chiefs, Chief Mangwende, to explain the purpose behind customary patterns of inheritance. To the great relief of all the women present, he replied that it was to care for and sustain the family of the deceased and that there was no estate until the surviving spouse or spouses died. This led to the Council of Chiefs' acceptance, in principle, of the reform and the legislation passed through Parliament." (Stewart and Damiso 2013, 464-465).

This example shows how activist African scholars, to develop appropriate strategies for research and action, used living law and legal pluralism as an analytical, political and legal tool.[16] It demonstrates how at that point in time they successfully used living law as a means of promoting women's human rights. But, as shown by other studies, the harsh reality is often

---

[16] Franz and Keebet von Benda-Beckmann in this book address the use of living law in contemporary South African customary law theory.

that the legal needs of women and girls are overridden or compromised in the local, national and international processes in which rights, culture and religious values are negotiated (Sithole 2007). Thus any consideration of the use of living law and legal pluralism as a strategy for promoting women's rights must be located and understood within a broader analysis of history, context, power and regimes of governance.

Women's human rights and legal pluralism in Africa: bridging the gap?

In the 1990s a number of African states ratified the Convention on the Elimination of All Forms of Discrimination against Women (CEDAW). In my doctoral work "Women's human rights and legal pluralism: Mixed norms and identities in infertility management in Zimbabwe", I set out to explore how the CEDAW's demand for gender-equal marriage laws was reconciled with women's experiences of the legal pluralities that informed their marriage and family relationships in everyday life (Hellum 1999). Rather than analyzing whether legal pluralism was compatible with human rights I was interested in how legal pluralities interplay with the promotion of women's rights.

To bring the concept of gender equality down from the plane of abstract international principles I examined it in relation to how different groups of childless women in Zimbabwe managed their procreative problems in everyday life. I wondered how different groups of women negotiated their position at the interface of the increasingly gender-neutral and equality-based family laws, and the prevailing patrilineal kinship norms that associated women's status with her childbearing capacity. To explore these questions I carried out fieldwork in urban middle class areas in Harare, a lower class high density area in Harare and in a peri-urban area. To describe and understand the circumstances under which the promotion of women's human rights was facilitated or hindered the study was framed by concepts such as the semi-autonomy of social fields (Moore 1973). It was used to draw a boundary around social entities that I assumed were affected by the equality principle embedded in international and Zimbabwean family law, but also had the capacity to uphold or generate rules internally (Hellum 1999,175-256).

To understand the normative interplay that took place through decision-making in the family, and consultations withtraditional healers and church ministers I examined the relationships and networks to which the childless women, family members, traditional healers and actors in court belonged. This provided a window into the complex process in which human rights were adopted or resisted through gendered power struggles taking place at the local level. Most women regarded the prevailing assumption that women were to blame for childlessness as a form of patriarchal power. Yet it was mainly urban middle class women who had social networks and resources that enabled them to take advantage of the protection offered by the increasingly fertility- and gender-neutral marriage legislation. Poor rural and peri-urban women, who were dependent for their survival on the entitlements arising from family relationships, pursued other paths, for example polygamous unions. Situating the CEDAW as a tool for change in a socially differentiated and pluralistic legal landscape I concluded:

> "An understanding of the bargaining power of different groups of women is crucial for understanding the process whereby patrilineal gender norms are reproduced or changed in their meeting with other norms (law reform aiming at gender equality in the family) in different contexts and settings." (Hellum 1999, 424)

To consider human rights progress I argued that human rights treaty bodies ought to acknowledge that adoption of their precepts is a long-term process, and that countries and communities respond at different rates and in different ways, and with different effects for different groups of women. Rather than analyzing whether or not legal pluralism was compatible with human rights I worked out a framework that examined an uneven and complex process in which norms and practices were changing at the local level. Regarding the disjunction between international human rights and the uneven normative development taking place on the ground I argued that it was an important task for the legal science s to provide a nuanced picture of custom and local law as a site of diverse and contested practices (Hellum, 2000, 60). To assess the extent of the emerging blend of human rights law, state law and local norms I suggested parameters addressing social, gendered, institutional and geographic space.

In this way I attempted to build a bridge between a descriptive approach, addressing the legal pluralities that operate in women's lives, and a normative approach embedded in international human rights law. In this endeavour Eugen Ehrlich's theory of living law provided a historical link to a holistic legal science, while the newer post-colonial anthropology of law theory helped me to come to grips with the complex and uneven situation on the ground. The normative and value-oriented women's law approach prompted my attempt to bridge the conceptual gap between human rights and legal pluralities through an approach that focused on the complex and uneven processes of socio-legal change.

Women's law and living law – a happy marriage?

We have seen how, by taking a broad interdisciplinary approach, which combines the methodological principle of taking women as the starting point and empirical studies of living law and legal pluralism, Scandinavian and African women's law scholars have anayzed the way women's rights claims are made and responded to at different levels and within different contexts. Scrutiny of claims-making processes initiated by women experiencing gender-based exclusion and inequality show that neither statutory, customary nor religious norms are static and bounded: they change in the face of challenges from individuals, group members and outsiders in a shifting and contested social, economic, and legal environment.

Eugen Ehrlich's theory of living law was a source of inspiration for Danish and Norwegian women's law scholars following this path, because it questioned the dominant state-centered notion of law propounded by Scandinavian legal realists such as Alf Ross and Torstein Eckhoff. To understand how women's rights claims were shaped and responded to in social fields where a multiplicity of norms were at work, such as the family and the workplace, concepts and theories that viewed law as a process of interacting normative structures, such as semi-autonomy, living law and local law were used. In an effort to change normative structures negatively affecting women's access to justice and equality women's law scholars moved beyond a purely descriptive approach to living law and legal pluralism.This normative and value-oriented perspective constitutes a delicate balancing act that calls for careful consideration of the options and limits of using living law and legal pluralism as an analytical, legal and political tool in diverse and shifting political and legal landscapes. Thus any consideration of the use of living law and legal pluralism as a strategy for promoting women's rights must be located and understood within a broader analysis of history, context, power and regimes of governance.

References

Bentzon, Agnete Weis (1968), *Familiens økonomiske administration og ejendelenes tilhørsforhold i de vestgrønlandske samfund – en retssociologisk undersøgelse.* Copenhagen: Nyt fra Samfundsvidenskaberne (Doctoral Dissertation awarded by the Faculty of Law at the University of Oslo in 1968).

Bentzon, Agnete Weis (1991), Sædvaneret, polycentri og legal pluralisme – en arbejdsnote. In: *Retsvidenskabeligt Institut B Årsberetning*. Copenhagen: University of Copenhagen, pp. 19-27.

Bentzon, Agnete Weis (1992), Anmeldelse av Hanne Petersen: Informel Ret på Kvindearbeidsplasser". *Juristen* 74:1988-1990.

Bentzon, Agnete Weis (1994), European Family Law Confronting the Extended Family in Developing Countries? The Case of Greenland and Mocambique". *Law and Anthropology* 7: 311-329.

Bentzon, Agnete Weis (1996), Some Useful Concepts in the Study of the Diversity and Change of Law in North and South. In: Signe Arnfred and Hanne Petersen (eds.), *Legal Change in North/South Perspective*. Occasional Paper no. 18. International Development Studies. Roskilde University.

Bentzon, Agnete, W., Hellum, Anne, Stewart, Julie, E., Ncube,Welshman and Agersnap, Torben (1998), *Women's Law: Pursuing Grounded Theory. South-North Experiences in Developing Women's Law.* Oslo/Harare: TANO/Mond Books.

Berg, Nina and Gundersen, Aase (1991), Legal Reform in Mozambique, Equality and Emancipation for Women through Popular Justice. In: Kristiane Stølen and Mariken Vaa (eds.). In: *Gender and Change in Developing Countries.* Oslo: Norwegian University Press.

Bolstad, Tove (1995), Kår-Contracts in Norway: Agreements Made Between Men Concerning Women's Work, Ownership and Lives. *Working Papers in Women's Law No. 46*. University of Oslo.

Børing, Hanne and Grannes, Annette (1991), Interview with Mary Maboreke. *Hefte for kritisk juss* 1:17-25.

Chanock, Martin (1985*), Law, Custom and Social Order. The Colonial Experience in Malawi and Zambia*. Cambridge: Cambridge University Press.

Dahl, Tove Stang (1987), Feminist *Jurisprudence. An Introduction to Womens Law*. Oslo: Norwegian University Press.

Damiso, Choice and Stewart, Julie (2013), Zimbabwe and CEDAW Compliance: Pursuing Women's Equality in Fits and Starts. In: Hellum, Anne and Aasen, Henriette Sinding (eds.), *Women's Human Rights. CEDAW in International,*

Regional and National Law. Cambridge: Cambridge University Press, pp. 454-481.

Derman, Bill, Hellum, Anne and Sandvik, Kristin (eds. 2013), *Worlds of Human Rights: Ambiguities of Rights Claiming in Africa*. Leiden: Brill.

Ehrlich, Eugen (1913), *Grundlegung der Soziologie des Rechts*. Duncker & Humblot, München.

Ehrlich, Eugen (1963), *Fundamental Principles of Sociology of Law*. New York: Russel & Russel Inc.

Fastvold, Marianne and Hellum, Anne (1988), *Money and Work in Marriage*. Studies in Womens Law No. 26. University of Oslo.

Gundersen, Aase (1992), Popular Justice in Mozambique: Between State Law and Folk Law. *Social and Legal Studies* 1:257-282.

Griffiths, Anne (1997), In *the Shadow of Marriage. Gender and Justie in an African Community*. Chicago: University of Chicago Press.

Griffiths, John (1986), What is Legal Pluralism? *Journal of Legal Pluralism* 24:1-55.

Hellum, Anne (1996), Women as Subjects in the Process of Law: The Use of Empirical Sources in Women's Law. In: Signe Arnfred and Hanne Petersen (eds.), *Legal Change in North/South Perspective*. Occasional Paper no. 18, International Development Studies. Roskilde University.

Hellum, Anne (1999), *Women's Human Rights and Legal Pluralism in Africa: Mixed Norms and Identities in Infertility Management in Zimbabwe*. Oslo/Harare: TANO Aschehoug/ Mond Books.

Hellum, Anne (2002), How to Improve the Doctrinal Analysis of Legal Pluralism: A Comparison of the Legal Doctrine about Custom and Local Law in Zimbabwe and Norway. *Retfærd* 89/23:40-62

Hellum, Anne (2012), CEDAW and the Discipline of Women's Law: Continuity and Change in the Understanding of Gender and Law. In Nielsen, Ruth and Tvarnø, Christina (eds.) *Scandinavian Women's Law in the 21st Century*. Copenhagen: DJØF Publishing, pp. 31-57

Hellum, Anne, Ali Shaheen, S., and Griffiths, Anne (eds., 2011), *From Transnational Relations to Transnational Laws. Northern European Laws at the Crossroads*. Farnham: Ashgate.

Holleman, John.F. (1952), *Shona Customary Law. With reference to Kinship, Marriage, the Family and the Estate.* Oxford: Oxford University Press.

Holleman, John, F. (1973), Trouble-cases and Trouble-less in the Study of Customary Law and Legal Reform. *Law and Society Review* 1973:585-609.

Ikdahl, Ingunn (2010), *Securing Women's Homes. The Dynamics of Women's Human Rights at the International Level and in Tanzania*. PhD thesis. Faculty of Law, University of Oslo.

Ikdahl, Ingunn (2014), Om rettsvitenskap og internasjonalisering: Fagutvikling ved kvinnerettsmiljøet i Oslo i perioden 1985-2013. *Retfærd.* 144/37:96?116.

Kalleberg, Ragnvald (2013), Om tverrfaglig samspill mellom rettevitenskap og sosiologi. In: Kirsti Strøm Bull and Marit Halvorsen (eds.), *Det juridiske fakultet gjennom 200 år. Kontinuitet og fornyelse*. Akademisk Publisering. Universitetet i Oslo, pp. 31-57.
Ketscher, Kirsten (1990), *Offentlig børnepass i retlig belysning*. Copehagen: Jurist og økonomiforbundets forlag.
Mathiesen, Thomas (2001), Huset med det rare i. *Kritisk Juss* 28:87-100.
Mathiesen, Thomas (1984), *Retten i samfunnet*. Oslo: Pax.
Mathiesen, Thomas (1997), *Retten I samfunnet*. Oslo: Pax.
Mathiesen, Thomas (2011), *Retten I samfunnet*. Oslo: Pax.
Mehdi, Rubya, and Shaheed, Farida (eds., 1997), *Women's Law in Legal Education and Practice in Pakistan*. Copenhagen: North South New Social Science Monographs.
Mehdi, Rubya, Petersen, Hanne, Reenberg, Erik, S. and Woodman, Gordon (eds., 2008), *Law and Religion in Multicultural Socities*. Copenhagen: DJØF Publishing.
Moore, Sally Falk (1973), Law and Social Change: the Semi-autonomous Social Field as an Appropriate Subject of Study. *Law & Society Review* 7:719-746.
Mir-Hosseini, Ziba, Vogt, Kari, Larsen, Lena, and Moe, Christian (eds. 2013), *Gender and Equality in Muslim Family Law, Justice and Ethics in the Islamic Legal Tradition*. London/New York: I.B. Tauris.
Ncube, Welshman (1986), Master thesis under the degree of philosophy of law, awarded by the University of Zimbabwe in 1986.
Petersen, Hanne (1991), *Informel ret på kvindearbejdspladser. En teoretisk og empirisk analyse*. København: Akademisk Forlag.
Petersen, Hanne (1996), *Home Knitted Law. Norms and Values in Gendered Rule-Making*: Aldershot: Dartmouth.
Sachs, Albie and Welch, Gita (1990), *Liberating the Law: Creating Popular Justice in Mozambique*. London and New Jersey: Zed Books.
Sieder, Rachel and McNeish, John (2013), Introduction. In: Rachel Sieder and McNeish, John (eds.),*Gender Justice and Legal Pluralities: Latin American and African Perspectives*. Abingdon:Routledge, pp. 1-30.
Sithole, Ellen (2007), Women's Burden: Women, HIV/AIDS and Home-based Care in Zimbabwe. In: Anne Hellum, Julie Stewart, Shaheen Ali and Amy Tsanga (eds.), *Human Rights Plural Legalities and Gendered Realities: Paths are Made by Walking*. Harare: Weaver Press, pp. 78-105.
Skirbekk, Gaute (1991), Rettsantropologi i norsk rettsvitenskap. *Tidsskrift for rettsvitenskap* 104: 449-479.
Stang, Fredrik (1934). *Innledning til formueretten*. Universitetet i Oslo.
Stewart, Anne (2013), *Gender, Law and Justice in a Global Market*. Cambridge; Cambridge University Press.
Stewart, Julie and Tsanga, Amy (2007), The Widow's and the Child's Portion: The

Twisted Path to Partial Equality for Widows and Daughters under Customary Law in Zimbabwe. In: Anne Hellum, Julie Stewart, Shaheen Ali and Amy Tsanga (eds.), *Human Rights Plural Legalities and Gendered Realities: Paths are Made by Walking*. Harare: Weaver Press, pp. 407-437.

Taj, Farhat (2013), *Legal Pluralism, Human Rights and Islam in Norway. Making Norwegian Law Available, Acceptable and Accessible to Women in a Multicultural Setting*. PhD dissertation, Faculty of Law, University of Oslo.

Tsanga, Amy and Stewart Julie (eds., 2011*), Women and Law. Innovative Approaches to Teaching, Research and Analysis.* Harare: Weaver Press.

Widerberg, Karin (2000), Harriet Holter: A Pioneer in Gender Studies and Sociology. *Acta Sociologica* 43:413-420.

Woodman, Gordon (1988), How State Courts Created Customary Law in Ghana and Nigeria, In: Bradford W. Morse and Gordon Woodman, (eds.), *Indigenous Law and the State*. Dordrecht: Foris Publication.

Zahle, Henrik (1986), Polycentri i retskildelæren. In: Torkel Opsahl and Magnus Aarbakke (eds), *Samfunn, Rett, Rettferdighet. Festskrift til Torstein Eckhoffs 70-årsdag*. Oslo: Tano, pp 752-756.

Zahle, Henrik and Petersen, Hanne (eds.,1995). *Polycentricity in Law.* Aldershot: Dartmoth Press.

A Voyage of Discovery: Eugen Ehrlich in Scandinavia

Knut PAPENDORF

Concept and idea

In a first version of this chapter I started by looking at how Eugen Ehrlich is presented in textbooks about the sociology of law in the Scandinavian countries. But I soon discovered that this approach was not in any way sufficient. With the exception of Sweden, as I will later show, sociology of law textbooks in the Scandinavian countries are marked – especially in the case of Norway – by an overwhelming absence of any presentation of Ehrlich and his living law concept. In other words, I had to start with a broader perspective, in which I both had to expand my time frame – the first textbook on sociology of law in the Scandinavian countries was not published until 1968 – and to include a broader discussion, and more research on issues connected to Ehrlich's suggestions on applying sociological method to legal science. In this regard I will start the second part of this paper with an examination of the famous Danish Greenland expedition of the early 1950s and the researchers' findings on the living law situation there (Betænkning 1950). Then – in the third part – following a suggestion made by the Swedish sociologist of law, Per Stjernquist, who identifies research on people's traditional legal perceptions primarily located in Norway (1986, 653), I will present three of these scholars: Fredrik Stang (1907 and 1935), Kristian Østberg (1914-39) and Erik Solem (1967; first edition 1933). Stang is most notable: his suggestions regarding customs and practice in trade relationships, with their particular emphasis on the practice of established trade organizations, seem to embody Ehrlich's living law concept and research. But Østberg's research on traditional (ancient) law relating to farmers (bonderett) too is quite close both to Ehrlich's methodological suggestions arising from his research on living law, and to his presentations of past surveys on living law relating to, for example the leasing of pasture, hay meadows or farmland (Ehrlich 1967, 55). This also applies to Solem and his research on the living law of the reindeer Same.

Part 1: Ehrlich in the Scandinavian textbooks on sociology of law

In Norway

Vilhelm Aubert was the first to write a textbook on sociology of law in Norway, and I think his was the first such book in all the Scandinavian countries (Aubert 1968). A cursory look at this book and the literature cited in it shows that Ehrlich does not seem to be of much importance. The same goes for his famous article of 1976, where he explicitly discusses the effectiveness of law (Aubert 1976, 308 pp). However, I will claim that this doesn't mean he is not discussing Ehrlich – but that he is doing so implicitly. In chapter 3 (ibid. 57 pp) of his textbook *Effects of laws* (*Lovgivningens virkninger*), his main interest is how far laws have any effect on people's willingness to obey them. In this context he presents and discusses the results of the 1952 Norwegian research on housekeeper law (hushjelpsloven) (Aubert, Eckhoff, Sveri). This work is very well known, so I can be quite brief here: The effects of this law were quite limited, both as regards the practical working conditions of servants, and as regards knowledge of the law. Since the level of knowledge about the law and the regulations was low, there was also a very limited connection between knowledge of the law and actual behavior. Tone Sverdrup (1984) later told us that the law relating to servants was applied to an area in which working conditions were predominantly personally based, and where the new law was bound to be seen as a foreign element; it was therefore not adapted to this very particular private and family-based context. A servant responsible for young children could not leave her place of work before the mother or father got back from work, even if she had already worked for the eight hours stipulated in the standard wage agreement.

Later in this chapter Aubert presents some results of Agnete Weis Bentzon's (1954) research on Danish law, and Greenland's customary law on marriage, and the property-relations between married couples. Because family structures differed from those found in Denmark, "the new Danish family law does not fit very well with the new Greenlandic extended family", as Aubert (1968, 64) says when summing up his presentation of Agnete Weis Bentzon's research.

Introducing some reflections from Per Stjernquist (1954), Aubert (1968, 65) goes on to ask if the whole question about the effects of laws is a good starting point. Is it not rather the case – as Stjernquist says – that laws alone never have any effects but must be seen as a part of "an area of social factors", and this is what one should examine. In other words, Stjernquist is quite skeptical about isolating the effects of law, or any other legal phenomenon. Aubert seems here to follow Stjernquist's arguments.

So we can conclude that the connection between Aubert and Ehrlich is Aubert's focus on the law's environment as a crucial condition for the law's effectiveness. But like Mathiesen (2011), in his textbook he contextualizes this not as a starting point, but more as a reactive perspective.

Thomas Mathiesen's textbook, *Law in society* (*Retten i samfunnet*) was first published in 1984. When one looks at the bibliography one finds that Ehrlich is not mentioned here either. But here the first glance does not give a correct picture. When Mathiesen discusses the ineffectiveness of law, he illustrates his findings with empirical research on the Norwegian prison law, the housekeeper act (hushjelploven) and on the availability of legal aid, with the main focus on marginalized persons and groups. In this context he presents the environment of the law as a vital condition for the effectiveness of law and its norms. Where state law comes up against the legal expectations of different social associations – to put it in Ehrlich's terms – Mathiesen conceptualizes this as "the social, political and economic environment". In Mathiesen's view "the social, political and economic environment" is crucial in determining whether or not the law has the intended effect. To put this in his own words: "The realization of the intended effects of the law in general depends on the social, economic and political surroundings in which the law is operating" (Mathiesen 2011, 75, my translation from Norwegian). If the social, political or economic environment conflicts with a law's intention, the law will not have the intended effect. To connect this conclusion to Ehrlich, we could say with Deflem: "Manifesting the practical consequences of his theoretical orientation, Ehrlich argues that legal propositions have to be consistent with the codes of living law to be effective" (Deflem 2009, 91).

In my view Mathiesen here – implicitly – introduces some of the main findings of Ehrlich, emphasizing the importance of the environment, or of social associations, we could say, for the effectiveness of state law. What Mathiesen does not do, is take the issue of the origin of law as his starting point, unlike Ehrlich. In this he seems to be more interested in a reactive perspective on the effectiveness of state law, or juridic law.

In Denmark

Before I take a look at Jørgen Dalberg-Larsen's textbook, a few words about his doctoral thesis (Dalberg-Larsen 1977, 309 pp). In the course of presenting a more ambitious analysis of the development of jurisprudence from the 18th to the 20th century (ibid. 109 pp), he also introduces Eugen Ehrlich in the context of the so-called "Freirechtsschule" (free-law school). Eugen Ehrlich is here presented as one of the key figures (besides Hermann Kantorowicz and others). Ehrlich is described by Dalberg-Larsen as a sociologist of law who identified a number of non-juridical norms in various parts of Austro-Hungary which were more important for how people behaved than juridical law. As examples of Ehrlich's famous research work Dalberg-Larsen cites among other things his *Grundlegung zur Soziologie des Rechts* (1913) and his *Recht und Leben. Gesammelte Schriften zur Rechtstatsachenforschung und zur Freirechtslehre*, published by Rehbinder (1973).

To return to my examination of textbooks. Dalberg-Larsen's textbook (first published in 1989 in a temporary edition) in its very title *Lovene og livet* (Laws and life) makes a kind of hidden reference to Ehrlich. When Dalberg-Larsen presents the concept of sociology of law, and discusses a sociology of law-based definition of law (Dalberg-Larsen 2005, 33 pp), he differentiates between two groups of definitions of law. The first defines law as a phenomenon with certain social functions (those of resolving conflicts, oppressing the lower classes, producing stability etc.). The second defines law as identical with some type of social phenomenon of a non-law character. Here Dalberg-Larsen introduces Ehrlich's concept of living law as an expression of informal law. Living law is understood as law in a sociological form, as opposed to "dead or formal law" (Dalberg-Larsen 2005, 36), that is to say juridical law. Dalberg-Larsen identifies Ehrlich's concept as important for understanding the effects of law in society on the basis of sociology of law. But Dalberg-Larsen also says that Ehrlich's definition of law as a social phenomenon "seems inadequate to formulating a precise theoretical issue or message" (ibid.).

But to go back to the question of the law's effects. At this point Dalberg-Larsen (ibid.) gives Ehrlich credit for understanding the limits of the law – especially in cases when state law aimed to regulate people's behavior in ways contrary to existing norms in a society. The parallel to Mathiesen's approach is obvious.

In chapter 2, which deals with general theories on the relation between law and society, Dalberg-Larsen (2005, 51 pp) introduces Ehrlich (along with Højrup and Foucault) in a law-pessimistic context. "Law-pessimistic" theories are defined as "giving law only quite a small significance as a regulator of society" (Dalberg-Larsen 2005, 82). To put it briefly: In real life the law cannot be isolated from other important influences: "In real life law always functions with a lot of other phenomena" (ibid.). The conclusion of such a law-pessimistic view is in Dalberg-Larsen's view – and he is again going back to Ehrlich – that the informal social norms in society are the central means of regulation, these being Ehrlich's "living law". And in Dalberg-Larsen's presentation of Ehrlich, the case of the Bukovina illustrates the failure of the Austro-Hungarian central power's attempt to establish laws valid for the whole empire. Living law or – in Dalberg-Larsen's terms – customary law successfully resisted these attempts.

In Sweden

In Per Stjernquist and Karin Widerberg's *Rätten i samhällsbyggandet* (Law in the building of society), published in 1980, we find the most detailed presentation and discussion of Ehrlich's work, especially in the first chapter of the book. One part of this chapter is in fact titled "written law and living law" (Stjernquist and Widerberg 1980, 13). The starting point of sociology of law is, according to the two authors, located in the former Austro-Hungarian double monarchy with its enormous political problems. South-Slavic movements, for example, regarded central state law as alien, and contrary to regional customary law traditions. Against this background Ehrlich is seen establishing his seminar for "living law" and studying it in a fieldwork project. His achievement is primarily seen as having identified the significance of customary law for society (Stjernquist and Widerberg 1980, 10). Ehrlich's concept is rooted in an earlier discussion initiated by Karl von Savigny (historic school). In von Savigny's view all positive law is "Volksrecht", based on people's particular, shared legal views. At von Savigny's time in the eighteenth century this was seen as an advance on concepts based on natural right.

But Ehrlich – as portrayed by Stjernquist and Widerberg – had a different political background from von Savigny. Von Savigny's approach was motivated by the desire to strengthen the nation state and its role after the French revolution, whereas Ehrlich lived at a time of political instability, and cultural and religious diversity. He was thus influenced by records of people's legal views, supported by and connected to the liberation movement of the time, which could be set against the positive law formulated at the centre of the Austro-Hungarian empire.

Juridical law, produced by the central state – which focused for example on tax, bureaucracy or the military – could be in agreement with living law. If not, it would be an unfamiliar or alien element in people's lives (Stjernquist and Widerberg 1989, 13-15). Stjernquist and Widerberg end their presentation of Ehrlich's thinking by stating that they feel his works lack any discussion from a class-based perspective, and therefore any account of possible class-related conflicts. They seem a little dissatisfied, summing up their presentation with the words "there was obviously no living law in the working class" (ibid. 15).

'Ehrlich in the Swedish woods' was a provisional title I suggested to Karin Widerberg when I asked her to do a lecture in our workshop; I thought it was in keeping with Stjernquist's (and her) research on the laws in the forest in Sweden. She could not join us for various reasons, but I still think that this title would have been a one for their research. This research, carried out in the early 1970s, is well known (Stjernquist/Widerberg 1989, 51 pp; Stjernquist 1973 and 1992; Mathiesen 2011, 137 p), so I can make this presentation quite short:

Stjernquist analyses the development of Swedish forestry from the early 1850s to the situation in the mid-1980s. I will here concentrate on the situation in the decades before 1960. In this period farmers were gradually drawn into a cash economy. To put it another way: private farmer forestry, which had for a long time remained outside the market economy, was drawn into the capitalist economic system. In order to pay their yearly running costs, farmers had to manage their forests by selectively felling single trees (or groups of trees) with the intention of getting natural re-growth. This development was supported by a governmental forest policy designed to protect the productive capacity of the forest and to prevent exploitation of the forest – a problem that occurred in the early industrialization of Sweden. A forestry board with field personnel was established in each district in Sweden, not primarily to control the farmers, but to provide training in, among other things, farming management. In his analysis Stjernquist talks about "co-operation in the forest, with the owner being shown how to manage the forest and being given an explanation of why things should be done in this way" (Stjernquist 1992, 32). This eventually resulted in farmers getting more and more interested in long-term forestry. Since the demand for timber from the wood industry was constantly increasing at this time, the farmers had to manage their forests in a restrained way, in order to deliver a steady supply of timber. The forests in Sweden thus had two important functions for the economy: firstly they were important for farmers as an additional source of income. Secondly, they were important as sources of raw material for the Swedish wood industry. Stjernquist and Widerberg sum up this development as follows: "reform legislation is effective if it functions in parallel with, or is in fact an expression of, an ongoing economic or politic process. In other words, changes that take place in society are not an effect of law alone, but of a whole process of which legislation only is one part" (Stjernquist and Widerberg 1989, 53).

Preliminary conclusion

My initial look at the Scandinavian textbooks on sociology of law concerning Eugen Ehrlich's 'living law' gives a varied picture: In the case of Norwegian books Ehrlich is conspicuously absent, while in those of Denmark, and of Sweden in particular, there is presentation and discussion of his theory. But in all the Scandinavian textbooks there is a strong focus on the relevance to the effects of law of the environment of legislation. This is also backed by empirical research – especially in the cases of Sweden and Norway.

Part two: the Greenland expedition of Agnete Weis Bentzon, Verner Goldschmidt and Per Lindegaard

When it comes to exploring the relevance of Ehrlich for Danish sociology of law, my first idea – of course – was to look at the basic preparatory work for the Greenland expedition of the early 1950s, a project for research on the living law in Greenland. In this context I had the fantasy that the researchers had been members of Ehrlich's living law seminar, and that he had told them what to do. But when one looks at the literature used by Agnete Weis Bentzon and Verner Goldschmidt, two of the most important researchers on the research expeditions, one finds no indication that they knew Ehrlich's work. Jørgen Dalberg Larsen, who has a wide-ranging knowledge of developments in sociology of law in Denmark, offers as an explanation the fact that both Weis Bentzon and Goldschmidt were more orientated towards Anglo-American literature. We now learn from Hanne Petersen's chapter in this book that subsequently, in the late 1980s and early 1990s, Agnete Weis Bentzon discovered the usefulness of the concept of "living law" for her later work in Southern Africa.

The starting point for the Greenland expedition was the decision, in June 1948, of the Prime minister of Denmark to send a group of researchers (all lawyers) – Verner Goldschmidt, Per Lindegaard and Agnete Weis Bentzon – to Greenland "with the aim to research the legal situation and submit proposals for the future regarding the Greenlandic system of law" (Betænkning, volume 1, I, my translation). To be more concrete, the instructions of 13 July 1948 formulated the brief for one year's research in Greenland as follows: It was to explore

> "... in what way and ... how far it would be possible to establish the rules of law in force in Denmark among that part of the Greenlandic population which is under so-called Greenlandic law. The research should concentrate on civil law, penal law, procedural law and that part of public law which deals with people's access to local democracy and possible future participation in the Danish parliament's legislative work" (ibid., II, my translation).

The sources for their research were mainly to be members of the local councils in Greenland involved in conflict-solving. Goldschmidt and his colleagues had the old Norse law-speaker in mind, which however they did not find in reality. So their task, to collect and describe the unwritten Greenlandic law, had to be accomplished in a different way. As their respondents, when answering questions, could often only refer to particular cases, and the conflict solution for them, the researchers acquired, "(t)hrough accounts of how conflicts and problems had been settled, an understanding of Greenlandic customary law" (Bentzon and Agersnap 2000, 376). That meant that they had to switch over to a case study method. The members of the expedition also focused strongly on describing the social background of the different fields of law. This was justified by the fact that

> "the proof of a connection between these social backgrounds and legal rules is necessary to fully understand the existing rules, and to an even higher degree the

absence of rules on many – from a West-European point of view – central legal areas" (Betænkning vol. 1, IV, my translation).

And the expedition was also clear about the fact that their report

"to a certain extent included information about Greenlandic judicial and administrative praxis, which goes beyond what is necessary to form an opinion about the legal situation in the area in question" (ibid., my translation).

In this regard the expedition studied and documented special areas of the unwritten law or customary law or – as the expedition sometimes is calling it – "Greenlandic law" on marriage and connected issues (inter alia, termination of marriages legitimate and illegitimate children and rules on names) (Betænkning vol. 1). Also covered were ownership and compensation outside contractual relationships (ibid. vol. 2); other debt law (ibid. vol. 3); inheritance (disputes) (ibid. vol 4). It is not possible to follow this up here. But I will just illustrate the method of the expedition by one example concerning Greenlandic inheritance customary law (ibid. vol. 4, 3 pp.). The expedition concludes their presentation in the following manner:

"Over all the regulation of legal inheritance in Greenland differs from Danish regulation in crucial respects ... The most essential difference between the Danish and the Greenlandic rules for the passing of an inheritance to the deceased's relatives is that the characteristic of 'Greenlandic law' is that there are actually no inheritance disputes, but rather a 'joint tenancy' (co-ownership or common ownership), a kind of community of heirs .... As long as Greenlandic living conditions are characterized by low average wealth and difficulties in getting one's own accommodation, even if one is of 'age', it could be said that the institution of joint tenancy achieves practical goals. Therefore it is not possible to abolish it today in favor of Danish legal rules" (ibid. 15, my translation).

Much later, in 2000, almost 20 years after the death of Verner Goldschmidt, Agnete Weis Bentzon and Torben Agersnap summarize their approach in the Greenlandic expedition, contrasting it to a reform strategy based on "technocratic experts' evaluations, as they may satisfy the interests of the ruling parties. However, Goldschmidt uses sociological studies from a bottom-up perspective to uncover existing norms in Greenlandic society, and to avoid legislation that does not respect existing ways of life; it is often irrational, and sometimes even destructive, to implement legislation in direct conflict with existing norms" (Bentzon and Agersnap 2000, 379).

It is not really surprising that their report never got published (see Petersen in this book).

Part three: Ehrlich and early contemporaries of the Norwegian customary law discussion

As we know, in Ehrlich's view, living law has to be set against the dominant school of legal science, which mainly focuses on legal propositions and their interpretation in legal literature and dispensations of justice. With the exception of usage and business custom in commercial law, customary law plays no role in the scientific discourse of lawyers (Ehrlich 2002, 486; 1913, 393).

Ehrlich is in this context not discussing customary law[1] as such, but the *facts* of customary law. For lawyers these facts are "all that is not or is not yet law and legal relationships; but these facts are already germinating as future rights and legal relationships ..." (Ehrlich 1907, 4, my translation). In his view customary law represents change, while the norms behind decisions (Entscheidungsnormen) represent what is permanent in the midst of change (ibid. 39). The principles of freedom of contract, association and testament constitute the framework,

> "which can almost completely absorb the fullness of modern life. ... all these contracts, associations and contents of will are social phenomena, like riverbeds in which the modern life of economy and society is able to flow calmly and in an orderly fashion. In such a way usage, the rule of life, circumvents the other sources of law" (ibid. 40, my translation).

In his *Fundamental Principles of the Sociology of Law* Ehrlich opens our eyes to what at his time were important fields for examples of living law, compared with, for example, "four meager sections" (ibid., 489; 1913, 396) in the Austrian civil code relating to the matrimonial community of goods (eheliche Gütergemeinschaft). Of much greater interest are agricultural usufructuary leases (landwirtschaftlicher Pachtvertrag), the system of agriculture (Agrarverfassung) in Germany and Austria and family law (Fami-

1 Customary law is defined by Ehrlich as "the forms of life, which without governmental intervention, just through life itself had become the basis of the organization of state, economy and society, ... " (Ehrlich 1907, 38, my translation).

lienrecht). Here, and only here, Ehrlich finds the ground for research on the living law as the object of sociology of law:

"This then is the *living*[2] law in contradistinction to that which is being enforced in the courts and other tribunals. The living law is the law which dominates life itself even though it has not been posited in legal propositions. The source of our knowledge of this law is, first, the modern legal document; secondly, direct observation of life, of commerce, of customs and usages, and of all associations, not only of those that the law has recognized but also of those it has overlooked and passed by, indeed even of those that it has disapproved of" (ibid., 493; 1913, 399).

A central area of interest for Ehrlich's research on living law is, as already mentioned, commercial law (Handelsrecht). Jurisprudence has, as Ehrlich tells us, included this, officially defining it as business custom or usage. And what is important here for Ehrlich as regards his idea of living law, is that:

"... the contract law of modern commercial law has not been taken over from the *corpus iuris*[3]; nor is it a product of the diligent reflection of its authors. What the commercial statutes and the commercial codes have to say about buying and selling, about commissions, about the forwarding of goods, about the insurance, the freight, and the banking business, is actually being practiced somewhere even though, possibly, not always to the extent set forth therein" (ibid., 493, 1913, 398).

With this concept in mind, we can now take a closer look at the Norwegian law professor *Fredrik Stang* and his discussion of and suggestions about commercial law and usage, custom and practice.

Stang's book (1907) has the Norwegian title *Handelskoutumer*, which could be translated into English as 'trading customs, usages or habits', or as 'business or commercial practice'. Stang starts by discussing the legal effect of usage. Referring to discussion in Germany, Austria and England, Stang presents usage as an interpretative method, or rule, and not as customary law, "because contracts regularly have to be seen as pointing to usage, when they do not clearly say something else" (ibid., 249, my translation from Norwegian). And he continues:

"if one supposes that usage and customary law are the same, is one forced to demand that usage should be old and that it should be exercised opinione legis;

2 No italics in the German version of 1913.

3 See note 2.

if it does not fulfill these requirements, it must be disregarded and has absolutely no legal significance" (ibid., my translation).

Here, Stang can also find support in Ehrlich's discussion of the relationship between the living law (in trade) and customary law:

"It is not true, therefore, that the investigation of the living law is concerned only with 'customary law' or with 'business usage' (Verkehrssitte). If one does any thinking at all when one uses these words – which is not always the case – one will realize that they do not refer to the concrete, but to that which has been universalized. But only the concrete usages, the relations of domination, the legal relations, the contracts, the articles of association, the dispositions by last will and testament, yield the rules according to which men regulate their conduct" (Ehrlich 2002, 501, 1913, 405).

Stang's project in his book is to show that this opinion, taken from the discussion in Germany, England and France, is right, and that the Scandinavian countries should follow. He identifies two big waves – the first in the Middle Ages in Northern Italian cities and the second in the age of industrialization – in the development of usages as an effect of the globalization of trade. And this is the starting point for Stang's research on established trade organizations, which is rather interesting when looked at with Ehrlich in mind (ibid. 254). In his research he looks at the development of usages, conflicts between different interests (wholesale and retail sale). He studies the practices of chambers of commerce with regard to reports in cases of conflict, again taking his starting point in the practice of Germany, England and France (ibid. 260 pp.). He also examines court judgment records, where he finds a lot of information on questions of usages. Again, he looks at practice in the countries I mentioned above, where he notes there are special commercial courts (ibid., 265 pp.). Finally he explores early codification of trade usages in the reports of various chambers of commerce (ibid. 268 pp).[4]

In addition Stang here exactly follows Ehrlich's suggestion that one should look into associations to find the real living law of trade: it is obvious that he – besides having a wide-ranging knowledge of German, French and

4 For example in the case of Germany, published by the *Kaufmannschaft zu Magdeburg* regarding "trade usages in wholesale and shipping" or in the case of *Der Aeltesten der Kaufmannschaft* in Berlin regarding usages in trade (Ibid. 264, note 2).

English juristic literature – had also read some studies by Ehrlich.[5] The title of one of these studies may sound quite legal and dogmatic, but the content may be seen as foreshadowing his later famous *Grundlegung der Soziologie des Rechts* of 1913. Ehrlich describes the content and method of his book as follows:

"I myself entertained this idea when about a quarter of a century ago I began to work at my book on the declaration of the will by silence. My intention was to study more than six hundred volumes of decisions of German, Austrian, and French courts, and on the basis of these decisions to present a picture of what judicial decisions had made of the declaration of the will by silence. Before long however my attention was arrested by, and occupied with, what actually took place rather than by the judicial decision. As a result my book contains, to a great extent at least, a statement of the facts on which the judicial decisions had been rendered, as they actually happened in life, and a statement of the significance of the silent declaration of the will in legal life. In this book, I actually, though unconsciously, applied the sociological method of legal science, for which I subsequently sought to establish a theoretical basis" (Ehrlich 2002, 494; 1913, 399-400).[6]

To conclude what I have to say with regard to the importance of the Norwegian lawyer Fredrik Stang as a follower and translator into practice of Ehrlich's living law concept: In his famous introduction to property law (*Innføring til formueretten*, 3rd edition, 1935), I found the following formulation of what Stang thinks is most important in the study of law: "The thousands of threads which connect the law's abstract world to the work and struggles of real lives" (ibid., VII, my translation from Norwegian). I should also mention Stang's important role in establishing an interdisciplinary institute of comparative cultural research in 1923 (Skirbekk 1991, 465).

The next Norwegian legal scholar I will consider is *Kristian Østberg*, also a law professor at the law faculty in Oslo, who was best known for his record of the customary law of Norwegian farmers, which he compiled in ten volumes and published between 1914 and 1935 (Østberg 1914 pp).[7]

[5] *Die stillschweigende Willenserklärung*. Berlin: Carl Heymanns Verlag 1893; *Das zwingende und das nichtzwingende Recht im bürgerlichen Gesetzbuch für das deutsche Reich*. Jena: Gustav Fischer 1899, and *Freie Rechtsfindung und freie Rechtswissenschaft*. Leipzig: C. L. Hirschfeld 1903.

[6] Ehrlich tells us later that he finally realized that this method alone was not sufficient. It had to be completed by "direct observation of life" (ibid, 495, German edition: 400).

[7] He published some general articles about the law relating to farmers. But his interest

Østberg is a contemporary of Ehrlich, and, while he does not draw on his theory, he does make use of his empirical method. Østberg discusses him indirectly by reflecting on Stang's suggestions on usages (Stang 1907).

As a starting point Østberg defines as customary law the old farmhouse rights based on custom.[8] He then goes on to discuss usages, and in this regard, we find an interesting discussion of Stang's suggestions in *Handelskoutumer* (1907). It seems quite interesting that, when he distinguishes himself from Stang, he at the same time also distinguishes himself from Ehrlich. In Østberg's opinion, uncodified usages which only serve to interpret and complete declarations of will, cannot be understood as customary law. But he agrees with Stang, albeit with different arguments, that most old law relating to farmers is customary law. Stang's argument here is that most of it is so old, that it qualifies as customary law. Østberg again makes a distinction between usages and declaratory customary law[9]:

> "Law relating to farmers however is not only usages. There is surely a great deal of customary law in it, of that a good measure of declaratory customary law. … People recognize and respect them as customary rules" (Østberg 1922, 16).

And as a final clarification of his own topic – the law relating to farmers – Østberg concludes that most of the rules in this area are to be seen as declaratory customary law: "Calling them customs or usages and only seeing them as means of interpretation makes the expression interpretation too comprehensive (ibid., 17).

What makes Østberg's contribution so important when one is thinking about Ehrlich is that he really empirically experienced what Ehrlich realized in practice only to a small degree – that is, he actually carried out a more or less complete piece of research on a field of living law important in his day, namely law relating to farmers in Norway.

My last Norwegian scholar is *Erik Solem*, who for eight years was a judge in Tana in the north of Norway (Finmark). He spoke the Samish lan-

is mainly concentrated on concrete issues like "saltwater fishermen's customary law" (vol. 8), "mountain pasture usages in Norway" (vol. 6)," customary law for neighbors" (vol. 5) or "logging" (vol. 4).

8 In this context he distinguishes between the customary law of laymen – the whole collected popular "Volksrecht" – and on the other hand lawyers' law: "a more scientifically justified customary law" (ibid., 3).

9 Declaratory law or customary law in the sense of mandatory law, means rules which only apply when the parties have tacitly, or not explicitly, agreed to something else.

guage and based his study on his contact as a judge with the Same and his experience of them. His study *Lappish*[10] *law study* (Lappiske rettsstudier) was first published in 1933[11]. He was, unsurprisingly, influenced by Fredrik Stang, who gave him help and advice on his study. What Solem was doing, was seeking out the legal perceptions of the Reindeer-Same in Finmark. He makes no reference to Ehrlich in his comprehensive bibliography, but the parallels are obvious. His starting point is to see legal rules in a dialectical relationship with material living conditions:

"In each society legal perceptions and legal propositions depend to a great extent on material living conditions; each particular industry demands its own rules. … It is life, which creates law, …" (ibid., 2-3).

Besides ancient sources of law, the sources for his study are Samish perceptions of law[12], custom and tradition, fairy tales, superstitions and sayings (ibid., 3). There is a rich literature on the Same in general, in former times often written by missionaries (or pastors), which meant that information about the legal perceptions of the Same was scanty. It is also obvious that the legal perceptions of the Same (like their culture and language in general) were influenced by their "host" states Norway, Sweden and Russia (ibid. 4 pp).

Solem sets out wide-ranging findings on subjects such as the social order of the Reindeer Same, or inheritance, marriage settlements and economic legal relationships (ibid., 41 pp). For my purposes I will particularly concentrate on the traditional *Sii' da*, which Solem translates into Norwegian as "sammenslutning", which in English can be translated as "(social) association". *Sii' da* can be understood both as a Same settlement in the mountains, and as an association consisting of two or more reindeer Sami families (up to a total of six)[13], which are often related. It is important that a *Sii' da* is not an economic community. The families composing a *Sii'da* have private property (tents, reindeer (ibid. 187). Each *Sii' da* has its own head – *ised* -, often the person with most reindeer and experience. The head

[10] Today it is more correct to use the term Same, since "Lappish" now has a deeply discriminatory connotation.

[11] The book was reprinted in a second edition in 1970 by Universitetsforlaget.

[12] As a judge Solem had the opportunity to study the Same's life and activities.

[13] This is because of the fact that effective maintenance of reindeer depends on a herd not exceeding a particular size due to limited willow (ibid. 184).

decides who must guard the reindeer, and when the herd is to switch from summer to winter willow. For reindeer management this seemed to be the most effective solution. Summer and winter pasture areas are used again and again by the same *Sii' da*, without any assertion of ownership – this "happened by itself" (ibid., p 190) and is respected by the other *Sii' da*. When a *Sii' da* wants to change to another summer willow area, they have to inform the head of the *Sii' da,* in whose area they want to graze their animals. This also goes back to traditional rules. To move from the summer to the winter willow areas, old traditional routes are used. It is a traditional rule that one *Sii' da* is not allowed to graze to the detriment of another *Sii' da* (ibid. 193).

When several herds feed in a relatively small area it sometimes happens that they get mixed up. There is an obligation in such cases that the *Sii' da* should help sort out the herds. This was already enshrined in law in 1888, but the law formulated only the traditional rules (customary law) of the Same (ibid. 195).

There is long-standing conflict between nomadic Same and farmers. On the one hand the nomadic Same have an obligation to keep their reindeer under supervision. But in practice it is quite challenging to stop reindeer eating hay belonging to farmers. In such cases compensation is paid to the farmers by the head of *the Sii' da.* The amount to be paid by the members of the *Sii' da* is calculated according to the number of reindeer they have in their herd (ibid., 200).

Solem's research, of which I can give only a few examples here, illustrates his methodological procedure, which could have been taken from Ehrlich's practice in his living law seminar, and applied to the social association *Sii' da* of the Reindeer Same.

I can only to repeat here what I said regarding Østberg's empirical research: Solem's work on the living law of the reindeer Same can also be taken as an embodiment of Ehrlich's idea of studying (living) law in real life.

Conclusion

It is obvious that Dalberg-Larsen's analysis is correct: Sociology of law in the Nordic countries after World War II was more orientated towards Anglo-American literature, as a consequence of the war, and the occupation of Denmark and Norway by the Nazis, who left an enduring moral disaster behind. So the absence of Ehrlich from Scandinavian textbooks on sociology of law should be seen against this background. But we must also realize that the situation in Germany after World War II meant that Ehrlich's work was not recognized there either. Stefan Machura tells us that it took decades after 1945 to rediscover Ehrlich in Germany (see Machura's chapter). The situation at the beginning of 19th century was quite different. At that time there were excellent scientific connections between Germany and, for example, Norway. Fredrik Stang says in his *Introduction to Property Law* (1935) "in the last 100 years German legal science (jurisprudence) has been preeminent, and in the last ten years has also influenced Norwegian (legal science) to a significant degree" (ibid. VII, my translation). But he also criticizes developments in Germany. German jurisprudence has focused exclusively on Roman law, and has lost interest in and appreciation for the Germanic law situation. And he concludes by saying: "(German jurisprudence) has removed legal doctrine (Rechtslehre) from life" (ibid.). That seems quite interesting to me: Fredrik Stang is criticizing – like Ehrlich more than 20 years earlier – German Jurisprudence for its failure to incorporate real life into their concept of legal science. In this way he presents himself as a follower or companion of Eugen Ehrlich: it is tempting to call the law professor Fredrik Stang the real first sociologist of law in Norway.

References

Aubert, Vilhelm, Eckhoff, Torstein and Sveri, Knut (1952), *En lov i søkelys*. Oslo: Akademisk forlag.

Aubert, Vilhelm (1968), *Rettssosiologi*. Oslo: Universitetsforlaget.

Aubert, Vilhelm (1976), Om lovers virkninger. *Samtiden* 85:308-320.

Bentzon, Agnete Weis (1954), Ægteskab og familie i Grønland. *Grønland* 14:41-46.

Bentzon, Agnete Weis and Agersnap Torben (2000), Verner Goldschmidt, Danish Sociologist of Law and Culture. *Acta Sociologica,* pp. 375-380.

Betænkning afgivet 6. september 1950 af den juridiske ekspedition til Grønland 1948-1949. Volumes 1-6. (cited: Betænkning, volume . . .).

Dalberg-Larsen, Jørgen (1977), *Retsvitenskaben som samfundsvidenskap*. København: Juristforbundets forlag.

Dalberg-Larsen, Jørgen (2005), *Lovene og livet*. En retssociologisk grundbog, 5th edition. København: Jurist- og Økonomiforbundets Forlag.

Deflem, Mathieu (2008), *Sociology of Law. Visions of a Scholarly Tradition*. Cambridge: Cambridge University Press.

Ehrlich, Eugen (1907), *Die Tatsachen des Gewohnheitsrechts*. Czernowitz: Selbstverlag der K. K. Universität.

Ehrlich, Eugen (1913), *Grundlegung der Soziologie des Rechts*. München and Leipzig: Duncker & Humblot.

Ehrlich, Eugen (1967), *Recht und Leben. Gesammelte Schriften zur Rechtstatsachenforschung und zur Freirechtslehre*. Ausgewählt und eingeleitet von Dr. Manfred Rehbinder. Berlin: Duncker & Humblot.

Ehrlich, Eugen (2002), *Fundamental Principles of the Sociology of Law*. Translated by Walter L. Moll, New Brunswick and London: Transaction Publishers.

Mathiesen, Thomas (2011), *Retten i samfunnet*. 6th edition, Oslo: Pax forlag.

Petersen, Hanne (1991), *Informel ret på kvindearbejdspladser – en retsteoretisk og empirisk analyse*. København: Akademisk Forlag.

Skirbekk, Gaute (1991), Rettsantropologi i norsk rettsvitenskap. *Tidsskrift for Rettsvitenskap* 104:449-479.

Solem, Erik Toralf (1933/1970), *Lappiske rettsstudier*. 2nd edition, Oslo: Universitetsforlaget,.

Stang, Fredrik (1907), *Handelskoutumer*. Kristiania: Særtryk af *"Tidsskrift for retsvidenskab"*.

Stang, Fredrik (1935), *Innledning til formueretten*. 3rd edition, Oslo: Aschehoug & Co.

Stjernquist, Per (1958), Gränsområdenmellan rättsvetenskap och samhällsvetenskap, *Statsvetenskaplig tidskrift* 61:141-150.

Stjernquist, Per (1973), *Laws in the Forest. A Study of Public Direction of Swedish Private Forestry*. Lund: Gleerup.

Stjernquist, Per (1986), Socialantropologiska infallsvinklar inom rättsforskningen. In: *Samfunn Rett Rettferdighet. Festskrift til Torstein Eckhoff*. Oslo: Tano, pp. 651-664.

Stjernquist, Per, and Widerberg, Karin (1989), *Rätten i samhällsbyggandet*. 3rd edition, Stockholm: Norstedts Förlag.

Stjernquist, Per (1992), *Forest Treatment: Relations to Nature of Swedish Private Forestry*. Stockholm: Almquist & Wiksell.

Sverdrup, Tone (1984), *Lovvern for arbeidstakere i private hjem*. Kvinneretslige arbeidsnotater no. 31, Universitetet i Oslo, Kvinneretten.

Østberg, Kristian (1914-1939), *Norsk bonderett i 12 bind*. Kristiania/Oslo: Grøndahl/Cappelen.

Østberg, Kristian (1922), Boderet og juristret. In: Kristian Østberg, *Norsk boderett*, 3rd edition. Hamar: Norsk skoletidendes boktrykkeri, pp. 1-41.

Sociology of Law at 'the Edge of Empires and Eras' – Reflections on Lawyers and Living Law 65 Years after the Legal Expedition to Greenland*

Hanne PETERSEN

Ehrlich, Goldschmidt and Bentzon – comparisons of lawyer-sociologists of the 20th century

Early one morning in September 2012, before attending the Critical Legal Studies conference on *Gardens of Justice* at the Royal Technical High School, I chose to pay a visit to the Royal Library in Stockholm in order to avoid the rainy weather. The encyclopedias were displayed in the entrance section, and I noticed to my surprise an encyclopedia called *Jüdisches Lexikon. Ein encyclopädisches Handbuch des jüdischen Wissens* published in the 1920s, which I had never seen before. I decided to look for an article on *"Get"* – the Jewish letter of divorce, which is sometimes rejected by orthodox Jewish men, thus denying their wives a divorce. By coincidence the book opened at Ehrlich, and to my astonishment I found a short entry on Eugen Ehrlich.

In the pre-Google Era of the 1980s I had read Ehrlich's book *Grundlegung der Soziologie des Rechts* of 1913, and I had been very inspired by his concept of 'living law', which I wrote about (Petersen 1991 and 1996).[1] However, I do not remember having found out at that time about his Jewish ancestry. Now, however, I was in the process of preparing a lecture on the relevance of 'living law' in relation to the Legal Expedition to Greenland 1948-49 – also called JUREX. This expedition was carried out by three young lawyers, Per Lindegaard (1918-1998), Verner Goldschmidt (1916-

* This title is borrowed from an article by Roger Cotterell: Ehrlich at the Edge of Empire: Centres and Peripheries in Legal Studies, Cotterell 2009.

1 My dissertation"*Informel ret på kvindearbejdspladser. En empirisk og retsteoretisk analyse*." was published in 1991. It was rewritten for an English-reading audience during a year as a Jean Monnet scholar at the European Institute in Florence 1993-1994 and finalized during my first period at the Home Rule University, Ilisimatusarfik in Greenland starting from 1995. Hence the title of the English edition, *Home Knitted Law. Norms and Values in Gendered Rule-Making*. (1996).

1982) and Agnete Weis Bentzon (1918-2013). Through this experience Verner Goldschmidt and Agnete Weis Bentzon (who were married from 1940-1959) both came to study sociology of law, and both later wrote their doctoral dissertations on the basis of this experience (Goldschmidt 1957; Bentzon 1968). They both stressed the importance of customary law both in the report on the expedition and in their later work. But as far as I knew, neither of them had dealt with Ehrlich's work or his ideas on this subject. I was trying to find a link between them which would make sense. And now one link seemed to have appeared.

I had known Agnete for 25 years, and I knew of course that her then husband, Verner Goldschmidt, whom I had never met, was of Jewish origin, and had to flee to Sweden in 1943. I had also many times heard Agnete retell the story of her own escape to Sweden in the summer of 1944, with her 16-month-old son, Per, who had been doped, so that he would not cause too much trouble during the escape, while she herself pretended to be the wife of the skipper of the boat.

I had myself gone to Greenland and lived and worked at the miniscule university in Nuuk, Ilisimatusarfik from 1995-1999 in part through the intervention of Agnete and her second husband, Professor Torben Agersnap (1922-2013), and first and foremost due to my interest in living law and legal pluralism, which I wanted to study in practice.

Experiences of background, exile and exclusion

In Stockholm I was struck by the similarities between Ehrlich and Goldschmidt, and to a certain extent also Agnete Weis Bentzon, and by the experiences they shared. Both men had a Jewish background but neither was a practising Jew. Ehrlich converted to Catholicism, as did many other Jewish intellectuals and businessmen.[2] Goldschmidt came from an agnostic culturally and economically privileged family and probably did not consider himself Jewish. However, the lives of both were influenced by their Jewish ancestry.

2 One of the important Jewish-German businessmen of 'Danish' origin, Albert Ballin (1858-1918) was a director of the world's biggest shipping company, Hamburg America Linien. His Jewish descent was an obstacle to his acceptance in both business and politics, but he refused to convert. See Wiborg 2007.

Agnete Weis Bentzon was of neither Jewish nor German origin. She was the second daughter of Asbjørn D. Bentzon (1887-1960), a judge, who after WWII was to become president of the Danish Supreme Court, and who happened to have been born in Munich. Her paternal grandfather, Viggo Bentzon (1861-1937) of whom she spoke often and with great affection, was a professor of law at the University of Copenhagen from 1892 to 1930. He had studied in Germany, Italy and Norway in the period 1887-1889, and her father was born during one of these study tours. Viggo Bentzon had been a pioneer in Nordic legal cooperation about harmonized family law, and was a supporter of women's rights. Agnete seems to have spent a great deal of time with her grandfather and to have had many discussions with him, thus also gaining access to information about what happened in Europe.

They all lived on the edge of eras – Ehrlich on that of the Austro-Hungarian Empire, which would fall apart in 1918 after World War I, and Verner Goldschmidt and Agnete Weis Bentzon on that of Hitler's Third Reich, which would collapse in 1945, after the end of World War II. They also both lived and worked on the 'edge of empires'. Cotterrell (2009, 76) mentions the importance of Ehrlich's "*own marginality or 'frontier' situation, which gave him a special viewpoint.*" The 'frontier experiences' of Verner Goldschmidt and Agnete Weis Bentzon, both in exile and in Greenland, surely also gave both of them a 'special' viewpoint – or perhaps allowed them to contribute to changing the 'normal' viewpoint.

Ehrlich (1862-1922) lived at the end of the Austro-Hungarian Empire and wrote on 'living law' just before World War I. The Jewish Encyclopedia mentioned that he had given a lecture about the question of Jews and farmers published in a small publication (Ehrlich 1909), which was available in the Danish Royal Library.

In the section in which he speaks about the farmers in Bukowina he describes their dismal situation: they suffered from hunger and undernourishment, and often died of starvation. The farmers from Bukowina who had emigrated to Canada however, were hardworking and had become very successful. He goes on to describe how two years before, in 1906, he had visited what he calls 'the paradise for farmers', which was Denmark. This was the only country with an agricultural sector which did not bewail its state, despite the fact that 100-150 years earlier Danish farmers had been in as miserable a situation as their later counterparts were in Bukowina.

What had changed the situation, writes Ehrlich, was the pietist movement of Grundtvig, which had focused especially on the education of farmers and farmers' sons during the six month winter periods. Ehrlich was especially surprised and impressed by the general libraries Danish farmers had in their homes, and the three daily newspapers to which they subscribed. He made detailed studies of the numbers of bookshops, subscriptions and prices. He also mentions the Danish agricultural cooperatives, which secured agricultural products of a very high quality. Danish farmers were not big farmers: they were generally comparable to farmers in Bukowina. Nonetheless they had become wealthy. In this lecture Ehrlich lays great emphasis on the importance of the modernization of the economy both for farmers and for the Jews.

He writes that he himself "belongs to a race (Geschlechte) for whom there is no other solution than complete absorption of Jews into Germanness."[3] But for many of the great mass of Jews, who lived in the East, it was not possible to become German, if the majority of the German people would not accept them. "The Jewish question in the East of Europe is, like the Russian Revolution [of 1905 – HP] an expression of the fact that Eastern society is undergoing a transformation"(Ehrlich 1909, 20, my translation).

If the Jews in the East of Europe – where most Jews were living in very wretched conditions – were able to find a peaceful solution, then they might foresee a time of economic and cultural success. Otherwise he did not doubt that they would bleed to death. Their economic living conditions were disastrous.

> "I will tell you the truth, so that you understand that the Jews are standing in front of a catastrophe that may be expected within at the latest ten to twenty years. Of the 100.000 Jews in Bukowina, perhaps 10.000 have positions and jobs which have an economic foundation and legitimacy. 90.000 have their jobs because of the backwardness of the country." (Ehrlich 1909, 25)

Ehrlich (1909, 22) also spoke about the *Intelligenzproletariat* and the fact that the Jews were fleeing into the learned jobs. What to do with the 90% of Jews, who are threatened by the catastrophe? he asks. He was not in favour of a Zionist solution, but was rather seeking to secure large scale industry

---

[3] "Ich selbst gehöre noch einem Geschlechte an, für das es keine andere Lösung der Judenfrage gibt, als ein vollständiges Aufgehen der Juden im Deutschtum" (Ehrlich 1909, 17-18, my translation).

for Bukowina. The role of social policy should be to educate (Ehrlich 1909, 31). He was a conservative, but clearly also a far-sighted social conservative.

Ehrlich was 'relegated' to the edge of empire. He had become a professor of Roman Law in 1897 in Cernowitz. At the beginning of WWI, when Russian troops occupied the city, he had to flee, never to return. He went to Switzerland for some years, where he could not get a job, and in 1921 planned to return to Cernowitz, where he would now have to teach in Romanian, as the city had become part of this country. However, he died of diabetes in 1922, so he never managed to return.

In 1934 Agnete Weis Bentzon (I will refer to her as AWB) read the novel "Slægten Oppenheim" ('The Oppermanns') by Lion Feuchtwanger,[4] a German-Jewish novelist and playwright, who in 1933 had to leave Germany, and whose novel *"Die Geschwister Oppenheim"* (later Oppermann) was translated into, amongst other languages, Danish, Finnish, Norwegian and Swedish within a year of its first publication in Amsterdam in 1933. The novel describes the fate of a Jewish business family who lived through the changes during the beginning of the 1930s and after Hitler's election. It was written in only six months to serve as a warning of what was to come to its readership. AWB mentions this novel in a later article[5], in which she also writes that she visited Germany on a scouts bicycle trip in 1934. Here she had first-hand experience of Nazi propaganda as expressed by children from a kindergarten (Bentzon 1987, 15). She also told me that she had visited Italy in the 1930s.

In October 1943, during a tense period for Europe and Denmark, when the catastrophe for European – and especially for Eastern European Jewry foreseen by Ehrlich – had been unfolding for a decade, Verner Goldschmidt had to go into exile. Within a few weeks about 7,500 Jews fled from Denmark over the narrow Øresund to various places in Sweden. Unlike the

4 Information from Ditte Bentzon Goldschmidt, June 2013. DBG stressed how strongly this novel had influenced her mother.

5 Bentzon (1987). When I read the novel in the summer of 2013 (in a German version from 1935) eighty years after its publication in Amsterdam, I was struck by its frightening foresight and not least by the descriptions of the rapid political changes followed by terrifying persecution of Jewish communities, which took place within a few months after Hitler's *Machtübernahme.* For those, who read this novel when it first appeared, it must have served as an alarming account of what was happening, and very clear warning of what the future might hold, reverberating Ehrlich's earlier warning

situation in the rest of Europe, 99% of the Jewish population in occupied Denmark were able to survive. There were several reasons for this: proximity to a neutral country, which had just changed its policy and opened up for refugees; a determination in Denmark not to abandon the Jewish population to concentration camps; and a cooperative German occupation administration (Bak 2010, p. 13). Perhaps the educational standard of the population, which Ehrlich had observed about 40 years earlier, may also have been of significance?

When the refugees returned to Denmark in 1945, their experiences in Sweden were described as 'nothing to talk about' (Bak 2010) – compared to the horrors experienced by Jews in the annihilation and concentration camps in Germany and Central Europe. It is thus only recently, in this century, that these experiences of exile have been described by historians. An exception is another novel by a Danish author and communist, Otto Gelsted, who as early as 1945 described his experiences of escape, and his first six months in a Swedish refugee camp in fictional form in a novel called *Flygtninge i Husaby* (Refugees in Husaby). The Jewish exiles were clearly not a united group, and Gelsted writes of orthodox, Danish national, and Eastern Jews, and even of 'Jewish anti-Semitism' (Gelsted 1945, 238). No matter how agnostic Verner Goldschmidt was, during the investigations at the reception centre in Malmö he would be categorized by the Swedish administration as M or MT – indicating 'Mosaic belief.' The reason for this categorization was unclear but it laid down an identification which was not recognized all who had fled (Bak 2010, 109).

Bak repeatedly writes about the negative sentiments towards Jews among both non-Jewish Danish refugees and Swedes in the communities where the (Jewish) refugees lived for shorter or longer periods (Bak 2010, 124 f.). Over time this developed into regular anti-Semitism (Bak 2010, 126) which was a constant shock and strain for the refugees (Bak p. 132). These experiences also influenced Goldschmidt.[6] The Stockholm-based administration for refugees from Denmark was led by a Jewish law professor from Copenhagen, Stefan Hurwitz – later to become the first Ombudsmand of the Danish Parliament in 1957, following the Swedish model. This leadership gave rise to considerable criticism and conflict among some of the refugees (Mogensen 2000, 150 f.).

---

6 Information from Ditte Bentzon Goldschmidt, June 2013.

Refugees who could get jobs, or who knew people who would guarantee their livelihood, could move out of the refugee camps. This was the case for Verner Goldschmidt, who ended up in Uppsala, in the home of Professor Torgny Torgnysson Segerstedt (1908-1999) (Bentzon & Agersnap 2000, 375). T. T. Segerstedt was the son of Torgny Segerstedt (1876-1945), who from 1917-1945 was editor-in-chief of Göteborgs Handels- och Sjöfarts-Tidning (GHT), a business and shipping newspaper of Sweden's second biggest and most liberal city, Göteborg. Segerstedt senior was a strong and open critic of Hitler from the beginning of 1933 and as a newspaper editor he constantly warned that the policy of the Third Reich would lead to war in Europe.[7]

Segerstedt junior became professor of philosophy at Uppsala University in 1938, and continued in this position until 1947, when he was by royal decree appointed to a special professorship as Sweden's first professor of sociology. He also was for a long period the Rector of the University of Uppsala, from 1955 to1978. He was influenced by the so-called Cambridge School of philosophy.

Verner Goldschmidt finished his law degree while he was in Uppsala. He could not fail to have been influenced by his connection with Segerstedt senior, a mythical figure in the Swedish press, or by the practical philosophy of his host, and by the community of exiles, of which he must also have become a part. His studies of law received had a 'marked sociological flavour' because of his stay at the home of Segerstedt junior (Bentzon and Agersnap 2000, 375).

Prof. em. Kjell Åke Modéer, Swedish professor of legal history, writes about the role of Swedish lawyers and their contribution to helping German and Danish exiled lawyers to Sweden. Amongst these lawyers were advocate Axel Forsmann, who was director of the board of the GHT newspaper, where Segerstedt senior was the editor, and Jewish lawyer, Ivar Philipson in

7 Segerstedt senior was a controversial figure, whose dissertation on the origin of polytheism had been turned down in 1903 by conservative forces at the University of Uppsala. In Lund in 1912 he was nominated for a professorship of theology specializing in the history and philosophy of religion. Because of strong protests from conservative circles who did not consider him a sufficiently convincing believer, he did not get this professorship. In 1913 he became professor of history of religion in Stockholm. In 1917 Segerstedt left this professorship to become editor-in-chief at GHT (Den Store Danske, n.d.; Wikipedia, n.d.).

Stockholm, who helped to save thousands of Danish Jews in 1943 (Modéer 2013a, 5; 2013b).

A recent biography of a Danish public intellectual, Poul Henningsen (1894-1967) (always called PH), describes PH's exile in Stockholm as highly important for his later political involvement and fight for democracy. The author, professor of literature Hans Hertel, writes that this part of occupation history – the exile in Sweden of a total of 18,000 Danes – Jews, communists, political activists, authors, artists and public intellectuals – has not yet been written (Hertel 2012, 241). Hertel however mentions the fertile Danish-Norwegian cultural environment and the importance of the Swedish debate. Stockholm during WWII was a 'unique intellectual environment', which was not only anti-Nazi but also anti-totalitarian (Hertel 2012, 247).

Amongst the exiled was the Danish author and participant in several expeditions to Greenland, Peter Freuchen, who was also a member of the resistance movement. He discussed ideas of anti-Semitism and racial superiority prevalent amongst exiles who felt themselves to be 'white men' (Hertel 2012, 253). PH himself also criticized racial superiority amongst the exiled Danes in some of the many speeches he gave in Sweden – "We think we are better than others, but we have abused Iceland, Greenland and the Faroe Islands" (Hertel 2013, 243).

Agnete Weis Bentzon and Verner Goldschmidt had met as students in 1936 and married in 1940. She had finished her law degree at the University of Copenhagen in 1942. During the next four years she had three children, Per in 1943, Ditte in 1945 and Jeanne in 1947. She fled Copenhagen in the summer of 1944, and arrived in Uppsala, where she had difficulties fitting into the exile community. She became pregnant immediately after she arrived and gave birth to Ditte in May 1945 before returning to Copenhagen with the family.[8]

In 1987, she wrote an article called "Glimt fra min tid som stud.jur. i 30erne. Strømninger fra Syd?" (Glimpses from my time as a law student in the 1930s. Currents from the South?). In this article she describes the very lively environment and discussions among the diverse group of students in the inter-war period in Copenhagen. Law students were generally more

8 Ditte Bentzon Goldschmidt, informed me that her parents had originally planned to call her Svea Viktoria, a name which clearly indicates the importance of their Swedish exile. Information from June 2013.

conservative than others, but avowed Nazis were rare. Foreign policy was important, and she describes the group of students she socialized with as

"mostly pink with sympathy for socialism and the Spanish anarchists, distrust of Stalin and his Moscow trials, and decidedly hostile to Hitler and Mussolini, to fascism/Nazism towards neighbouring states and to race persecutions and concentration camps. This was well known from contact with refugees from Germany and from literature, for instance *The Oppermann*, which was published in Denmark in 1934." (Bentzon 1987, 7 – my translation).

She also writes that the nazification of the Faculty and its teachers at this time was not very far advanced. Her article is built around three conceptual pairs in German of importance for the 'currents from the South':

Übermensch – Untermensch; Kirche – Küche – Kinder and *Gemeinnutz geht vor Eigennutz.*

These were ideologies to do with racial, ethnic and gendered hierarchies, as well as with the superiority of the collective over the individual. They were also influences which would impact on herself as a woman, on Jews, to whom she was related by marriage, and on Greenlanders, with whom she became connected through her participation in JUREX.

Amongst the of course many differences between Ehrlich and the couple Goldschmidt – Bentzon, was the fact that Ehrlich was never married. He lived most of his life in the period before women entered the public sphere as voters, workers with economic rights, and individuals with higher educations. Modernity is strongly linked to the deconstruction of gender hierarchies – which totalitarian systems mostly tend to reinstall in practice if not always in theory. Bak describes the breaches in and changes to Jewish norms and traditions in the Swedish exile – which impacted not least on gender relations (Bak 2010, 135 f.).

From centre to margins of a kingdom under reconstitution

The Bentzon-Goldschmidt family did not stay long in Copenhagen after their return in the summer of 1945. Agnete was (formally) employed in the Ministry of Justice from 1943-46[9], and worked at the prosecutor for

[9] Information from Dansk Biografisk Leksikon (n.d.), which does not mention that she fled to Sweden.

Sjælland (Zeeland), from 1947-48. Verner Goldschmidt worked from 1945-47 as a prosecutor with the police dealing with cases of traitors. Both of them thus must have been involved in what was called the *retsopgør* – the painful 'showdown over law' in the early years after WWII which dealt with cases concerning former Nazi-collaborators. One of these collaborators declared that he would not be examined by a Jewish interrogator such as Verner Goldschmidt.[10] In 1947 Verner Goldschmidt was employed by the Department of Greenland, and only a year after sent out on the expedition to Greenland – on the 'edge of the empire'.

Greenland was certainly on the edge of the remains of the Danish mini-empire. This medium-small empire had gradually shrunk during the 19th century. At the Treaty of Kiel of 1815, Norway was transferred to Sweden after the defeat of Napoleon in 1813. After the war between the remains of the Danish empire and Prussia in 1864-66 the Duchies of Schleswig-Holstein were lost, although a smaller part was returned in 1920 after a referendum. During WWII the Kingdom of Denmark had been under several occupation forces. The United States of America occupied Greenland and in 1941 took over Iceland after the British: A few years later Iceland became independent from Denmark in 1944. In 1940 the United Kingdom occupied both Iceland and the Faroe Islands, which later got Home Rule in 1948. Hitler's Germany occupied Denmark from April 9, 1940 until May 5, 1945. However, before the end of the German occupation, the Soviet Union occupied the island of Bornholm and kept it occupied from 1945-1946. 'The Kingdom' was thus a fragile entity, which had barely survived as an 'independent' country, and was gradually being reconstituted. This was by no means an experience peculiar to European powers, countries and citizens. Countries emerged and disappeared, and borders came and went.[11]

After WWII the Danish Kingdom was involved in the general process of decolonization that followed in the wake of the establishment of the United Nations. Acknowledgment of Home Rule in the Faroe Island was at least indirectly part of this process, and the initiative to change the status of Greenland was a direct consequence. This led first to integration of

10 Ditte Bentzon Goldschmidt – information June 2013.

11 Czeslaw Milozs (1911-2004), who received the Nobel prize for literature is considered a Polish writer, despite the fact that he grew up in what is now Lithuania, during the time before the Russian revolution, when his birth place was part of the Russian empire. He got asylum in France in 1953, and later emigrated to the United States.

Greenland into the Kingdom of Denmark – formally on a par with 'any' other municipality in the realm, established through a change of the Constitution in 1953, and later to first Greenlandic Home Rule in 1979, and then to expanded Self Rule in 2009.

In 1948, Greenland was isolated by thousands of kilometres of sea, limited and expensive air traffic, and a policy of exclusion, which had made it difficult for anybody to enter the country without specific official acceptance. Now it had to be modernized, to remove the appalling stain on the Danish state, which wanted to keep Greenland as an integrated part of the Kingdom. To that end several reforms were to be undertaken, amongst them a reform of the judiciary, and an introduction of a 'modern system'. The legal expedition was meant to come up with suggestions for this modernization, which amongst other things was to take the form of new legislation by the Danish legislator designed to bring Greenland 'on a par' with the rest of the country.

It is interesting to note that originally the Ministry of Greenland only sent out the two men, Lindegaard and Goldschmidt, as members of the expedition. Probably the Danish authorities did not consider women, mothers of infants and babies, suitable for participation in such an expedition. It was only when the expedition reached Greenland, where a nomadic population was used to families travelling with both women and children, that AWB became part of the expedition through the intervention of the Greenlandic authorities (Petersen 1998, p. 25).

The attraction of Greenland and living law?

What was the attraction of Greenland for Goldschmidt and Bentzon? We do not really know, as the couple never either wrote or spoke about it.[12] But in the period after WWII many young people, who had been unable to travel during the years of war and occupation felt an urge to leave the country and see the world.

We know that the couple had encountered other cultures including legal cultures, while in Sweden, and that they had been living through very difficult times for more than a decade. They were both rather young. Like everybody else they knew about the work and writings of the Greenlandic-

12 Information from Ditte Bentzon Goldschmidt, June 2013.

Danish explorer Knud Rasmussen (1879-1933). His many Polar and literary expeditions were famous and known to the general public. When he died in 1933 the funeral was a big event in Copenhagen. Agnete later said that she had read his descriptions of some of the expeditions as a teenager. [13]

The process of decolonization was going on all over the world and was part of an important progressive movement. Expeditions also attract adventurers, and Goldschmidt and Bentzon may have become adventurous through their earlier experience of forced exile. It was no doubt a challenge to move to Greenland to live and work under comparatively primitive conditions with three infant children. But they had faced hard existential challenges already. Going that far away might perhaps also have offered an escape from the tense post-war situation in Copenhagen, and a freedom unavailable there.[14] The expedition travelled primarily by boat, as this was the usual and most practical way of travelling in Greenland. It visited settlements and villages and interviewed local people. It seems that the Danish participants in the expedition had learned some Greenlandic, but they also travelled with an important Greenlandic female translator, Guldborg Chemnitz, with whom they continued to work and write for many years. Both became fascinated by Greenland, and continued to work on it for decades to come, and to draw upon their experiences for the rest of their lives. The encounter with a Greenlandic legal culture and tradition also underlined the sociological interest which they had already developed during their stay in Sweden. Many lawyers who went into exile later became comparativists.

It is highly likely that in the late 1940s feelings about state law and statutory law of young lawyers with the experiences of Goldschmidt and Bentzon would have been at least ambivalent, if not actually disillusioned. This was especially the case in Germany, where the German legal philosopher, and former Social Democratic Minister of Justice during the Weimar Republic, Gustav Radbruch, in 1946 introduced a formula intended to reconcile positive law and ideas of justice. The formula argued that where statutory law is incompatible with the requirements of justice to an intolerable degree, statutory law as *unrichtiges Recht* ('wrong law/right/justice')

13 According to Anne Hellum the couple was supposed to to go England for preparation of the trip to Greenland to get informed about English legal anthropology. I have not been able to verify this information.

14 When I interviewed Per Lindegaard in October 1997 for my article on Agnete's role in the expedition (Petersen 1998), he told that she seemed quite nervous during their stay.

must yield to justice (Petersen 2008).[15] The couple may not have known the work of Radbruch, but they knew about the concerns and catastrophes which had given rise to reassessments of totalitarian modern positive law.

This very general unease with, and experience of the role of statutory law turned against minorities may have been indirectly reflected in the report of the legal expedition to Greenland, which clearly recommended that Greenlandic tradition should be considered when establishing a new and 'modern' law, which would govern decolonized Greenland. Amongst these recommendations were suggestions that it should include the Greenlandic understanding of law, and that a judiciary with lay judges trusted by local communities and familiar with both Greenlandic culture and normative culture, and not least with the Greenlandic language should be established. This was not the highly modern approach to a unified legal system, which (parts of) the administration might have expected. The report, which the members of the expedition presented,[16] was never published unlike other reports by other commissions. As the third member, Per Lindegaard remarked, when I interviewed him in 1997 in an untranslatable pun: "Den blev ikke trykt, den blev undertrykt" – "It wasn't published, it was suppressed" (Petersen 1998, 28).

Both Goldschmidt and Bentzon later wrote their dissertations[17], and Verner Goldschmidt wrote an insightful article in the Nordic Legal Journal *Retfærd* in a special issue on Greenland in 1981 about the move from

---

15 Radbruch lost his job after the introduction of *Gesetz zur Wiederherstellung des Berufsbeamtentums* (Act on Reestablishment of the Civil Service) of April 7, 1933. This legislation was mostly aimed at Jews, but also at opponents of the Nazi regime. Radbruch, who was not Jewish, was the first German professor to be dismissed from his post, on May 8, 1933.

16 *Betænkning afgivet 6. September 1950 af den juridiske ekspedition til Grønland 1948-49* (utrykt); [Report of September 6 1950 by the legal expedition to Greenland – unpublished).] The bibliography of this six- volume stencil report is quite short, and does not contain any international references. Amongst the references to Danish law professors is a reference to Viggo Bentzon's Family Law I & II of 1924 and 1926.

17 In Goldschmidt's dissertation of 1957 there are references to a few German authors, but mainly to English-speaking authors in the original languages including references to Theodor Geiger (in German), Georges Gurvitch, Llewelyn & Hobel, Malinowski, Merton, Parsons, Roscoe Pound, T.T. Segerstedt, Timasheff and Weber (in English). The postwar orientation towards North American social and legal theory is very clear.

This is also the case in Agnete Weis Bentzon's dissertation from 1968 on family issues. Here the international references are all in English, and the sociological reference is to Parsons.

unwritten to written criminal law in Greenland. In this article Goldschmidt underlines the importance of what he came to describe as *the Arctic Peace Model*, where the important thing was "that the demand for *peaceful coexistence* was set above a demand for people to behave in the same way and in general *be in conformity* with each other and with some type of system of norms" (Goldschmidt 1981, 118 – emphasis in original).

The 'model of conformity' is contrasted to the model of peace, and in case of conflict the former is characterized by attempts to "*pressurize the parties in the conflict or one of them to be in conformity with valid norms*" (Goldschmidt 1981, 118 – emphasis in the original). He continues that conformity requires a tier of leaders and a state apparatus, and first and foremost expresses a repressive tendency, even if conformity may be achieved through ideology. This model is "related to inequality in society" (Goldschmidt 1981, 118).

Goldschmidt goes on to say that Greenlandic legal practice in his view was undoubtedly more important for future Greenlandic legislation than Danish criminal law, which reflects the interests and values of modern industrial societies. He writes that the inspiration for the legislation on Greenlandic criminal law, which he came to work on later, came from a draft criminal law of 1921 by the Italian socialist, Enrico Ferri.[18] This draft however was to have no practical impact in Italy, as Mussolini came to power shortly afterwards. But it became the basis for the original Russian criminal law, and was a source of inspiration when the Greenlandic criminal law was being considered (Goldschmidt 1981, 122-123). According to Goldschmidt both Danish and Swedish criminal policy in this period in the early 1920s developed along the same lines as the Italian draft.

Goldschmidt rejects what he calls the European Conformity Model in this quote:

> "When I prepared the first draft for the Greenlandic Criminal law, I was strongly engaged in the wish not only to keep the Greenlandic 'peace model' for solution of those conflicts we today call crime; I also wished to protect it [the peace model HP] against the European 'conformity model', which I did not think had anything to do with the living conditions of Greenlandic small communities and their consciousness of solidarity." (Goldschmidt 1981, 123 – my translation)

---

[18] See Goldschmidt 1986, 122, note 12, which refers to: Relazione sul Progetto Preliminare di Codice Penale Italiano, ed. Ministero Della Guistizia, Roma 1921.

It is clear from the writings of Bentzon and Goldschmidt that they did not know the work of Ehrlich on 'living law' around the time of the expedition, and that they drew their inspiration from other sources. Agnete Weis Bentzon and her later husband Torben Agersnap wrote in an article in 2000

"The expedition planned to base their descriptions of Greenlandic customary law mainly on information from those Greenlandic members of local councils who dealt with conflicts, limited to the cases they remembered. They also planned to attend a number of meetings of the councils and witness the settlement of disputes and quarrels.

The members of the expedition had in their minds a picture of the old Norse law-speaker (*logsobur madr*) active around the beginning of the millennium. While the moot assembled, he would find an account of the content of the laws relevant to the strife to be settled. These conflicts could be personal strife between individuals but also matters of more general importance.

However the expedition found no law-speakers even though they started out by contacting people of high in the local communities. They soon discovered that it would be impossible to achieve this goal – a fairly coherent description of the unwritten law of Greenland – by asking questions, but they would sometimes refer to a specific case and relate how it had been solved. This experience led to another procedure (well-known to common-law jurists): the case study method." (Bentzon and Agersnap 2000, 376)

Agnete Weis Bentzon – customary and living law in the post-colonial and post-communist era

It is difficult to assess the importance of the experience of exile, but there is no doubt that the Greenlandic experience was of paramount importance to both Agnete and Verner. Agnete lived for almost a generation longer than Verner, and the last section of this article will briefly discuss the way she came to absorb and integrate this experience at the end of another era – after her formal retirement in 1988, and not least during the post-communist era after 1989 when a new active period for her – and for living law – began in the Nordic countries.

As already indicated, Agnete Weis Bentzon came from a privileged family background and a line of lawyers. Her older sister also became a lawyer, and Agnete herself became the first Danish woman to obtain a doctoral degree in law, though not a degree from Denmark. She delivered her dissertation in Oslo, which had a more open-minded attitude towards socio-legal approaches to law than the Law Faculty at the University of Copenhagen, and she got her degree there in 1969 with Torstein Eckhoff and Vilhem Aubert on the committee. The lists of references in the dissertations of both spouses reflect the influence of American sociology of law. The only reference to a German book in Agnete Weis Bentzon's dissertation is to a book by another exiled German sociologist, who lived in exile in both Denmark and Sweden: Theodor Geiger's *Vorstudien zur Soziologie des Rechts.* Both Agnete's first and second husband worked together with Theodor Geiger. The few other references in her dissertation to authors originally writing in German are to English texts by Bert F. Hoselitz, Paul Lazarsfeld, Max Rheinstein, Max Weber and others. The turn towards the United States and its theory and literature is a general trend for Scandinavian academics after World War II.

Agnete Weis Bentzon never applied for a professorship *in law* in Denmark, and no woman was granted a professorship in law in Copenhagen before 1990.[19] The University of Copenhagen may at that time have considered her topics: family issues in Greenland, approached from a socio-legal perspective, as both marginal and controversial. However, her work was both in terms of topic, as well as theoretically and historically, clearly influenced by and linked to the work of her grandfather and professor, Viggo Bentzon at the University of Copenhagen. One of her first chapters deals with the Danish law on the legal implications of marriage and its societal background – the legal reform her grandfather was closely involved with in the first decades of the 20th century. Her own work also dealt with the topic of legal reform though in the postcolonial context and period, and her question was to what extent an introduction of the Danish law on the implications of marriage would make sense. She answered this question mainly in the negative because of the very different social conditions in the two parts of the Kingdom. While nuclear marriage had become the norm in Denmark, the economic role of the *household* consisting of different generations and relations, was much more important in Greenland.

[19] In 1990 the Faculty of Law in Copenhagen employed the first female law professor, Eva Smith, the daughter of a former Social Democratic minister. She was the third Danish woman to get a doctoral degree in law in 1986. The second after AWB was Inger Dübeck, who obtained her degree in 1978, and was appointed professor of family law at Århus University in 1991.

In 1974 AWB became professor of sociology of law at the modern Roskilde University – established in 1972. She was an early member of the Commission on Folk Law and Legal Pluralism – as it was originally called. The Commission was established in 1978 by the International Union of Anthropological and Ethnological Sciences, and affiliated with the International Association of Legal Science. She attended several of its conferences and established an international network. When she retired in 1988 she became an adjunct professor at the Faculty of Law at the University of Copenhagen. During this period I was writing my dissertation on informal law at women's workplaces, and I had many very valuable discussions with her. As already mentioned I was very inspired by Ehrlich's work, as well as by Sally Falk Moore's work on legal pluralism and law as process.[20] It became clear, especially in later work by Agnete, that the concept of 'living law' was very useful to describe some of the experiences of the members of JUREX in 1948-49. In the 1990s, when she became involved with projects in Southern Africa particularly, the case method, customary law and the concept of 'living law' turned out to be very useful, and her Greenlandic post-colonial experiences were extremely valuable.[21]

During the Ehrlich-seminar in Oslo in November 2012, the participants discussed the present attraction of legal pluralism. Keebet von Benda Beckmann suggested that it might be due to 'disillusion with state law'.[22] That was certainly my own experience when I defended my thesis (Informal Law in Women's Workplaces – An Empirical and Theoretical Investigation) in the summer of 1991, when the Soviet Union was on the verge of collapse. The insecurity of the political and legal situation made it possible to argue for understandings of law other than black letter state law. The collapse of state socialism in Eastern and Central Europe, started a period of intense focus on human rights, which had already taken off after the two – East and West oriented – UN treaties on Human Rights had entered into force in 1975.

20 I have not been able to find references to Ehrlich's work in her own writings, and I do not think that Agnete knew about him before around 1990. She became a member of my dissertation committee, and she would have known of his work before 1991.

21 In the collectively written book by Agnete Weis Bentzon, Anne Hellum, Julie Stewart, Welshman Ncube and Torben Agersnap (1998), there is a reference to Ehrlich's work in the joint references.

22 Author's notes from workshop, Oslo, November 2-3.2012.

Agnete Weis Bentzon had dealt with the role of the family in Greenlandic society since her 1968 dissertation and in 1975 she wrote an article called "Hvad styrer retten?" [What governs/steers law?] in the first formal publication in Denmark on women's law, *Jura og kvinder* (Law and Women) published on the occasion of the centenary of women's access to legal education in Denmark. Women's law was clearly in need of a new socio-legal theory of law to explain the changes and realities in women's lives, and in 1986 she wrote a piece called "Comments on women's law in Scandinavia".

During her period of work with post-colonial African societies, which was especially concerned with the changing role of gender in these societies, she combined her Greenlandic experience with her new experience. One example is what she called a worknote on customary law, polycentricity and legal pluralism (1991). Here she describes customary law in 'the North', in 'the South' and in modern societies. She discusses the ambivalence towards customary law of the newly independent African states, where the ideal of politicians is legal unity and state monopoly in regulation. The choice of a definition of law is important in a number of respects, and the ideal of legal unity has clearly been used as part of a fight to consolidate the nation state, she writes. The goal of legal pluralism and legal polycentricity may be more unclear, she writes, but those holding it are often critical of traditional views of law, which represent an oppressive ideology (Bentzon 1991, 26).

An even clearer example of the comparisons of periods and forms of law is an article called *European Family Law Confronting the Extended Family in Developing Countries – the Case of Greenland and Mocambique* from 1994.

This is an interesting comparison over both considerable time spans and spaces. Agnete Weis Bentzon was the secretary of the Greenlandic Law Reform Committee from 1951-87, which meant that she followed the Greenlandic development from colony to incorporation in 1953 into the Kingdom in Denmark as an equal part, with the subsequent establishment and implementation of Home Rule in 1979. In both Greenland and Mozambique the presence of lay judges at the lowest level of the judicial hierarchy was of the utmost importance. In the last part of the article, she writes in the '*Summary of the Two Countries' Unification of Law and Adoption of Customary Norms*' about the case of Mozambique:

"The source of law prescribed for the locality courts is 'common sense and local sentiments of justice and official ideology'. However, this could as well be labelled *living customary law*. Although state law is not a formal source of law, the usage of the courts displays a mixture of formal and traditional sources in the arrangements solving disputes." (Bentzon 1994, 325 – emphasis as shown)

And half a page later she writes "... even so customary law applied by lay judges would be living law which changes with changing local conditions." (Bentzon 1994, 326)

Her major contribution is to the above mentioned collective work *Women's Law: Pursuing Grounded Theory. South-North Experiences in Developing Women's Law* of 1998. This is the only work in which there is a reference to Eugen Ehrlich. During this period she had a very close collaboration with Anne Hellum. Since 1989 Anne Hellum has been involved in cooperation in teaching and research with the Southern and Eastern African Center for Women's Law at the University of Zimbabwe (SEARCWL), and in 2000 she became professor of women's law, at the University of Oslo. Another important co-author and collaborator of both Agnete and Anne Hellum was Professor Julie Stewart, originally Australian, but who has lived in Zimbabwe for many decades.

What this brief comparison over lifetimes and over one and a half centuries seems to indicate is the relevance of broader understandings of law – not least when eras come to an end and the 'edges' of a round planet become increasingly interconnected. The work of Ehrlich, of the Greenlandic juridical expedition, and Agnete Weis Bentzon's last involvements and work underline the relevance of what has in the 20th century often been considered 'outsider' perspectives of 'law'. It demonstrates the importance of living law, customary law, legal pluralism and socio-legal as well as socio-cultural perspectives on and understandings of 'law' in periods of change in legal landscapes and of political and legal maps. These are processes which were highly characteristic of the 20th century, and they are likely to continue in the 21st century.

References

Bak, Sofie Lene (2010), *Ikke noget at tale om. Danske jøders krigsoplevelser 1943-45*. [Nothing to talk about. War experiences of Danish Jews 1943-45]. Copenhagen: Dansk Jødisk Museum. The Danish Jewish Museum.

Bentzon, Agnete Weis (1968), *Familiens økonomiske administration og ejendelenes tilhørsforhold i de vestgrønlandske samfund – en retssociologisk undersøgelse*. Copenhagen: Nyt fra Samfundsvidenskaberne 11. (Doctoral Dissertation awarded by the Faculty of Law at the University of Oslo in 1968).

Bentzon, Agnete Weis (1975), Hvad styrer retten. In: Inger Dübeck, Jytte Lindgaard and Ruth Nielsen (eds.), *Jura og kvinder,* Copenhagen: Juristforbundets Forlag, pp. 266-281.

Bentzon, Agnete Weis (1986), Comments on Women's Law in Scandinavia. *International Journal of the Sociology of Law* 14:249-254.

Bentzon, Agnete Weis (1987), Glimt fra min tid som stud.jur. i 30'erne. Strømninger fra Syd? (Glimpses from my time as a law student in the 1930s. Currents from the South?) *Retfærd* 39:6-18.

Bentzon, Agnete Weis (1991), Sædvaneret, polycentri og legal pluralisme – en arbejdsnote. In: *Retsvidenskabeligt Institut B (ed.), Årsberetning 1991,* Copenhagen, pp. 19-27.

Bentzon, Agnete Weis (1994), European Family Law Confronting the Extended Family in Developing Countries – the Case of Greenland and Mocambique. *Law and Anthropology* 7:311-329.

Bentzon, Agnete Weis, Anne Hellum, Julie Stewart, Welshman Ncube, and Torben Agersnap (1998), *Women's Law: Pursuing Grounded Theory. South-North Experiences in Developing Women's Law.* Oslo/Harare: TANO/Mond Books.

Bentzon, Agnete Weis, and Torben Agersnap (2000), Verner Goldschmidt: Danish Sociologist of Law and Culture. *Acta Sociologica* 43:375-380.

Betænkning afgivet 6. September 1950 af den juridiske ekspedition til Grønland 1948-49 (utrykt); Report of September 6, 1950 by the legal expedition to Greenland (unpublished).

Cotterell, Roger (2009), Ehrlich at the Edge of Empire: Centres and Peripheries in Legal Studies. Queen Mary, University of London, School of Law. *Legal Studies Research Paper* No. 3/2009. Electronic copy available at http://ssrn.com/abstract=1330365 (accessed June 2013).

Dansk Biografisk Leksikon (n.d.), Agnete Weis Bentzon, http://www.denstoredanske.dk/Dansk_Biografisk_Leksikon/Samfund,_jura_og_politik/Samfund/Sociolog/Agnete_Weis_Bentzon (Last accessed July 2013).

Den Store Danske (n.d.), Torgny Segerstedt, http://www.denstoredanske.dk/Samfund,_jura_og_politik/Massemedier/Kreative_mediefolk/Torgny_Segerstedt.

Ehrlich, Eugen (1909), *Die Aufgaben der Sozialpolitik im österreichishen Osten insbesondere in der Bukowina. Mit Besonderer Beleuchtung der Juden- und Bauernfrage.* Vortrag gehalten im Sozialwissenschaftlichen Akadem. Vereine an der Czernowitzer Universität im Wintersemester 1908/09, Zweite Auflage. Im Selbstverlage des Vereines, Czernowitz.

Ehrlich, Eugen, (1913), *Grundlegung der Soziologie des Rechts*. München: Duncker & Humblot.
Ehrlich, Eugen (1936/2002), Fundamental Principles of the Sociology of Law, translated by Walter L. Moll. New Brunswick/London: Transaction.
Feuchtwanger, Lion (1935), *Die Geschwister Oppenheim*. Amsterdam: Querido Verlag (first published 1933, Danish translation 1934).
Gelsted, Otto (1945), *Flygtninge i Husaby*. Copenhagen: Athenæum.
Goldschmidt, Verner (1957), *Retlig Adfærd. En analyse af retsmyndigheders adfærd med eksempler særlig fra den kriminelle retspleje i Grønland*. Meddelelser om Grønland 90, no. 4.
Goldschmidt, Verner (1981), Fra uskreven til skreven kriminalret i Grønland. *Retfærd* 16:116-129.
Hertel, Hans (2012), *PH – en biografi*. Copenhagen: Gyldendal.
Mogensen, Michael (2000), Det danske flygtningesamfund i Sverige og "jødespørgsmålet" 1943-45. In: Johnny Laursen, Michael Mogensen, Thorsten Borring Olesen and Søren Hein Rasmussen (eds.), *I tradition og kaos. Festskrift til Henning Poulsen*. Aarhus: Århus Universitetsforlag, pp. 150-160.
Modéer, Kjell Åke (2013a), *Det svenska rättsarvet. Om beredskapstidens historisering och dess rättsliga uttryck ur ett law & literature – perspektiv*. Edited lecture given at Nordiska Rättshistorikardagerna i Uppsala 24-26 April, 2013.
Modéer, Kjell Åke (2013b), Äreminne över två av beredskapstidens advokater. *Juridisk Publikation* No. 1/2013.
Petersen, Hanne (1991), *Informel ret på kvindearbejdspladser. En teoretisk og empirisk analyse*. Copenhagen: Akademisk Forlag.
Petersen, Hanne (1996), *Home Knitted Law. Norms and Values in Gendered Rule-Making*, Dartmouth, Aldershot.
Petersen Hanne (1998), 50 år efter Den Juridisk Ekspedition – Spredte refleksioner over kolonier, køn og ret. In: Peter Blume and Kirsten Ketscher (eds.), *Ret og skønsomhed i en overgangstid*. Copenhagen: Akademisk Forlag, pp. 21-39.
Petersen, Hanne (2009), Legal Cultures on the Move. *Retfærd* 31: no 4/123: 3-22.
Wiborg, Susanne (2007), Alfred Ballin. Hamburg: Ellert & Richter Verlag.
Wikipedia (n.d.), Torgny_Segerstedt, http://sv.wikipedia.org/wiki/Torgny_Segerstedt.

Ehrlich's Concept Applied to Non-Western Countries

Organizing a Community: The “Living Law” of the Don Cossacks

Olga LITVINOVA and Stefan MACHURA

Studying the works of Eugen Ehrlich, the Austrian founder of the sociology of law, can be helpful in understanding the old legal culture of South Russia, especially of the multi-ethnical Don area. In 1913 the population at the Don numbered 2.6 million, and half of these were Cossacks (Shpagin 1997), which makes their laws an important subject of any analysis. Ehrlich (1936/2002, Foreword, 486-488, 491-493, 498) famously states that to understand the law of a society, the “living law” representing the inner order of the “associations”, the various groups people live in, had to be studied. It cannot be found in law books alone. Concerning himself mainly with civil law, Ehrlich suggests that one should employ methods such as observation of daily activities, interviews and – above all – analyses of legal documents. Contracts to do with marriage and land use would be examples of what should be studied. Furthermore, Ehrlich always finds society made up of different “associations”. His birthplace, where he later held a professorship, belonged to Romania after World War I and now forms part of Ukraine. It was characterised by a plethora of ethnic groups, all with their own special (living) laws (Ehrlich 1912/1967, 43). The same was true for South Russia. In the Don area, as can be learnt from the novel *Steppe* by Anton Chekhov (1887/1985), one passed through Russian, Jewish, Cossack, Ukrainian, and Armenian settlements on the journey from a village near Slavianoserbsk to the city of Taganrog, with its Greek merchants.

In one of his last publications, Ehrlich (1920/21/2007, 197-198) concerns himself with the principle of the “nationality of law”. In the Roman Empire, non-citizens were treated according to their respective “national law” and medieval law generally followed this pattern too. Only the modern territorial state imposes its universal law on all. Nevertheless, in reality, different nations (which for Ehrlich are just another form of “associations”) inside a state follow their own laws. As we have seen, “law” for Ehrlich means “living law”; it is not necessarily codified, and in many cases deviates from written law. A nation, for Ehrlich, is a “cultural community independent of the ethnic origin of its members" (Vogl 2003, 322, our translation). The Cossacks indeed exemplify this description, as they first had to form a community, and later to constantly integrate large inflows of migrants, along the way creating their own laws.

The law of the Don Cossacks initially develops from the challenge of organizing life in a forbidding environment. According to Ehrlich (1907/1986, 108 f.), in early stages of social development people feel that the existential struggle against nature and other humans can be survived by forming groups. From this arise feelings that bind people together. Communities at first only grant legal protection to individuals seen as full-fledged members: those who can take part in its defence and are themselves able to help others (Ehrlich 1907/1986, 110). Later, political intervention produces large land holdings for the ruling political class with groundbreaking legal and social consequences (Ehrlich 1907/1986, 113). This happened later in Cossack history.

In the USSR the ideas of Eugen Ehrlich stood no chance of becoming known to scholars. The government followed the concept of the dictatorship of the proletariat through centralized powers, including a state monopoly on law (Pashin 2003). Ehrlich's writings on the self-organisation of society were thus unwelcome. The Austrian law professor had after all called the socialist ideology a "social alchemy" (Ehrlich 2005, 226). Only in recent years have brief overviews of Eugen Ehrlich's legal concepts at last been published in Russian (Rumjanzeva 2005; Antonov 2012).

Nevertheless, in the pre-revolutionary Russian Empire, with its huge variety of legal systems, one publication of the Chernovtsy law professor was accessible in Ukrainian (Bihun 2005). At that time a range of Russian legal philosophers, sociologists and historians explained the origin of law in the same way as Ehrlich: the whole society provides the legal norms[1]. Hundreds of Russian ethnicities, with their native customs, supplied examples supporting the theory. The last half of the 19th century saw a blossoming of the study of customary law in the Russian provinces[2]. Mikhail Kharusin (1887) as Secretary of the Russian Imperial Geographic Society developed a questionnaire for the collection of data on legal customs which covered issues that would also have interested Ehrlich. Answers came in from all

[1] Ehrlich 1936/2002, Foreword and 493, Kharusin 1885, 1; Timashev 2004, 108.

[2] Efimenko 1869; Kovalevskij 1886; Mainov 1885; Kovalevskij 1890; Sagoskin 1891.

Russian provinces. The unprecedented surveys were commissioned by the Tsarist government with the aim of collecting data about the customary law used by local communities. Despite the introduction of an all-Russian “bureaucratic” law in the 1870s, the Don area courts of first instance nevertheless worked mainly on the basis of time-honoured legal traditions (Krasnov 2011, 49, 57).

This article aims to demonstrate that some of Ehrlich’s findings apply to the specific local law of the Don Cossacks. Thanks to Ehrlich’s sociology of law we are able to shed light on certain features of the Cossacks’ law, and to highlight the peculiarities of their legal culture. Russian intellectuals, especially classic writers of the 19th and 20th century, have been fascinated by the freedom displayed by Cossack society, which compared favourably with Tsarist oppression. To appreciate their work, therefore, an understanding of Cossack society is indispensible. The legal culture of the Don Cossacks does not entirely belong to history, as it is a subject of contemporary interest and even survives in places. Like other local ethnic traditions, those of the Don Cossacks are remembered with nostalgia, reconstructed to serve political interests, and at times utilised in the context of a less than perfect post-Soviet social and legal system (Machura 1998).

The Don Cossacks and their Settlements

In the Middle Ages the Russian verb “to cossack” meant “to get free,” or “to escape from Russia to no-man’s land”. The noun “Cossack” indicated a decisive and independent person, someone who is making a fresh start far away from his previous habitat and social environment.

Between the 14th and the 17th century, numerous escapees, mostly young single men had fled from central Russia to the thinly populated banks of the Don, Dnepr, Ural and Volga rivers on the margins of the empire. By far the largest and strongest Cossack community developed from the early 14th century on the Don basin (Rigelmann 1846, 1-3). Who were they? Firstly, there were thousands of peasant-serfs running away from their landlords. A second significant group consisted of prosecuted members of non-official Christian sects (Markedonov 1998, 104-105). During the tyranny of Ivan the Terrible (1533-1584) a major uprising of escapees took place (Markedonov 2005, 96). In addition, former Russian aristocrats also took refuge on the Don, because of reprisals by the Tsar (Tulaeva 2010, 67).

How was it possible to survive, within a rough Cossack brotherhood, in the harsh conditions facing them in the wild, far away from any Russian towns, and, on top of that, in close proximity to equally militant Moslem and Buddhist tribes? The Cossacks organized their territory by forming new social bodies that provided an alternative to the Russian state (Bykadorov 1930, 4; Tulaeva 2010, 68).

Historians and ancient Don folk songs claim that the Cossacks could turn to the local forests and rivers for their sustenance: "From the beginning their favourite activities were hunting and fishing." (Kharusin 1885, 4). Strong, mostly single, males formed *vatagas*, bands of 10-50 men, who lived close to the river in temporary dugouts, surrounded by a simple earth wall planted with impassable thorn thickets. These first Don Cossack settlements were called *gorodki* (meaning "small fenced settlements"). In 1593 there were about fifty such primitive encampments, which were used just for one season or even less than that (Korolev 1999, 1-3). Later these morphed into larger permanent fortified Cossack *stanizas*. By about 1720 some of these, such as Gnilovskaya (now part the South Russian capital Rostov-on-Don), became proper walled Cossack fisher communities on the Don estuary (Avakov 2012), mainly living off selling fish and caviar to Russian and Turkish merchants.

The best protected *stanizas*, like the first Cossack capital, Rasdory, were built on islands in the Don river (Dolgopolov 2007). The later capital *staniza*, Cherkassk, was similarly situated. In 1644 about 20,000 armed warriors and their families lived there, protected by tall, strong walls (Ev. Astapenko 2003, 188). Taking part in guarding the settlement was a compulsory duty for all males. In exceptionally dangerous times the *stanizas* were also defended by the women (Georgi 1799, 201; Saveljev 2010, 376). This might in part explain the special status of Cossack women, who were much more emancipated than women in Central Russia. For example, in contrast to women everywhere else, and even to aristocratic ladies, according to Cossack law they and their brothers inherited equal shares (Kharusin 1885, 130).

In the 18th century Cossacks mostly lived with their families in relatively comfortable *stanizas*. They protected themselves against enemy attack in ways that influenced the organization of community life. Inside the walled area, which was surrounded by four to eight towers with canons on their tops, there were generally *kureni* (warrior barracks for 20-50 persons),

Turkish-style dwelling houses, a community arsenal, a well and community storage space. Later, by the beginning of the 19th century, nearly every *staniza* had an Orthodox church. Inside the protected area the maidan was the place used for the settlers' general assembly *Krug* (meaning "circular place"). All of these were in community ownership (Georgi 1799, 209). Behind the Cossack *staniza* there was invariably a *zimovnik*, a protected area for cattle, this too owned communally, together with community meadows (Korolev 1999, 13). In addition, the *duvan* on a hill in front of the typical *staniza*, was the place set aside for the public distribution of bounties from military expeditions (Svatikov 1924, 94). Nowadays, even if the original *staniza* layout has been lost, people still call the areas of their towns by the traditional Cossack names: *maidan, zimovnik, duvan* etc. (Losev 2013). The local dialect preserves the phrase "Duvan duvanitj," that means "to share the spoils in a brotherly way, fairly and informally" (Svatikov 1924, 94).

Between the 16th and 17th centuries, camping on the main trade routes between Turkey, Persia, Lithuania and Russia, armed Cossack bands regularly attacked merchant ships under all flags on the Don and the Black and Caspian Sea (Rigelmann 1846, 40-43). Cossacks plundered neighbouring Russian, Lithuanian, Turkish or Persian towns (Saveljev 2010, 204-224). As a consequence of war, an important part of the Cossack economy was based on the slave trade (Rigelmann 1846, 9). The prisoners taken in several Cossack wars were sold on the slave markets of neighbouring Turkish Black Sea ports. Selling thousands of slaves annually, with no exemption for those of a Slavic background, by now formed the backbone of the Cossack economy (Larionov 2007, 102).

In the 1850s Leo Tolstoy became familiar with Cossack culture during his military service, when he fought alongside them in the Caucasian and Crimean wars. He witnessed a specific kind of benefit Cossacks gained from the military campaigns: the collection of ransoms for the dead bodies of their enemies. Once they received money from Tatar families their dead were delivered in time for a Muslim funeral, which had to be held on the same day (Tolstoy 1863/1980, 22).

From the 14th to the 18th century generations of Cossacks were on the lookout out for dangerous adventures promising rich bounties: "In the old days they were mostly unmarried young men and didn't settle down anywhere, but constantly undertook violent attacks on their neighbours," wrote a local historian. "They shared the spoil equally, and lived together like brothers" (Saveljev 2010, 166, our translation). The Cossack raids on foreign towns were targeted, and described by them as "a campaign to take clothing", "a campaign to kidnap wives" etc. It should be pointed out that the practice of kidnapping women for marriage was common to nearly all of the neighbouring Caucasian and Crimean tribes (Lermontov 1839; Rigelmann 1846, 10). As a legal historian, Ehrlich (1907/1986, 111) notes that women of defeated enemies had an economic and sexual value and their lives were spared in early times. The abduction of oriental women explains why, even up to the middle of the 19th century, some women in the Don area conversed among themselves in Turkish (Saveljev 1908, 12). Even today the local dialect contains a lot of Turkish vocabulary and many places have Turkish names (Beznochenko 2008). Many traditional Turkish dishes are common in the locality.

Up to the beginning of the 18th century the Don Cossacks were not involved in large-scale livestock and poultry farming or agriculture. They would not commit to such long-term activities. "Any peaceful activities there were well-nigh impossible due to the continuous military struggles of the Cossacks with their Turk and Tatar neighbours" (Pronstein and Mininkov 1983, 86, our translation). Such activities would also have been less profitable for the Cossacks than war, and for a time were even forbidden by the local assemblies, which wanted constant readiness to go to war (Sukhorukov 1892, 22). Indeed, robbery and war formed the foundation of the Cossack economy. Soon the armed Cossacks troops based on the main trading routes became a force to be reckoned with, capable of destabilising the relations between countries (Rigelmann 1846, 211; Svatikov 1924, 49-83; Saveljev 2010, 211-224).

The ancient maps gave the name "Don Host Land" to the Cossack areas on the Northern Coast of the Black Sea, around the Don basin up to the Caucasian mountains in the South, and to the Russian border in the North (Korolev 1999, 1). In modern Russian the meaning of "Cossack" has become "an armed, reckless, extremely dangerous man who may be encountered unexpectedly". On the Don, a man who does not want stable relationships with women is referred to as a "Cossack".

Up to the 15th century, no neighbouring country had accepted Cossacks as compatriots (Svatikov 1924, 22; Korolev 1999, 2). On the other hand, the Steppe warriors were often sought out as strong allies in armed conflicts (Korolev 1999, 2). It should be mentioned that the Don Cossacks themselves often cooperated with their Ukrainian counterparts, the Dnepr Cossacks, who also lived as a paramilitary community. Even the ancient Don Cossack capital, Cherkassk, many researchers argue, was constructed by Ukrainian Cossacks according to the layout of their main castle on the Dnjepr island Hortiza (Rigelmann 1846, 201; Saveliev 1915a, 20; Bykadorov 1930, 4).

Be this as it may, the Russian Tsar’s court gradually established diplomatic contacts, initially through Orthodox missionaries, with the dangerous Cossack *stanizas*. In the second half of the 16th century the Cossacks were paid on a regular basis by the Russian treasury for military services (Rigelmann 1846, 12-16; Saveljev 1915b, 16-17; Svatikov 1924, 22).

The general assembly of staniza settlers as a hub of decision-making

Attending community assemblies was obligatory for Cossacks (Sukhorukov 1892, 16). All aspects of community life were discussed. Each family was represented by one member, male or female. The assembly took place in the middle of the town in a special place called the *maidan* between the church and the *staniza* office. The latter, the *stanichnaya izba*, was the meeting place in winter. In some *stanizas* the meeting house could hold up to 1,000 people. As a rule, an annually elected official, the *esaul*, assistant of town chief, chaired the meeting.

> “He stood in the circle and managed the crowd using a small hand bell. The participants took off their hats, faced the icons and religious flags, taken out from the church for the general assembly. Resolutions of the *Krug* were taken by majority voting, the votes being counted by the ayes and the noes forming two separate groups.” *(Kharusin 1885, 285*, our translation)

The *Krug’s* responsibilities included the annual election of leaders, of the *ataman*, the *esaul*, and of judges. It also organized the town’s defence, the supply of weapons and food, and decided on attacks against enemies. It also sorted out local conflicts (Rigelmann 1846, 201). Until the end of the 18th century, the *Krug* also elected a lay priest, skilled in the interpretation of the *Evangelium* who had to take part in assemblies. Later, the Muscovite Orthodox Church took over and professionalized the clergy (Kharusin 1885,

285). Up to the 1920s, holders of most public offices continued to be democratically elected in the *Krug* by a wide spectrum of the Cossack population, in contrast to the long-standing "leadership committee", nominated by aristocrats in the Russian towns (Nebratenko 2006, 4). From the Middle Ages up to the 1920s another hugely important matter decided by the *Krug* was the regular distribution of the town's land between community members (Kharusin 1885, 36-37). Every seven, or in some settlements, ten years, the assembly re-allocated meadows and fields to Cossack farmers[3].

Only the *Krug* could decide on the inclusion of new members into the community[4]. Up to the 19th century new community members had two possible statuses. Ukrainians and other Slavs often refused to do military service, and therefore had a lower status and no voting rights in the *Krug,* and had to pay tax. Baptized Tatars and Kalmyks usually agreed to all Cossack duties, above all that of serving as warriors (Saveliev 1908, 8). Only those new members who were able (and willing) to fight were also given economic privileges in the *staniza*, namely a salary for military training and engaging in war. They were also exempt from paying tax. The *Krug* also decided on the form and amount of financial support for widows and children of deceased members (Kharusin 1885, 49).

Up to the 1920s in accordance with a binding Cossack rule, in case of war each *staniza* family had to provide their male members with a battle-trained horse, arms and other war equipment (Kharusin 1885, 142). Clearly, not all families could follow the rules. The *staniza Krug* therefore annually allocated money to equip poor community members with horses and weapons (Kharuzin 1885, 144). It is interesting to note that at this time neighbouring nomadic tribes also had community assemblies and took collective responsibility for poor members. Thus, for example, the whole Kalmyk clan paid money for a clan member who was not able to service debts or pay court penalties (Kovalevskij 2002, 136). Like the Cossacks, the neighbouring Caucasian people (such as the Chechens and the Ingushs) also had assemblies for community matters, *Mekh–khel*, but without female participation (Arsanukaeva 2009, 103).

---

3 As an unwelcome consequence of a growing population, the economic situation worsened as the plots of land got ever smaller.

4 Unless they converted to Christianity, Jews were mostly excluded from living in the Don Host area. They could, however, receive permission to settle in the larger harbour cities Taganrog and Rostov, and in the Donbas.

Because of the war economy, the *staniza Krug's* competence extended to the affairs of the local Cossack regiment. It decided the number of soldiers and the details of their equipment (Saveliev 2010, 381). The election of the leader for a war campaign – *pokhodny ataman* – also took place in the town's *Krug*. For the civil administration of the town a different *ataman* was chosen[5].

The institution of elected *atamans* on the Don was not always as beneficial for Moscow, as in the case of the Cossack leaders who with their men conquered Siberia and the Far East for the Russian Crown. Several times in Russian history the elected *atamans* headed extremely dangerous Cossack insurgencies, which turned into long-term civil wars against the Russian ruling aristocracy. On their way to Moscow the rebellious Cossacks abolished the local authorities and replaced them with new ones elected in the Cossack manner.

Marriage and family were less strictly regulated among the Don Cossacks compared to central Russia. Notably, children born outside of marriage were accepted in the community (Kharuzin 1885, 109-115). A prime example of Cossack customs was the marriage ritual in the *Krug*. The bridegroom, wearing an elaborated community bridal kaftan (Kharusin 1885, 64), stepped out in front of the *Krug* assembly and introduced his bride-to-be with the words: "Dear *staniza*-people, this is ... (name of the woman)." – Then, repeating her name, the groom asked her: "Would you like to be my wife?" After her agreement, it was the bride's turn to ask her groom. When both partners announced their union to the community and had kissed each other, the crowd chanted: "*Lubo, lubo*!" (Well done, well done!") (Sukhorukov 1892, 16-17; Saveljev 2010, 376; Kharusin 1885, 48). In some *stanizas*, the marriage ritual was completed by the headman leading the couple around a tree, or a horse-drawn carriage brought into the middle of the *Krug* (Savielev 2010, 270), substituting for a church altar. This voluntariness compared favourably with the marriages arranged by Russian landlords for their un-consenting serfs (Kharusin 1885, 48).

While divorce was unavailable in Russia, among Cossacks it took place in the town *Krug*. Again, the couple was asked about their intention to separate. Not only men, but women too could demand a divorce, which was very

5 Saveliev 2010, 366. This pattern of a second leadership for times of war was highlighted by Max Weber (1922/1968, 1111) as a prime example of charismatic leadership, though he used the example of North American Indian and Teutonic tribes.

rare elsewhere at the time. Some Cossacks "married and divorced up to four or five times", so the Russian Tsar in 1745 asked that Cossack men should not marry more than four times if their ex-wives were alive (Saveliev 2010, 269-270). When a divorce had been declared, in the same *Krug* another man might immediately ask the divorced woman to be his wife. After she expressed her agreement in front of the whole community, the new husband kissed her and covered her with his coat, literally, "to cover her disrepute" (Kharusin 1846, 49-50; Saveljev 2010, 269). By chanting, the crowd again expressed its agreement with the new partnership. The ease of this procedure was explained by the extreme shortage of females in the Cossack area and by the essentially civil (rather than religious) nature of Cossack marriage (Kharusin 1885, 49).

Until the end of the 18th century, marriage, and divorce too, took place in front of the *Krug* only, often without a priest, or in the presence of a priest elected by the *Krug*. Both procedures were based on the verbal agreement of man and woman and on verbal community assent (Kharusin 1885, 48-50). Tellingly, there is a similarity between these customs on the Don and those of North Russian Novgorod, which until the 17th century maintained its independence from Moscow. Novgorod was ruled by an elected ruling body, the *Veche*. Some similarity in town names can also be found, so a significant group of Novgorod migrants might have found asylum on the Don (Saveljev 1908, 1).

In the 18th and 19th centuries the local *Krugs* decided whether persons of other nationalities should be allowed to settle on *staniza* territory (*yourt*). Foreigners had to pledge to carry out a specified service, which was not necessarily a military one. For example, in the 18th century the Cossack *Krugs* admitted thousands of Ukrainian peasants to farm on land rented from Cossacks (Kharuzin 1885, 15-17; Sulin 1905, 68-74; Tereshchenko 2000). At the beginning of the 19th century, thousands of Armenian and Greek merchants gained permission to settle and trade. Later, people from such diverse places as the Balkans and Germany settled after the *Krug* had given assent (Pirko 2003, 46-97). In the second half of the 19th century, the competence of the *Krug* was limited to local affairs. Hughesovka, a British colony founded in 1869 around a metallurgical plant was permitted by the Don Cossack government of the time (Friedgut 1994, 17). In 1913, the year in which Ehrlich published "*Grundlagen der Soziologie des Rechts*", half of the population in the Don area had no Cossack status and lived under separate legal regulations (Shpagin 1997).

In practice, the implementation of what Ehrlich calls the principle of nationality of law, led to the isolation of the non-Cossack population from the Cossacks, who with their rules and rights formed special associations in the Don area. The differences in legal status between the Cossacks and the rest of the population of the Don area only disappeared after the Socialist revolution of 1917, which finally declared the equality of all citizens and abolished all the old social classes and statuses (Turoverov 1952, 4).

The local self-government of the *stanizas* had been almost completely abolished by the Tsarist government in 1891, with elected officials replaced by nominated ones (Svatikov 1924, 4). In its session from 28 April to 5 May 1917, the Cossack *Krug* in Novocherkassk declared the democratic election of *atamans* (Savchuk 2007). Later, in January 1918, it granted equal rights to non-Cossack settlers. This included compulsory military service for every male (Turoverov 1952, 5). During the civil war, all men were needed for the military effort. Equal rights were intended to silence any revolutionary opposition in the area, to "save the Silent Don" (Turoverov 1952, 4).

Today, although the population has other governmental bodies, the local assemblies in the former Don Cossack settlements are once more called *Krug* (El. Astapenko 2012; Teleradiokompaniya Don TR, 2013).

The election of leaders

At the centre of Ehrlich's theory are the "associations" and the law that constitutes their internal order. One of the most important aspects of social life is the choice of leaders and the definition of their powers. The Don Cossacks developed a particular pattern of leadership selection. Although there were numerous changes as regards detail, until the 1920s democratic election was the norm at local level. This feature sets Cossack culture clearly apart from central Russian Provinces.

Among the Cossacks, leadership was traditionally originally strictly temporary and always democratically legitimated. This would only change at the end of the 18th century, when the Tsar finally succeeded in splitting off the absolutely top-level leaders from their followers by creating a Cossack nobility (Svatikov 1924, 3). It was already the case that, since 1728, the head *ataman* of the Don Cossack host was nominated by the Tsar (Avakov

2002). As mentioned above, one of the oldest forms of associations, the *vataga* was formed for a certain enterprise only, such as fishery, hunting, or collecting the honey of wild bees etc[6]. The *vataga* members elected a particular leader for the activity in hand – the *vatachnyj ataman*. His role was to organise the activity and the fair distribution of the spoils between *vataga* members[7]. After the task was completed, the *ataman*'s leadership ended (Suchorukov 1892, 88). For military enterprises, *pokhody*, Cossacks also formed parties and elected a *pokhodnyj ataman* as their head (Saveliev 2010, 374). The legendary Don *ataman* Yermak, the conqueror of Siberia, was chosen in this way to lead the Cossack troops (Saveliev 1904, 39). Elected leadership has to be understood in the context of almost constant war.

The word *ataman* has Turkish origins and means "father of the folk". *Atamans* not only led military action, fishery or hunting, but also administered the local affairs of Cossack groups, visited foreign countries on diplomat missions or organised the safe passage of merchants who paid for this on the river Don. The *ataman's* decision was binding for all (Suchorukov 1882, 86). Nevertheless, sometimes temporarily elected Cossack rulers were punished by the ordinary members of the *Krug*, if they did not carry out their responsibilities properly. For example, when they shared the gains from hunting or fishing unfairly, *atamans* were beaten by the "whole brotherhood". Thereafter they could never be elected as an *ataman* again (Rigelmann 1846, 9-10).

When it came to electing the *ataman* for a whole *staniza*, literate, industrious candidates with life experience were sought out (Kharusin 1885, 289). For the period of a year, the *ataman* was responsible for the administration of the *staniza*. All community members were absolutely subordinate to the *ataman* (Saveljev 1917, 2). He received the symbols of *staniza* power – a special sceptre (*naseca*) from the also elected *esaul*. The Don Host *ataman's* sceptre was made from more valuable materials than the wooden sceptre of the *staniza atamans*, who sometimes used theirs for corporal punishment of badly behaved members of the public.

Signifying a change in the position of the *ataman*, the sceptre of the

---

6 Ehrlich (1936/2002, 241) mentions the Russian enterprise community *artele* when emphasizing "the influence of collectivism in Russian law".

7 According to Sulin (1905, 44), fair distribution meant proportionate to individual contribution.

Head *Ataman* of the Don Cossack Host, donated by the Russian Tsarina Ekaterina II, was gold and decorated with gemstones[8]. From 1728 the highest *ataman* was no longer democratically elected, but nominated by the Tsar (Svatikov 1924, 3; Avakov 2002). With *ukas* from 1775, the Tsar introduced a new government body for the Don Host area and partially Tsarist law. From 1795, serfdom began to be slowly and partially introduced by the allocation of mostly Ukrainian serfs to the new aristocracy of Cossack leaders. Their large land holdings were taken from communal lands. As in the whole of Russia, serfdom was abolished in 1861. But Cossacks were never serfs (Svatikov 1924, 2-3).

After the abolition of the monarchy, in Spring 1917 the Cossacks freely elected a Host *ataman* again (Svatikov 1924, 4; Turoverov 1952, 52). The Cossack capital Novocherkassk became a centre of anti-Bolshevik resistance, notably it was the headquarters of the staff of the All Russian Voluntary Army. Well-organized Cossack troops formed the core of the White Movement (Venkov 1997). When a number of Cossacks went into exile in 1921, they continued to organize themselves abroad in the traditional way in *stanizas* with elected *atamans* (Budanov 1957, 41; Kasachij Krug sarubeshija 1974, 27 and 32). After the end of the Soviet Union, Russia saw a revival of Cossack culture and nowadays the highest *ataman* of the Don area is an appointee again: the Deputy Governor of the Rostov Province (Teleradiokompanija Don TR 2013).

Judgment and Courts

Around the end of the 18th century, "when the Cossacks' life became more complex" (Krasnov 2003, 5), besides the *ataman*, the general community of the *stanizas* also had elected local judges. Like their elected temporary leadership this feature also distinguished Cossack life from other Russian areas, as Rigelmann (1846, 201) noted in his contemporary survey of the Russian population.

During the major uprisings against Moscow at the end of the 18th century, the Cossacks introduced elected local courts and the separation of powers in the conquered areas, which did not exist in central Russia (Pushkin 1984, 43-44; Svatikov 1924, 93). For instance, in the second half

[8] It is now on display in the Don Cossack Museum in Novocherkassk.

of the 17th century, in the neighbouring Russian Belgorod Province judges were appointed by the local aristocrats from their own class (Dudina 2010, 85).

Cossack community judges, *stanichnyie sudyi*, were elected from experienced and, as a rule, older people (Saveliev 1917, 4). Usually judges were literate and seen as able to make their legal rulings on the basis of the New Testament (Kharusin 1885, 297). Although punishments for crimes could be extremely severe, including gruesome versions of the death penalty, in civil actions compensation for wrongs suffered was the main solution. An interesting provision of traditional Russian communal justice is even mentioned by Ehrlich (1936/2002, 141): "If the court cannot make up its mind what decision it is to render, it divides the damage equally between the parties." Among the Cossacks, this would have happened if neither of the parties could bring sufficient evidence, or if the damage done turned out to be unintentional (Kharusin 1885, 163).

In the 1880s, Kharusin collected several interviews with the Don settlers about why the communal courts newly introduced by Moscow were not effectively used by the locals. According to them, the aldermen of each Cossack community always set out to regulate all conflicts internally without a court. For example, if a Cossack had verbally abused someone, the aldermen ordered him to go that same evening to the victim of the abuse, and fall on the floor in the front of them and ask for pardon. Usually this took place in the presence of witnesses (Kharusin 1885, 298). If the parties involved in a conflict couldn't make peace, the case was then a matter for the community courts. These courts dealt with civil as well as criminal cases, except those for which capital punishment could have been imposed (Shshelkunov 1907, 168; Sukhorukov 1892, 60).

An interesting example of an alternative form of dispute resolution should be mentioned, here. If two parties in a civil case could not reach agreement locally, despite all the efforts of the local judges and aldermen, they were sent to the Cossack capital Starocherkassk by boat. The journey would take a long time, as Starocherkassk is located on the Don Estuary. On top of that, the two parties were required to travel on their own in the same boat, with food and wine, all provided by the community. While rowing together and sharing their rations, reputedly, the parties often decided to lay their quarrel to rest. The local court was then only left with the task of noting the agreement (Kharusin 1885, 283; Sukhorukov 1892, 43).

A court procedure at the *Krug* could sometimes proceed without judges. It resulted in instant decision and followed a standardized pattern. The accuser verbally explained his accusation in front of the judges and the whole community. The crowd ordered the defendant to step forward, asked him about the details of the accusation and took a decision about the punishment. The rulings of the court were immediately enforced.

If the community court dealt with a criminal case, the accuser’s statement was followed by two to three speeches from witnesses for the prosecution in front of the crowd, after which the *Krug* questioned the defendant. In cases when the *ataman* had known about the crime before the court sitting, he himself carried out an investigation and shared the result with the *Krug* (Kharusin 1885, 299).

After the court reform of the 1870s, *staniza* courts became more bureaucratic, with written records, although they were still conducted publicly in a court house and with elected lay judges. Even so the courts followed local customary law, not the Russian codified law (Kharusin 1885, 147; Krasnov 2011, 49). While the courtroom interior was quite similar to European courts, the walls of the courtroom were not decorated with the monarch’s portrait but with depictions of famous Cossack *atamans* (Kharusin 1885, 152).

Some sources idealized the orderly conduct of the trials. In 1913, however, an elected lay judge, Fedor Kryukov (1913/2009), described irregularities such as biased judges, or carelessness in conducting their investigation. Earlier, it had been observed that some judges preferred to convene in a tavern rather than in the court building (Kharusin 1885, 151-152; Krasnov 2011, 53). Up until the beginning of the 19th century legal cases exceeding the competence of the *staniza* courts were subject to trial by the Don Host *Krug* in the Cossack capital Cherkassk. The leaders of the three Cossack uprisings, however, despite having had the right to be tried in the Don Host *Krug*, were put on trial in Moscow, reflecting the prevailing power relations (Svatikov 1924, 124).

Conclusion

How much of the above has any relation to the work of Ehrlich? His oeuvre is mainly concerned with the inner order of the associations formed within a society. Ehrlich mainly covers civil law and has little interest in state law, including criminal law. Students of the living law of the Cossacks would be very likely to notice the special features of leadership selection and criminal procedure. With his focus, Ehrlich would, however, have observed the formation of associations for economic enterprises and the rules around marriage and land use. The time-honoured principle of "nationality in law" which distributes rights according to group membership is quite central to Ehrlich's theory. It was decisive for life in pre-revolutionary South Russia. In an extreme case, a Cossack who took part in a crime in central Russia could see his accomplices punished there while he himself was sent to be tried by his local court.

The development of law in the Don Host Area also confirms the theory of Ehrlich (1922, 123), that a legal system can exist without codified law. The society develops norms for its life long before laws are formulated which specifically instruct decision-makers such as judges and administrators. Ehrlich observes (1922, 138) that judges and other officials first need to have the trust of the community they serve, and as a rule are appointed by the state only at a later stage and this rings true for Cossack legal history. The locally selected decision-makers tend to be ignorant of state legislation. Even more, where disputes arise, they are "often settled in a friendly manner (...) because the parties have reached compromise", as Ehrlich (1922, 141) writes, and what a perfect example of this the boat journey of quarrelling parties on the river Don provides!

As Ehrlich (1922, 144) points out, the study of the living law requires "the greatest possible knowledge of the whole structure of society". Independently of Ehrlich, Russian and Ukrainian scholars have assembled an impressive array of insights into the social and legal history of the Don Cossacks. The development of Cossack legal culture can now be seen with its peculiarities, but also its similarities with that of other people. Our analysis affirms Ehrlich's (1922, 144) idea that law has to be looked upon "as a function of society".

Literature

Antonov, Mikhail V. (2012), Putj i perspektivy pravovogo uchenija Ojgena Erlikha. *Zhurnal rossijskogo prava* 1:121-127.

Arsanukaeva, Madina S. (2009), Obychnoe pravo chechenzev i ingushej (XIX-nach.XX vv.) *Pravo. Zhurnal Vysshej Shkoly Ekonomiki* 3:111-130.

Astapenko, Elena (2012), *Stoliza Donskogo kasachestva prinimala gostej so vsego mira.* Rostov-on-Don: Parlamentskij Vestnik Dona. No. 10 (35). http://www.vestnikdona.ru/article/detail.php?ID=5784\&sphrase_id=3426 (Accessed 12 August 2013).

Astapenko, Evgenij M. (2003), *Gorod Cherkassk – stoliza semli Vojska Donskogo: XVI- nachalo XIX veka. Avtoreferat kandidata istoricheskich nauk.* Rostov-on-Don: Izdateljstvo Yuzhnogo Federaljnogo Universiteta.

Avakov, Petr A. (2002), *Elita Vojska Donskogo v 1738 godu: borjba za vojskovuyu naseku.* Rostov-on-Don: Donskoj Vremennik. http://www.donvrem.dspl.ru/Files/article/m5/2/art.aspx?art_id=1195 (Accessed 3 April 2013).

Avakov, Petr A. (2012), *Novoe o Gnilovskoj stanize.* Donskoj Vremennik. http://www.donvrem.dspl.ru/Files/article/m1/22/art.aspx?art_id=58 (Accessed 3 April 2013).

Beznochenko, Anatolij I. (2008), *Imena donskikh rek.* Rostov-on-Don: Donskoj Vremennik. http://www.donvrem.dspl.ru/Files/article/m9/0/art.aspx?art_id=484 (Accessed 3 April 2013).

Bihun, V. S. (2005), Evgen Erlikh: zhittja i pravoznachna spadshchina (aktualjnyj naukoznavchij naris). *Problemy filosofii prava* 3, 1-2:105-126.

Budanov, Ivan P. (ed., 1957), *Kasachij istorisheskij sbornik.* Paris: Izdanije Kasachjego Sojuza.

Bykadorov, Isidor F. (1930), *Istorija kasachestva. Kn. 1. Proiskhoshdenije kasachestva. Vosniknovenije respublik voljnogo kazachestva – Donskogo, Volchskogo,Yaizkogo i Terskogo vojsk. Osnovnyje cherty ikh bytija v period gosudarstvennoj nesavisimosti (1549-1671 g.)* Prague: Biblioteka voljnogo kasachestva – viljnogo kosatztva.

Chekhov, Anton P. (1887/1985), *Stepj. Istoriya odnoj poezdki. Polnoje sobranije sochinenij i pisem v 30-ti tomakh. Sochinenija*, Vol. 7. Moscow: Nauka.

Dolgopolov, Sergey A. (2007), *Sagadki pervoj kasachjey stolizy. Part 1. Kogda pojavilisj Rasdory?* Rostov-on-Don: Donskoj Vremennik. http://www.donvrem.dspl.ru/article/m1/18/art.aspx?art-id=438 (Accessed 3 April 2013).

Dudina, Olga V. (2010), Sudji v Belgorodskov rasryade vo vtoroj polovine XVII veka. *Vestnik Voroneshskogo Gosudarstvennogo Universiteta. Istoriya. Politilogiya. Sociologiya* 2:85-87.

Efimenko, Petr S. (1869), *Sbornik narodnykh juridicheskikh obychajev Arkhangeljskoj gubernii.* Arkhangelsk: Gubernskaja tipografiya.

Ehrlich, Eugen (1907/1986), *Die Tatsachen des Gewohnheitsrechts*, Reprinted in Eugen Ehrlich, *Gesetz und Lebendes Recht*, edited by Manfred Rehbinder, Berlin: Duncker & Humblot, pp. 104-132.

Ehrlich, Eugen (1912/1967), Das lebende Recht der Völker der Bukowina. Reprinted in Eugen Ehrlich, *Recht und Leben*, edited by Manfred Rehbinder, Berlin: Duncker & Humblot, pp. 43-60.

Ehrlich, Eugen (1913/1967), *Grundlagen der Soziologie des Rechts*, 3rd edition. Berlin: Duncker & Humblot.

Ehrlich, Eugen (1920/21/2007), Über das 'lebende Recht', Reprinted in Eugen Ehrlich, *Politische Schriften*, edited by Manfred Rehbinder, Berlin: Duncker & Humblot, pp. 191-200.

Ehrlich, Eugen (1922), The Sociology of Law. *Harvard Law Review* 36:130-145.

Ehrlich, Eugen (1936/2002), *Fundamental Principles of the Sociology of Law,* translated by Walter L. Moll, New Brunswick/London: Transaction.

Ehrlich, Eugen (2005), Karl Marks i problemi suspiljnogo pitannya. Translated from Romanian into Ukranian by Toronchuk I. G. *Problemy filisofii prava*, Vol. 3, 1-2:221-226.

Friedgut, Theodore H. (1994), Iuzovka and Revolution. *Politics and Revolution in Russia's Donbass, 1869-1924*, Vol. 2. Prinston, New Jersey: Princeton University Press.

Georgi, Iohann G. (1799), Donskie kasaki. In: Georgi, I. G (ed.), *Opisanije byta vsekh obitayushchikh v Rossijskom gosudarstve narodov. Ikh zhiteiskikh obryadov,obyknovenij, odezhd, zhilishch, uprazhnenij, zabav, veroispovedanij i drugikh dostopamyatnostej*. Sankt Petersburg: Isdanije pri Akademii Nauk, pp. 200-260.

Kasachij Krug sarubeshija (1974), Kasachje Slovo. Cossack World, Vol. 19. Cleveland.

Kharusin, Mikhail (1885), *Svedeniya o kasackikh obshchinakh na Donu*. Moskva: Tipografiya M. P. Shchepkina.

Kharusin, Mikhail N. (1887), *Programma dlja sobiranija svedenij ob juridicheskikh obychajakh.* Moscow: Tipografiya E. G. Potapova.

Korolev, V. N. (1999), Donskie kazachji gorodki. *Donskaya arkheologiya* 1:1-29.

Kovalevskij, Maksim M. (1886), *Sovremennyj obychaj i drevnij sakon; Obychnoje pravo osetin v istoriko-sravniteljnom osveshenii*, Vol. 1-2. Moscow: Tipografiya V. Gatzuk.

Kovalevskij, Maksim M. (1890), *Sakon i obychai na Kavkase*, Vol. 2. Moscow: Tipografiya A. I. Mamontova i Ko.

Kovalevskij, Maksim M. (2002), Klan u aborigennykh plemen Rossii. *Sociologicheskie issledovaniya* 5:129-138.

Krasnov, Sergey Y. (2003), *Obychno-pravovoye regulirivanie imuchshestvennykh otnoshenij u Donskikh kazakov vo vtoroj polovine XIX veka: istoriko-pravovoj aspekt. Avtoreferat dissertazii kandidata yuridicheskikh nauk.* Volgograd: Isdateljstvo Volgogradskogo Gosudarstvennogo Universiteta.

Krasnov, Sergey Y. (2011), Stanichnyj sud kak odin is vidov obychnykch sudov u Donskikch kasakov vo vtoroy polovine XIX veka. *Vestnik Volgogradskogo gosudarstvennogo universiteta*. Serija 5. Yurisprudenzia 15, 2: 49-58.

Kryukov, Fedor D. (1913/2009), *Na Tikhom Donu (letnie vpechatleniya i sametki)*. Rostov-on-Don: Donskoj Vremennik. http://www.donvrem.dspl.ru/Files/article/m18/2/art.aspx?art_id=662 (Accessed 3April 2013).

Larionov, A. N. (2007), Ekonomicheskije osnovy sushchestvovanija Vojska Donskogo. *Ekonomicheskij Vestnik Rostovskogo Gosudarstvennogo Universiteta* 2, 5:100-109.

Lermontov, Mikhail Y, (1839), *Geroj nashego vremeni.* http://ilibrary.ru/text/12/p.\,5/index.html (Accessed 25 June 2013).

Losev, Petr P. (2013), *Progulka po rodnoj stanize: istoricheskij ocherk o stanize Veshenskoj Sholochovskogo rajona*. Rostov-on-Don: Donskoj Vremennik. http://www.donvrem.dspl.ru/article/m1/18/art.aspx?art-id=569 (Accessed 3 April 2013).

Machura, Stefan (1998), Rußlands Umweg zum Rechtsstaat. *Zeitschrift für Rechtssoziologie* 20:211-229.

Mainov, V. (ed.,1885), *Ocherk juridicheskogo byta Mordvy: Otvety na programmu Russkogo geograficheskogo obchestva.* Sankt Petersburg: Tipogafiya ministerstva vnutrennikh del.

Markedonov, Sergej M. (1998), Donskoe kasachestvo i Rossijskaya imperiya (istoriya politicheskikh otnoshenij). *Obshchestvennye nauki i sovremennostj* 1:103-111.

Markedonov, Sergej M. (2005), Rossijskaya zivilisaziya. Kasachestvo: edinstvo ili mnogoobrazie? Problemy terminologii i tipologisacii kasachjik soobscchestv. *Obscchestvennye nauki i sovremennostj* 1:95-108.

Nebratenko, Gennadij G. (2006), Obychnoje pravo Donskikh kasakov: vchera, segodnya, savtra. In: Nebratenko, G. G. (ed.), *Obychnoje pravo narodov Severnogo Kavkasa: itogi i perspektivy issledovaniya.* Rostov-on-Don: Isdateljstvo SKAGS, pp. 40-49.

Pashin, Sergej (2003), Kratkij ocherk sudebnykh reform i revoluzij v Rossii. *Otechestvennye zapiski* 2:1-22.

Pirko, Vasylj O. (2003), *Saselennya Donechchini u XVI-XVIII st. (korotkij istorichnyj naris i urivki s dzherel)*. Donezjk: Skhidnyj vidavnychnyj dim.

Pronstein, Alexandr. N., and Mininkov, Nikolaj A. (1983), *Krestjanskije vojny v Rossii XVII-XVIII v.v. i Donskoe kasachestvstvo.* Rostov-on-Don: Isdatelstvo Rostovskogo Gosudarstvennogo Universiteta.

Pushkin, Alexandr S. (1984), *Kapitanskaya dochka.* 2nd edition. Leningrad: Nauka.

Rigelmann, Alexandr I. (1846), *Istoriya ili povestvovanie o Donskikh kasakakh, otkolj i kogda oni nachalo svoyo imeyut, i v kakoe vremya ii z kakikh lyudej na Donu poselilisj, kakie byli dela ikh i chem proslavilisj i proch.* Moskva: Universitetskaja tipografiya.

Rumjanzeva, V. G. (2005), Sociologicheskaja interpretazija prava v ucheniji E. Erlikha. *Istorija gosudarstva i prava* 1:12-14.

Sagoskin, M. V. (1891), *Otvety na programmu Russkogo geograficheskogo obch-*

estva dlja sobiranija narodnykh juridicheskikh obychajev. Irkutsk: Gubernskaja tipografiya.

Savchuk, Galina V. (2007), *Vlastj v marte-iune 1917go. Vojskovoj Kazachij sjeyd I Perwyj Bolshoj Voiskovoj Krug*. Rostov-on-Don: Donskoj Vremennik. http://www.donvrem.dspl.ru/Files/article/m3/0/art.aspx?art_id=95 (Accessed 3 April 2013).

Saveljev, Evgraf P. (1904), *Kto byl Ermak i ego spodvizhniki*. Novocherkassk: Oblastnaya Tipografiya VD.

Saveljev, Evgraf P. (1908), *Tipy donskikh kasakov i osobennosti ikh govorov*. Novocherkassk: Oblastnaya Tipografiya VD.

Saveljev, Evgraf P. (1915a), *Istoriya kasachestva s drevnejshikh vremen do konza XVIII veka: istoricheskoje issledovanie v trekh chastyakh, Vol. II: Rosyskanie o nachale russkogo kasachestva*. Novocherkassk: Oblastnaya Tipografiya VD.

Saveljev, Evgraf P. (1915b), *Istoriya kasachestva s drevnejshikh vremen do konza XVIII veka: istoricheskoje issledovanie v trekh chastyakh, Vol. III: Don sluzhit russkim zarya*m. Novocherkassk: Oblastnaya Tipografiya VD.

Saveljev, Evgraf P. (1917), *Vojskovoj Krug na Donu kak narodopravlenie. Istoricheskij ocherk*. Novocherkassk: Oblastnaya Tipografiya VD.

Saveljev, Evgraf P. (2010), *Drevnyaya istoriya kasachestva*. Moscow: Veche.

Shchelkunov, Sakhar Z. (1907), Prestupleniya protiv "Vojska" po drevnemu kasachjemu pravu. In: *Sbornik Oblastnogo Vojska Donskogo statisticheskogo komiteta*, Vol. 8 Novocherkassk: Tipografiya OVD.

Shpagin Sergej A. (1997*), Oblastj Vojska Donskogo 100 let nasad. K itogam Pervoj Vseobscchej Perepisi Naseleniya Rossiyskoy Imperii 1897 g*. Rostov-on-Don: Donskoj Vremennik. http://www.donvrem.dspl.ru/Files/article/m5/2/art.aspx?art_id=117 (Accessed 5 April 2013).

Sukhorukov, Vasilij D. (1892), *Obshchezhitie Donskikh kasakov v XVII i XVIII stoletiakh. Istoricheskij ocherk*. Novocherkassk: Oblastnaya Tipografiya VD.

Sulin, Ivan M. (1905), Akty, otnosyashchiyesia k bytovoy istorii Donskikh kasakov. In: *Sbornik Oblastnogo Vojska Donskogo statisticheskogo komiteta*, Vol. 4 Novocherkassk: Tipografiya OVD, pp. 60-80.

Svatikov, Sergej G. (1924), Rossija i Don (1549-1917). *Issledovanie po istorii gosudarstevennogo i administrativnogo prava i politicheskikh dvizhenij na Donu*. Belgrade: Isdanie Donskoj Istoricheskoj Komissii.

Teleradiokompanija Don TR. Vesti (2013), *Viktor Goncharov stal atamanom Vsevelikogo Vojska Donskogo*. Rostov-on-Don: 8 June 2013. http://dontr.ru/%D0%B2%D0%B5%D1%81%D1%82%D0%B8 – (Accessed 9 June 2013).

Tereshchenko, Alexandr G. (2000), *Ukrainisaziya v Severo-Kavkasskom krae. Ukrainzy na Donu i Severnom Kavkase do revolyuzii*. Rostov-on-Don: Donskoj Vremennik. http://www.donvrem.dspl.ru/Files/article/m2/2/art.aspx?art_id=84 (Accessed 3 April 2013).

Timashev, Nikolaj S. (2004), Chto takoje sociologija prava? *Sociologicheskije issledovaniya* 4:107-112.

Tolstoy, Lev N. (1863/1980), *Kasaki. Kavkasskaya povestj 1852 goda.* Polnoye sobranije sochinenij v 22 tomakch, Vol. 3, pp. 151-300: http://rvb.ru/tolstoy/01text/vol_3/01text/0023.htm (Accessed 2 July 2013).

Tulaeva, S. A. (2010), Donskoe kasachestvo v XVI-XVII v.v. kak avtonomnaya ochrannaya organisaziya. *Poliitya* 57, 2:66-74.

Turoverov, Nikolaj N. (1952), *Osnovnyje Sakony Vsevelikogo Vojska Donskogo.* Paris: Izdanije Kasachjego Sojusa.

Venkov, Andrej V. (1997), *Dobrovolcheskaya Armiya.* Rostov-on-Don: Donskoj Vremennik. http://www.donvrem.dspl.ru/Files/article/m6/0/art.aspx?art_id=132 (Accessed 3 April 2013).

Vogl, Stefan (2003), *Soziale Gesetzgebungspolitik, freie Rechtsfindung und soziologische Rechtswissenschaft bei Eugen Ehrlich*, Baden-Baden: Nomos.

Weber, Max (1922/1968). *Economy and Society. An Outline of Interpretive Sociology*, translated by Ephraim Fischoff et al., edited by Guenther Roth and Claus Wittich. New York: Bedminster Press.

Between the Power of the State and the Guardianship of the Church: Orthodox Copts Seeking Divorce

Monika LINDBEKK

> *"But I say unto you, That whosoever shall put away his wife, saving for the cause of fornication, causeth her to commit adultery: and whosoever shall marry her that is divorced committeth adultery."* (MT5;32)[1]

The point of departure for this contribution is a verse from the New Testament on the basis of which Pope Shenouda III, patriarch of the Orthodox Coptic Church, issued a decree making illicit sexual relations (*zina*) the only ground for divorce. In the following, I investigate the situation of Egyptian Orthodox Copts in pursuit of divorce and critically engage with Ehrlich's theory of the living law in light of this specific context. In approaching the subject I adopt a joint perspective where analysis of court records is combined with the actor's perspective from below based on interviews with Copts in pursuit of divorce.

In his book "Fundamental Principles of the Sociology of Law", Eugen Ehrlich (1975, 493) presented a concept of law based on the distinction between judicial decisions and statutory enactments, on the one hand, and 'living law' defined as "the law that dominates life itself, even though it has not been printed in legal propositions". The living law does not depend on the state but is linked to the inner ordering of various social associations. Ehrlich's work here points toward legal pluralism: the concept of a plurality of normative orders co-existing and sometimes conflicting in the same society. In this contribution, I highlight some main strengths and weaknesses by reflecting on Ehrlich's work along two lines. In Ehrlich's vision of social orders, society consists of various social associations which denote "a plurality of human beings who, in their relations with one another, recognise certain rules of conduct as binding, and, generally at least, actually regulate their conduct according to them" (Ehrlich

1975, 39). As a consequence, it has been argued that Ehrlich did not lay enough emphasis on the role of normative disagreement and human agency. Elaborating on this, I begin this chapter by showing how Orthodox Coptic legislation concerning marriage and divorce developed under the influence of political and legal factors. A recurrent theme in this article is that the Coptic laity, the church, and courts are not homogenous entities: rather there is considerable disagreement within them. With an emphasis on the role of women and men's agency, I also explore how Orthodox Copts and members of the judiciary deploy the Islamic and Christian normative repertoires in a manner which suggests that they are not the exclusive property of their respective communities. Furthermore, individuals change their religion and Christian denomination.

The second line of inquiry deals with Ehrlich's fundamental distinction between state law and informal norms. It has been argued that Ehrlich's theory of the living law did not anticipate the great expansion of state intervention in many aspects of social life through legislation and the courts during the 20th century (Nelken 1984, 211). While this criticism may have some merit, Ehrlich stressed the close relationship between state law and society on several occasions. With Ehrlich's important insight in mind, I seek to elucidate how actors use courts belonging to state structures in their interactions and how the enforcement of Coptic Orthodox law by state courts impacts on people's lives. In looking at judicial practice, I also highlight diversity among the judiciary by looking at how judges draw upon a multiplicity of factors, including Islamic shari'a (recognized as the general law of the state), the Bible, and conservative social norms concerning gender relations and sexuality. Based on this I argue that it is very difficult to establish a line of demarcation between state law and 'rules of conduct' when engaging with the concept of living law. Rather, as indicated by Ehrlich, the two may sometimes be inextricably intertwined.

This chapter is divided into three sections. I begin by providing an outline of the legal developments toward greater centralization in the 20th century. I then outline key laws by which the rights to divorce among Muslims and Orthodox Copts have been codified. This will be followed by a section entitled 'The courts between the state and the church'. In particular, I will examine how courts presided over by Muslim judges have interpreted the 2008 amendment which made illicit sexual relations the sole reason for divorce. I end by considering developments in the aftermath of the Egyptian revolution, focusing on the period between the ousting of Mubarak in February 2011 and of his successor Muhammad Mursi in July 2013. This period witnessed unparalleled Coptic activism and I will highlight the role played by a group called 'Copts 38' which sought to negotiate citizenship rights in a changing political terrain. During the period analyzed, the group navigated between the church and the state, a state that – until the July 2013 military coup – was increasingly influenced by political Islam. The study of divorce among Orthodox Copts provides a window on how legal actors, individuals and groups deploy norms of different provenance. However, while fully recognizing the plurality of norms invoked, I also intend to show that they were limited by the constraints of the political context. In the case of the group under examination, this refers to a normative discursive field where struggle was either waged in terms of citizenship within an Islamic framework, or in terms of a normative repertoire which assigns a prominent place to fighting lust and illicit sexual relations.

Citizenship and religious affiliation

Egypt has a system of law that is based upon the French civil law tradition, except in personal status matters which are subject to Islamic *shari'a.* Personal status law, also known as family law, is the law that governs family relations, including marriage, divorce, custody, and inheritance. Egypt took over the Islamic system of interreligious law in which the Muslim, Christian and Jewish communities are governed by their own laws in matters of family law. However, during the 20th century this domain came increasingly under the control of state authorities which developed a centralized and hierarchical legal system based on formal equality before the law for all citizens, regardless of religion, gender, class, or ethnicity (Berger 2001, Shaham 2010, 410).

Until 1956, non-Muslim communities in Egypt enjoyed judicial and legislative autonomy in the field of personal status law. They had their own personal status regulations, most of them drafted by their respective community councils.[2] These councils also had judicial competence capable of

[2] The Orthodox Copt community council (*majlis al-milli*) was established with the man-

enforcing these regulations on their members. However, since the Nasserite regime viewed the community councils as a legacy of Ottoman imperialism (Sezgin 2011, 1008), their powers were curbed and religious courts replaced by a unitary legal system. Meanwhile, the legislative autonomy enjoyed by the non-Muslim community councils was restricted to matters of marriage and divorce and other areas such as inheritance codified on the basis of Islamic *shari'a* in laws that apply to all Egyptians, Muslims and non-Muslims alike. [3] Further, personal status legislation for non-Muslims applies only if the two spouses share the same denomination and community (e.g. both are Coptic Orthodox) (Bernard-Maugiron 2011, 358-361).

Although the church has competence to enact laws pertaining to marriage and divorce, these rules are enforced by courts belonging to state structures. The national family courts are overwhelmingly presided over by Muslim judges. Although Egypt's family courts include a handful of Christian judges, the Cairo Appeal Court handed down a landmark decision in 2009 in which it stated unequivocally that all judges must be Muslims in matters pertaining to the stipulations of *shari'a* (*ahkam shari'a*) and where the parties are Muslims. In the view of the court, this decision was based on consensus among Islamic legal scholars together with the Quran and the Sunna according to which a non-Muslim cannot exercise power (*wilaya*) over a Muslim.[4]

Although the power of the state has increased, Egyptian citizens nonetheless experience their relationship to the state as mediated through religious communities, and religious membership is specified on citizens' ID cards (Joseph 2000, 11; Tadros 2013). In effect, Orthodox Copts are connected to the state through the church, to which the state has delegated the control of family law for its members, putting it into the position of their guardian (*wisaya*). At the end of this chapter, I show that the role of the church as representative of Copts in their relations with the state has been challenged since the 2011 revolution.

---

date to oversee Coptic endowments (*awqaf*), schools and other institutions besides the religious courts (Lawrence 2013, 300).

3 Egyptian law recognizes legislative autonomy for fourteen religious groups. These include three Christian communities (*milla*) composed of one or more denominations (*ta'fa*). The Orthodox communities include four denominations: the Coptic, Greek, Armenian, and Syrian. See Bernard-Maugiron (2011, 260) for more information.

4 Cairo appeal court, case no. 3611, judicial year 125, 4 March 2009.

Divorce according to personal status law for Orthodox Copts and Muslims

Among the enduring legacies of Ehrlich's sociological approach to law, is his advocacy of a legal pluralist perspective. Ehrlich's attention was focused on the life of the groups, institutions and associations, and he portrayed rules of conduct as engrained in individual behaviour. *"Organisation is the rule which assigns each individual his position and his function"* (Ehrlich 1975, 85). Similarly, he remarked that *"[t]he great mass of law arises immediately in society itself in the form of a spontaneous ordering of social relations"* (Ehrlich 1922, 136). According to Webber (2009), Ehrlich's tendency to present norms as emerging out of human interaction also typically presents non-state normative order as natural and non-contentious. Following Shaham (2010) and Melcangi (2012), I aim to show that, rather than emerging spontaneously, the Orthodox Coptic rules pertaining to personal status were subject to conflict and resistance. Their formulation was also heavily influenced by religious and political developments in Egypt, including the greater involvement of state institutions and Islamic resurgence.

Meanwhile, according to classical Islamic jurisprudence, marriage is seen as a contract, with repudiation (*talaq*) a prerogative of the husband, while the wife has a more limited right to judicial divorce (El-Alami 1992). Notwithstanding this, as Islam and Christianity developed side by side in Egypt for several centuries, there has been interaction and mutual influence between the two religions in areas such as marriage and divorce. In 1938, *majlis al-milli* (the Coptic community council) issued a legal decree. In addition to illicit sexual relations (*zina*), which was explicitly mentioned in the Bible, the 1938 code allowed divorce for the following reasons: conversion to another religion, absence for a period of five years with no sign of life, a sentence of imprisonment for at least seven years, insanity or incurable illness for at least three years, impotence for at least three years, mistreatment, vice, or neglect of marital duties leading to separation for at least three years, or a spouse joining a monastic order (Bernard-Maugiron 2011, 363; Hatem 2003, 41).

The above-mentioned provisions were largely based on a compilation of Coptic Orthodox family law from the 1200s (Shaham 2010, 415). With the exception of illicit sexual relations (*zina*), the 1938 code was also heavily influenced by the nationwide codification of personal status law for

Muslims in the 1920s. Unlike Coptic personal status law, the personal status codes pertaining to Muslims are enacted by the state. From the 1920s onwards the Egyptian legislature enacted personal status laws for Muslims that were designed to make marriage a more permanent bond than envisioned by traditional Islamic jurisprudence, by curbing men's right to repudiation. It was also believed that giving women more marital rights, including wider rights to petition for judicial divorce, would strengthen the marital bond. Although personal status laws promulgated in the twentieth century sought to make marriage a more permanent bond than envisioned in classical Islamic law, the legal codes nonetheless reify a hierarchical relationship between the spouses (Kholoussy 2010, 95-96, 2005, 317-350, Lindbekk 2013).

The grounds on which divorce may be obtained by Orthodox Copts were restricted after the election of Shenouda III as patriarch in 1971. He upheld the biblical verse which stated that divorce could only be permitted in cases of adultery. While the 1938 code was based on medieval sources, the idea underlying these legal policies was Shenouda's intention to return to the 'true' and 'fundamental sources' of lawmaking in Christianity (Shaham 2010, 412). This took place during a period of increasing sectarian tension and Islamization of public sphere which was exacerbated when president Anwar al-Sadat introduced Article 2 to the constitution in 1980. Article 2 read as follows: *"Islam is the religion of the state. Arabic is the official language and the principles of Islamic shari'a are the principle source of legislation"*. This constitutional amendment had profound implications. While the description of Islam as the religion of the state was not new, the stipulation that the principles of Islamic shari'a are the main source of legislation represented a significant shift from earlier constitutional discourse and conferred on the state a more pronounced Islamic character.

While the preceding legal order had restricted the role of religious law to the familial arena, the religion of the majority was now becoming the foremost source of state legislation. In politicizing religion and religious institutions, the amendment also reinforced the church and its conservatism (Hatem 2000, 54). According to Shaham (2010, 409), an important aim behind Shenouda's decree was to strengthen the Coptic family, considered the basis of the Coptic community, which had to be protected in the face of political Islam and Islamic *shari'a* as the general law of the state. In addition to attempting to make the Coptic community more autonomous, the above shows the narrowing of grounds for the dissolution of marriage were accorded considerable symbolic value for the Orthodox Church as a measure of authenticity and difference vis à vis political Islam.

This was the beginning of a long-standing normative disagreement between the Egyptian state courts and the Coptic Orthodox Church (Bernard-Maugiron 2011, 364). The papal decree was not applied by the state courts, which continued to follow the 1938 regulations. Meanwhile the church refused to recognize divorce rulings issued by the courts on any grounds other than *zina*. Consequently thousands of couples divorced before the courts were considered by the Church to be still married (Hatem 2000, 55 and Bernard-Maugiron 2011). In order to end the conflict between what the Coptic Orthodox Church regarded as divine law and the law applied in courts, the Community Council amended the 1938 code in June 2008 following a political conflict between secular and religious authorities (Bernard-Maugiron 2011). In particular, Articles 52 to 58, which allowed divorce on several grounds, were abrogated, leaving only Articles 50 and 51, which allow divorce in case of adultery and change of religion.

In addition to adultery caught in the very act, the concept of adultery was expanded by the amendment to include acts which *indicate* betrayal (*khiyana*). Unlike adultery caught in the act, the presumption of adultery is subject to the discretionary power of the judge. Revised, article 50 gives examples of such acts. These include (among others): the presence of a strange man or woman with the spouse in a suspicious situation, or a husband who incites (*tahrid*) his wife to commit adultery or debauchery (Bernard-Maugiron 2011, 370). In the following I am going to look at the interpretations of the 2008 amendment as given by Muslim judges on Egypt's family courts.

The courts between the state and the Church

Whereas the church has maintained legislative autonomy in the field of marriage and divorce, it does not have authority to adjudicate in personal status disputes involving Orthodox Copts. Following the nationalization of the courts in 1956, Orthodox Coptic personal status legislation is enforced by the hierarchical judicial structure of a modern state where the majority of judges are Muslims trained in modern law schools. The transfer of jurisdiction over Christian family law disputes to the centralized national courts has been described as a severe blow to the Coptic Orthodox Church (Shaham 2010, 411). An important objective behind the 2008 amendment was therefore to bring the courts under the control of the church.

Egyptians frequently resort to the courts to claim their rights as regards personal status matters, ranging from alimony to divorce, child custody, and visitation (Lindbekk 2013). Saba Mahmoud (2001, 212) encouraged the conceptualization of agency as not only "resistance to relations of domination, but as a capacity for action that specific relations and subordination create and enable". In the following, I am going to look at how the plurality of normative orders recognized by the Egyptian state enables the deployment of agency among members of the Orthodox Coptic laity in terms of the capacity to deploy as well as subvert the amended 1938 regulations based on individual strategies. This also underlines the importance of showing the dynamic nature of the 2008 amendment through different interpretations offered by Muslim family court judges of them in spite of the church's efforts to control them.

Accusations of illicit sexual relations are a serious matter in Egypt, for legal and social reasons. Legally, they constitute a reason for divorce, and the person found guilty of *zina* will not be granted authorization by the church to remarry. Socially, they are considered very shameful for the perpetrator and his/her family (Kamal 2006). Nonetheless, since 2008 a considerable number of cases have been filed for judicial divorce due to *zina* before Egyptian family courts in areas of Cairo where many Orthodox Copts reside. This illustrates the fact that, rather than a clean division between rules of decision and living law, there is often interaction between state structures and people.

This complex interplay between state law and social law was also acknowledged by Ehrlich. Any form of law can become part and parcel of daily life, including statutes enforced by courts, but living law is not *confined* to them (1975, 502). Although critical of the belief that legal institutions develop only through state-created norms, Ehrlich encouraged investigation into the''influence of the state upon social law" (Ehrlich 1975, 504, see also Vogl 2009, 102). Further, when one explores the notion of agency informing Ehrich's theories, it becomes clear that, while he did not sufficiently stress its role in the context of social associations, he acknowledged the presence of agency in juristic law, that is, state law as enforced by judges. An important insight offered by Ehrlich was that much legal development occurs through the influence of informal norms on judicial decision making. *"Compared with these revolutionary changes [in legal meaning over time], the changes brought about by legislation are negligible"* (Ehrlich 1975, 501). When people pose new problems for the courts to solve, judges modify the law to accommodate new situations (Ehrlich 1975, 399). Attention devoted to non-statutory developments and the ways in which legal actors use state law depending on their individual interests shows the continued relevance of Ehrlich's sociological approach to law. This may be illustrated by the following analysis of the relationship between state law (Islamic shari'a), church law, and informal social norms.

I begin by telling the story of "Sawsan", an Egyptian Coptic Orthodox woman in her forties who lives in a slum area on the outskirts of Cairo. Although still beautiful, she is visibly marked by more than twenty years of abuse by her husband and easily begins to cry when she recounts the most painful events in her life which led her to file for divorce from him. Her eldest daughter "Nermine" sits by watching silently, but sometimes intervenes to fill in her mother's story or to show me her own scars, caused by the abusive father. At the age of 14, before finishing her secondary education, Sawsan was forced by her family in Upper Egypt to marry her cousin on the mother's side. One month after getting married she learnt that her husband was an alcoholic and drug addict. They later moved to the outskirts of Cairo where he used to drag her by the hair in the street, which she claims made her hair very thin. He also burnt her with cigarettes and repeatedly beat her head against the balcony railing of their apartment. Once when he was intoxicated he also tried to sexually molest Nermine, the eldest of their three children. Yet neither her family, neighbours, nor the police intervened to help.

Sawsan told me that most of her life she obeyed the orders of the men in her family and, later, those of her husband. However, she gradually underwent a personal change and became more independent. *"After having been subjected to a lot of pressure, I eventually exploded",* she said. Sawsan reported her husband to the police three times, but they said there was nothing they could do, since this was a domestic problem. Next, she turned to the clergy in an attempt to solve their problems. Officially holding marriage to be a sacrament, not to be broken by anything except illicit sexual relations (*zina*), the Orthodox Coptic church attempted to work out a reconciliation agreement between the spouses. However, the church could not put a stop to his violent behaviour, and during one such session, the husband even attempted to stab a bishop. The church also attempted to help the husband financially in setting up a project to start a business, but it was all to no avail due to his addictions.

After having exhausted all mechanisms for reaching a solution at the level of family and local community, Sawsan eventually resorted to the state's judicial authorities and filed for judicial divorce due to *zina* in 2008. According to Sawsan her husband was in the habit of inviting friends over to their house and making Sawsan serve them alcohol. During one of his drunken brawls, Sawsan had to escape and seek refuge at her neighbours' apartment while scantily dressed. On the basis of this, she later petitioned for judicial divorce on the basis of incitement (*tahrid*) to illicit relations. Although her neighbours testified to what happened in court, the family court dismissed her case because *zina* could not be proved (Interview with "Sawsan", 3 October 2012). At the time of this research she was living alone in a flat in a slum area on the outskirts of Cairo where she worked as a hairdresser, while her youngest children lived with her sister. Although her husband was unaware of her whereabouts, she lived in constant fear that he might find her. Her independent way of life was difficult for her family to bear, and she had no contact with them, although they lived only a few blocks away. She was also frustrated by the fact that she had become too old to enroll in a public school to complete her secondary education. This made it difficult for her to commence a new life. I am going to return to Sawsan's story later in this chapter, since it bears living testimony to the wide range of normative orders that shape the lives of Egypt's Orthodox Copts. In addition to these concrete constraints, Sawsan's story highlights the importance of an individual's own choices, which is a central aspect of this discussion of Ehrlich's "Fundamental Principles of the Sociology of Law".

In what follows, I analyze a sample of judicial decisions dealing with judicial divorce on the basis of illicit relations (*zina*) by paying attention to how different legal actors use normative repertoires. Although the 2008 amendment provided ample room for judicial discretion, most judges appear to exercise caution in enforcing it. This should be viewed in relation to a trend in other areas of family law where judges punish husbands and wives for making accusations prejudicial to the honour and reputation of their spouses. Judges interviewed also appeared keenly aware that Orthodox Copts are manipulating the law. In the word of one family court judge:

> "There are many cases of judicial divorce due to illicit relations filed before this particular court, and most of them are rejected because illicit relations cannot be proved. In addition to witnesses, the parties bring internet footage, SMS, CDs, and pictures. Sometimes couples make a deal before they come to court to obtain divorce due to zina. Others bribe witnesses to give false testimony in court. Sometimes women even confess to illicit sexual relations".[5]

Judging from analysis of court records and of interviews with judges and lawyers, Muslim family court judges tend to give the 2008 amendment a restrictive interpretation. Some judges in the Cairo Appeal Court go so far as to challenge the legislative autonomy of the Orthodox Coptic church. By way of example, I am going to consider a case brought by an Orthodox Coptic man before a family court in 2008. He petitioned for divorce on the basis of the abrogated article 57 of the 1938 code, accusing his wife of leaving the conjugal home and of filing false police reports in which she accused him of beating her, and which made his life an "unbearable hell". This was followed by separation for three years and during these years the husband was not allowed to see their daughter The case was reviewed by the court of first instance, which decided to dismiss it, on the basis of the papal amendment which only permits divorce due to illicit sexual relations or change of religion.

Next, the husband appealed the ruling to the Cairo Appeal Court in 2009, which granted his request for judicial divorce. The ruling of the appeal court is of interest for several reasons. Firstly, the court declared that the 2008 amendment had no legal value since it had not been submitted to the legislature (the parliament or the President) for adoption according to the procedures laid down in the constitution. For this reason, the appeal court found the amendment to be flawed and decided to disregard it and rely on the 1938 code instead. The court based its ruling on the abrogated article 57, and said that spousal mistreatment that leads to aversion (*nufur*) and separation for more than three years is a sufficient reason for judicial divorce. Consequently, the court ruled for judicial divorce on the basis of the impossibility of marital life.[6] Meanwhile, the Coptic Orthodox

5 Interview with a judge in the family court of Ain Shams, 1 November 2012.

6 Cairo appeal court, case no. 1620, judicial year 126, 26 January 2011.

Church denied any legal value to the 1938 code, which, in its view, violated fundamental principles of Christianity. This shows that some judges still challenge the hegemony of the Coptic Church in the context of judicial divorce due to illicit sexual relations. In addition to invalidating the 2008 amendment, the Muslim judges on Cairo Appeal Court offered a dynamic interpretation of Christianity. Although not explicitly invoking Islamic *shari'a*, the court stated that animosity (*nufur*) prevents the realization of the goals of marriage which, according to "the heavenly religions", are "amity and mercy" (*mawadda wa rahma*).[7] Instead of relying on the papal decree which prohibits divorce on the basis of other reasons than *zina* or change of religion, the court endowed Christianity with the same model of marriage outlined in judicial practice based on Egypt's personal status laws for Muslims (Lindbekk 2013).

As we have seen, the 1938 code was significantly influenced by the Muslim laws of personal status enacted by the legislature in the 1920s. The twentieth century witnessed unparalleled penetration of the Egyptian family by the state, which promoted a model of companionate marriage and deep affection as a condition for successful marriages. Contemporary Egyptian Muslim judges are reinforcing an increasingly hegemonic discourse of companionate marriage through their redefinition of marriage as an eternal contract or pact based on emotions of amity and mercy distinguishable from other contracts (Lindbekk 2013). Indeed, this ruling shows that hegemonic interpretations of Islamic *shari'a* continue to influence the interpretation of non-Muslim personal status law, in spite of attempts by the Orthodox Coptic church to bring the courts under its control.

Regardless of the attitude taken to certain controversial provisions, it is important to bear in mind that the judges' approach is largely orientated to procedural and legal relevance, because of their aversion to the possibility of being overruled (Dupret 2007). The sources of law used by family court judges include statutory legislation and precedence. Instead of a clear hierarchy between sources, a study of court decisions leaves the impression that sources intersect and interplay, although legislation usually takes precedence over other sources of law. Egyptian judicial practice is also influenced to a considerable extent by local custom, since the laws empower judges to exercise considerable discretion (Lindbekk 2013). Al-

7 Cairo appeal court, case no. 1620, judicial year 126, 26 January 2011.

though Egyptian judges share a similar background, they bring different perspectives to the bench in a manner which demonstrates the presence of further agency and fluidity within the law's formulation. Hence, while most judges exercise caution in enforcing the 2008 amendment, some are disposed to accept petitions for judicial divorce due to illicit sexual relations. Some judges are also prepared to accept what appears to be rather flimsy evidence, including hearsay, as evidence of illicit sexual relations. In May 2010, a wife applied to the court for judicial divorce on the basis of *zina*. According to the documents of the case, the wife brought forward two witnesses who testified that they had heard from the wife's brother that the husband used to bring women to the house. The family court of Al-Helwan dismissed her petition since the witnesses did not see the incident with their own eyes. However, the Cairo Appeal Court took a different position:

> "The court thus feels confident with respect to the testimonies of the appellant's witnesses even if they are based on hearsay, since they emphasized that the defendant has had numerous relationships with women and ran the risk of perpetrating an abomination (irtikab l-l-fahesha) when he took a woman to the marital and enjoyed privacy (ikhtila') with her there."[8] (my translation)

By admitting hearsay evidence, the Cairo Appeal Court set an astoundingly low *threshold of evidence for establishing illicit relations. The judge gave the testimonies by the wife's witnesses decisive weight and* ruled the wife should be irrevocably divorced from her husband. In so doing, the judge justified his decision by referring to the Bible in a manner which stands in marked contrast to the previously-mentioned verdict issued by the Cairo Appeal Court in 2011.

> "Zina is a clear basis for judicial divorce in the Bible, where the marriage bond is stated to be sacred (rabeta muqadesa) and unbreakable, except for adultery. Jesus said: 'But I say unto you, That whosoever shall put away his wife, saving for the cause of fornication, causeth her to commit adultery: and whosoever shall marry her that is divorced committeth adultery.' Jesus was asked another time: is it lawful for a man to put away hiswife for every cause? 'And he answered and said unto them, Have ye not read, that he which made them at the beginning made them male and female, And said, For this cause shall a man leave father and mother, and shall cleave to his wife: and they twain shall be one flesh? Wherefore they are no

[8] Cairo Appeal Court, case no 5071, judicial year 129, 9 April 2013.

more twain, but one flesh. What therefore God hath joined together, let not man put asunder"'[9] (my translation).

The above excerpts show that interpreting the religious sources of Christian family law is not solely the province of the Coptic Orthodox Church: Muslim judges too claim the right to interpret Christianity in an authoritative manner. In another fascinating case, a husband petitioned for judicial divorce, accusing his wife of illicit sexual relations and of abandoning the marital home, a matter that had led to their separation for more than three years. He also alleged that his wife's family beat him up.

In this case, the Cairo Appeal Court (case no. 2686, judicial year 126, 18 May 2011) described the events as follows:

"Neighbours told the appellant [husband] that his wife was apt to come home late at night, looking drunk and bumping into cars in the parking area. (...) One night the appellant discovered the defendant [wife] in Sonesta hotel at 1:30 am with a strange man for no reason (dun sabab) drinking wine and smoking water pipe in a suspicious situation in the hotel's coffee shop. The appellant brought a tourist officer with him to the coffee shop. The wife and stranger were both surprised when the officer burst on the scene and inquired what they were doing. The man told the officer that he was the wife's lawyer and they were preparing papers for a case. He [the strange man] left the hotel afterwards. The defendant [wife] claimed that the man was her lawyer and that they were discussing legal matters" (my translation).

We learn from the case documents that neighbours saw the wife come home late looking intoxicated, and reported this to the husband. This suggests that neighbours felt it was their duty to report on her to the husband and agreed to become actors in the legal sphere by testifying in court. After discovering his wife in the hotel café with another man, the husband proceeded to file a police report about the matter, which he claimed was evidence of *zina*. He also claimed the wife returned to her house at 4:30 with two men, who she claimed were friends of her brother. The family court of Al-Nuzha reviewed the case, but dismissed it. The husband then decided to appeal the ruling to Cairo Appeal Court on the basis of misapplication of law. Unlike the family court of Al-Nuzha, Cairo Appeal Court viewed his claim with favour, and in May 2011, it ruled on the basis of the available evidence that the wife's

[9] Cairo Appeal Court, case no 5071, judicial year 129, 9 April 2013.

behaviour constituted *zina*. When delivering its decision, the court dwelled on the subject, saying that:

"The strange man (al-rajul al-gharib) should have remained by her side if he was her lawyer and not run away like a mouse. (...) The defendant lives in an Oriental society which does not allow a wife to be out with male strangers in public places. She was not innocent by virtue of meeting them in these places; she met them late at night in suspicious situations where there was smoking and drinking. This is considered a reason for judicial divorce. The court rules the defendant should be irrevocably divorced from the appellant."[10] (my translation)

Based on the wife's meeting with male strangers under what the court considered "suspicious" circumstances, it found that there were grounds for the dissolution of the marriage. The quoted passage from the judgment shows that some judges rely on their personal values when judging. In formulating the above ruling the judge linked the strict divorce rules to the protection of public morality by seeking to regulate public space in a manner which excludes women who are socializing with male strangers. This interpretation of the 2008 amendment was shaped by certain assumptions about women's nature, and their relations with men who are not their husbands or family members. Cairo Appeal Court also institutionalized contemporary discourses which pit east against west by defining the expanded concept of *zina* as a means of authenticity. The above ruling shows that judicial practice is not only influenced by legislation and precedence, but by customs and other social forces which reinforce conservative perceptions of gender relations and sexuality.

The above cases show that courts do not interpret the 2008 amendment in a consistent manner. In dealing with cases of judicial divorce due to *zina*, judges refer to a number of formal and informal legal sources, including statute, Islamic law, the Bible, and custom. While an aim of the 2008 amendment was to bring the state courts under the control of the church, the strict divorce laws of the Orthodox Church remain a contested issue in the state courts which are mainly presided over by Muslim judges. The inconsistent case law of the Cairo Appeal Court demonstrates the presence of agency and fluidity within the law's formulation. This is all the more noteworthy since, following the establishment of family courts in 2004, it is very difficult to alter decisions issued by the appeal courts. Some judges in the

10 Cairo Appeal Court, case no. 2686, judicial year 126, 18 May 2011.

Cairo Appeal Court continue to challenge the Orthodox Coptic church, relying on an interpretation of Christianity influenced by the hegemonic interpretation of Islamic *shari'a*, the general law of the state. Meanwhile, Pope Shenouda III's puritanical view of marriage has struck a chord with some Muslim judges who endorse conservative views and punish presumed sexual transgressions outside the confines of marriage. In the process some appeal court judges reinforce social norms which engender public space.The above case studies provide a clear indication of what this paper is setting out to demonstrate with respect to the relation between state law and society, namely that informal norms interweave with judicial practice. This is in line with Ehrlich's account of dynamic social-legal change and shows the continued relevance of his work.

The vexed issue of conversions

As previously mentioned, family legislation for non-Muslims applies only if the two spouses share the same denomination and community (e.g, both are Coptic Orthodox) and it its rules do not contradict public order. If two spouses do not belong to the same denomination, the court will apply Islamic shari'a, which is the "general law" (*al-qanun al-?amm*) of the country. As a resistance strategy, members of the Orthodox Coptic community have long been able to circumvent church laws: there have been numerous cases of conversion to other denomination or to Islam with the intention of obtaining divorce. In this connection it is also worth mentioning that the 2008 amendment has attracted disagreement and contention from certain members of the clergy (Kamal 2006, 86).

Male members of the laity have long resisted the church by means of conversion to other denominations, or to Islam, simply to obtain the right to end their marriage by repudiating their wives unilaterally, as Muslims do. As for a Coptic Orthodox wife who wishes to terminate her marriage, she may request a judicial divorce though khul'. Male members of the laity have long resisted the church through conversions to other denominations or Islam merely for the sake of obtaining the right to end his marriage by repudiating his wife unilaterally, as Muslims do. As for a Coptic Orthodox wife who wishes to terminate her marriage, she may request a judicial divorce though khul'. Under the so-called khul' law a woman can go to the national family courts and obtain swift and irrevocable divorce, on condition she forfeits all her financial rights.[11] In a surprise turn of events in March 2012, "Sawsan's" violent husband converted to Islam. This was not the first time he had done so; he had previously twice converted to Islam in return for money from pious Muslims who wished to set him on the straight path. Little did they know that he used the money they gave him to finance his drug addiction, and that he soon returned to his original religion. The previous times Sawsan had not been able to procure a copy of the conversion certificate from al-Azhar in time. However, after his third conversion to Islam she succeeded in obtaining a copy of the certificate and hurried to the court where she lodged a petition for judicial divorce through khul'. However, at the time of writing, her husband had once again converted to Christianity, an act which called into question her right to resort to the personal status laws of Muslims (Interview with "Sawsan", 15 August 2013). Thus Sawsan's story bears living testimony to the multiple normative orders that shape the lives of Egypt's Orthodox Copts, ranging from kinship and communal relationship structures that discriminate against women to codified statutory law based on Islamic *shari'a.*

Conversions to Islam take place for many reasons, but the motivation is often to obtain divorce on the basis of Muslim family law (Al-Ahram Online 2012). Many Christians who convert to Islam seek to return to their original religion once they have received a divorce. Suffice it to note here that in these cases the courts face difficult questions concerning the boundaries around religious communities, the circumstances in which individuals may abandon Islam without being considered apostates, and their ability to change the religion appearing on their identity cards (for more, see Berger 2002, 584). In practice, courts have agreed to change the religion stated on identity cards in individual cases. However, citizens who are born Muslim and attempt to convert to Christianity meet several obstacles (Ibrahim 2010, Bernard-Maugiron 2011).

For the church, the provision which stipulates that Islamic law should be applied if the litigants are not of the same community or denomination, has represented a challenge to its authority and control over the Coptic community. Conversions are also problematic since they have served as a pretext for subsequent inter-religious conflict (Osman 2013). For fear that

11 This law challenged the authority of the husband over his wife in fundamental respects and sparked considerable controversy after it was passed in 2000 (Lindbekk 2013; Sonneveld 2012).

the 2008 amendments might lead to an increase in conversions to other religious faiths to escape application of the revised 1938 code, the practice of conversions from one denomination to another has increasingly been met with resistance from the three officially recognized Christian communities (Orthodox, Catholic, and Protestant) and a great deal of corruption surrounds certificates of conversion (Leila 2010). It has therefore become almost impossible for all but the elite to convert to another denomination. Consequently Rafiq Fuad, the leader of 'Copts 38'? a civil society group campaigning for a return to the 1938 code? summarized the plight of Copts seeking divorce as follows:

> "There are currently three paths to divorce. 1) Accuse your spouse of illicit sexual relations, something which is difficult to prove in court. 2) Pay L.E. 30,000 for a certificate of conversion to another denomination in order for Islamic shari'a to be implemented. The Coptic Orthodox Church tells its members they may change their community or denomination and obtain divorce. But in practice, officials from other churches have been forbidden to issue certificates of conversion because they are controlled by the Orthodox Coptic Church. Only the sons of priests, the rich, and celebrities are allowed to change their religious denomination. This represents a form of manipulation. I myself was asked to pay L.E. 25,000 in order to convert. 3) Leave the religion and convert to Islam. However, if we convert to Islam, we will be accused of causing sectarian tension."

The above quotation shows that the legal avenues available to Orthodox Copts seeking divorce became increasingly narrow subsequent to the 2008 amendment. The following section on activism by Copts 38 sets out to show that the scope for political contestation remains similarly constrained in the aftermath of the 2011 revolution.

Christian activism outside the framework of the church after the 2011 revolution

A battle over the identity of Egypt has been taking place since the 2011 revolution, and Christians are struggling to find their place within the emerging political order. It has been argued that public debate in the wake of the Egyptian revolution has not involved serious reflection on the concept of citizenship, including the role of the church as mediator between the Coptic citizenry and the state. There are, however, exceptions to this, and this section is devoted to one such initiative. The period after the ousting of

Mubarak saw the emergence of a number of civil society organizations and coalitions outside the framework of the church (see Tadros 2013).

One such group was Copts 38. Although established prior to 2011, Copts 38 mobilized more forcefully for a return to the 1938 regulations after the revolution (Shams El-Din 2012). In the process, they challenged the role of the Coptic Church as the political representative of 10 million Copts in relation to the state. In the light of the importance of the divorce laws for questions surrounding citizenship, the arguments which Copts 38 presented deserve to be examined in some detail. Members of the group I interviewed defined themselves not only from a religious viewpoint, but also in relation to the state and the larger international community. Yet the type of arguments put forward by the group leaders reflected the constraints of the political environment. Their decision to build on these repertoires highlights the fact that normative plurality is limited by the political constraints faced by individuals and groups wishing to participate in power. Their space of contestation is confined to normative repertoires which are compatible with authorized religious frameworks, a situation which Dupret (1999, 40) calls "a closure of the normative field". For example, the repertoire of Copts 38 includes, but only peripherally, human rights norms. This is due to the fact that the political authorities are critical of human rights conventions and human rights organizations, considering them tools of western imperialism. Instead of developing a secular discourse, the group has therefore framed its demands within the framework of two dominant normative discourses: Islamic *shari'a* and the Church-authorized discourse of fighting against lust and illicit relations.

Initially, Copts 38 sought a solution through the church, in the belief that it held "99% of the cards", as they put it. However, they later changed tactics and criticized the church's hegemony over the religious and personal status of Copts. Many social movements have an iconic moment around which they rally. In the case of many of the members of Copts 38, this was a dramatic situation which came to be known as "the Battle of the Dog" after its leader Faruq Fuad chanted against the church's divorce laws inside Abbasiya cathedral in the centre of Cairo (Shams El-Din 2012). According to the group's spokesperson Nader al-Serafi (interview, 23 October 2012): *The church did not want to speak to us on equal terms, since they had no interest in doing so and let loose dogs on us. This led us to change strategy and address the state, not the church.*" In the opinion of group members, the church had abandoned its role of serving and protecting the Copts and, relying on the principle of equal citizenship, they therefore considered the intervention of a central power to be necessary. Their decision to appeal to the state authorities could probably also be seen as connected with the ambiguous role played by the church hierarchy in the early post-Mubarak era, when it was excluded from power- sharing (Tadros 2013, 13).

In the following section, I focus on the attempt by Copts 38 to re-negotiate their citizenship rights under the constitution in the context of the drafting of the 2012 constitution, a critical juncture in Egyptian history. The Muslim Brotherhood emerged from the 2011 revolution as the strongest and best organized political force. Because of this, the Brotherhood, together with the Salafists, won Egypt's first free parliamentary elections and used their majority to set up a constituent assembly dominated by Islamists. This provided the political backdrop for Copts 38's articulation of a discourse on citizenship in which they emphasized the role of the principles of Islamic *shari'a* as the main source of legislation, and reduced Egypt to a single aspect of its identity, Islam. In an attempt to appeal to Egypt's (then) Islamist leaders, the group issued a manifesto in which they justified their demand to have Islamic *shari'a* applied in the familial domain with reference to Quranic sura *ma'idah* verse 49: *"And judge, [O Muhammad], between them by what Allah has revealed and do not follow their inclinations and beware of them, lest they tempt you away from some of what Allah has revealed to you."* In the group's interpretation of this verse, Islamic *shari'a* guarantees Christians the right to resort to Islamic *shari'a* in matters related to personal status. They also approached legal scholars at the Sunni-Islamic university al-Azhar who conferred religious legitimacy on their demands (Copts 38 2012, 1). A manifesto issued by Copts 38 and presented to President Mursi and the constituent assembly can be seen as yet another example of the fact that the Islamic normative repertoire is not an exclusive property of Muslims, but is a normative resource in the hands of other actors too.

The manifesto was created in response to a leaked constitutional proposal designed to reinforce the political and spiritual hegemony of the church. Copts 38 continued by arguing that the proposed article was unconstitutional since it contradicted the proposed article 2, which reaffirmed that the principles of Islamic *shari'a* are the principal source of legislation, and actually emptied it of its content. They continued by arguing that this article would turn Orthodox Copts into second-rate citizens by forcing them to convert to Islam in order to have their affairs adjudicated in accordance with the principal source of legislation. They also claimed that the leaked article had been included by the constitutional assembly in response to threats by the clerical leaders, who asserted that, unless the article was added, the West would believe Copts were persecuted and unable perform their religious rituals. Ultimately, they claimed, this was part of a western plot to enflame Egypt in sectarian strife in cases where Christians converted to Islam for the sake of divorce and returned to their religion after obtaining it (Copts 38 2012, 1). Instead, the 38 group argued that all Egyptians should be subject to the principles of Islamic *shari'a*.

Not surprisingly, the group's invocation of article 2 as a tactic to influence the Islamist government and constituent assembly caused outrage among the larger Coptic community in a political and social climate where Christians were increasingly marginalized, and some feared the application of Islamic *shari'a* to every aspect of their lives, including the familial domain (El-Gergawi 2012). Unlike Egypt's previous constitutions, the 2012 constitution did not recognize the equality of all citizens irrespective of religion, gender, class, and ethnicity. However, the political authorities in the assembly decided to preserve article 2 of the 1971 constitution so that the principles of Islamic *shari'a* remained the principal source of legislation. Eventually the constituent assembly tasked with drafting the constitution proved more inclined to appease the church over a small, but rather vocal group. This was also in line with the 2011 election programme of the Muslim Brotherhood's Freedom and Justice Party which endeavoured to make personal status laws for Muslims comply with Islamic *shari'a*, while reserving the right of Copts to resort to their own personal status laws (Freedom and Justice Party 2011, 25). Hence, for the first time in Egypt's history, the Church was constitutionally designated the guardian of Christians in matters of personal status laws, religious affairs, and the selection of their spiritual leaders.[12] The article hinged on an assumption that Egyptian Christians are members of internally homogenous communities led by the churches. This reinforcement of the political role of the Church was criticized by Copts 38, who argued that the constituent assembly divided

[12] Article 3 of the 2012 constitution stipulated that "the canon principles of Egyptian Christians and Jews are the main source of legislation for their personal status laws, religious affairs, and the selection of their spiritual leaders".

the country into different religious communities based on assumed homogeneity, rather than building the post-revolutionary legal order on ideals of universal and equal citizenship. However, they did not waste time reflecting on the reasons for their defeat. After their demands failed to be accommodated in the 2012 constitution, Copts 38 swiftly shifted their strategy away from state institutions and once again focused their attention on the church leaders.

In the end the 2012 constitution was suspended by a constitutional declaration issued by interim president Adli Mansur, following the ousting of Muhammad Mursi by the armed forces in July 2013. This controversial article was retained with some modifications in the 2014 constitution, and it remains to be seen what impact it will have in practice.

Toward a new family law for Orthodox Copts?

In post-revolutionary Egypt family law emerged as a contentious area among Muslims as well as Orthodox Copts. During Mubarak's presidency the vast majority of law proposals were initiated from above, by the executive. Similarly, Copts 38 criticize Patriarch Shenouda III for the top-down manner in which he drafted the laws pertaining to marriage and divorce. To some extent this changed in the post-revolutionary period, when several civil society organizations approached members of the parliament and the executive in a bid to see their aims realized (Lindbekk and Sonneveld 2014). Having said this, it is too early to say whether relations between society and the state at the level of lawmaking need to be reappraised in the context of the ongoing Egyptian revolution. The Orthodox Coptic church was not entirely exempt from this tendency, as will be shown in the following section.

In November 2012, Tawadros II was elected the 118th pope of the Orthodox Copt church. Partriarch Tawadros II stressed the spiritual rather than the political role of Egypt's Christian church (Egypt Independent 2013). In March 2013 the Ministry of Justice formed a committee with representatives from the Egyptian churches who were charged with drafting a unified law for non-Muslims in personal status matters.[13] Such a unified per-

[13] This coincided with the establishment of another committee tasked with drafting a proposal for a unified family law for Muslims. See Al-Sanhuri 2013.

sonal status law would mean that marriage between Christians from different communities or denominations would no longer be subject to Muslim personal status laws. Concomitantly, the Orthodox Copt Holy Synod (*al-majma' al-muqades*) convened a conference in a monastery in Wadi Natrun at the beginning of April 2013. The conference included leaders of the church, the church's legal advisors, and, most notably, three representatives of Copts 38. In the winter of 2013 the group leaders also met with Patriarch Tawadros II himself. According to Nader al-Serafi, the subject of the talks between Copts 38 and the newly elected pope was the church's regulations concerning divorce and conversions connected with divorce (Interview with Nader al-Serafi, 7 May 2013). Tawadros' decision to initiate dialogue with chosen members of the laity could be viewed as an effort to assuage Copts 38, in response to the challenge inherent in their loud calls for application of Islamic *shari'a* in matters of marriage and divorce.

Copts 38 viewed this as a highly significant step, arguing that the church had never entered into dialogue with members of the laity at such a high level. In the course of the conference the 38 group presented a law proposal, which was subsequently leaked to the press (Fares 2013a and interview with Nader al-Serafi, 7 May 2013). The proposal included several grounds for dissolution of marriage, most notably mistreatment and physical separation for a period of three years. The proposal also retained the article on divorce for illicit relations (*zina*), but added that judicial divorce on this basis should not be accepted unless proved by "proper legal evidence" (article 64). Although the proposal bore a close resemblance to the 1938 regulations, the group's proposal did not advocate a complete break with the model according to which illicit relations is the only ground for the dissolution of a marriage. At the level of their religious community the group tried not to disrupt the dominant discourse of the Church, and incorporated the additional grounds for divorce by expanding the concept of incitement (*tahrid*) to illicit relations in the 2008 amendment. According to Nader al-Serafi, the group's law proposal emphasized the importance of fighting *fitna* (disorder), that arose from uncontrolled sexual lust occasioned by a spouse's abandonment, defect, or bad treatment, and which threatened to undermine the stability of the community. The proper remedy was therefore to grant judicial divorce for these reasons. This discourse was intended to appeal to conservative members of the clergy who shared the ideas of the late Pope Shenouda III.[14]

The church quickly moved to clarify the fact that the leaked proposal was merely one among several, and that the conference held in bishop Bishoy's monastery had not produced a decision or any recommendations. While the Holy Synod was open to reviewing the laws, the opportunities for Copts 38 to achieve their aspirations depends on the legal policies of the church and the political opportunity structures offered by post-revolutionary Egypt. The Orthodox Coptic church headed by Pope Tawadros II is waiting and assessing the consequences of political change, and is perhaps not able to make critical decisions. Although members of the clergy are divided on the issue of divorce due to illicit relations, it could also be difficult for the Church to change its stance on an issue on which the late charismatic Patriarch Shenouda III so clearly articulated his views. In the political sphere of post-revolutionary Egypt, Orthodox Copts are also becoming increasingly marginalized. As indicated earlier, during previous periods of great political turbulence and sectarian tension when the Copts have felt threatened, the Coptic Church has believed it essential to protect its community, whose basis is the family. It is also worth mentioning that a large part of the Coptic laity supports the restrictive divorce laws of the church.[15] These factors are possible reasons for maintaining the current normative order and shelving the law proposal by Copts 38. Yet during an interview Nader al-Serafi maintained that the situation was still open and that Copts 38 expected the church to change its normative stance. Otherwise, he said, the group would reconsider its strategy of cooperation with the church (Interview with Nader El-Serafi, 5 December 2013).

---

14 Similarly, in 2008 the suppression of the grounds of divorce allowed by the 1938 regulations was criticized because the limitation of divorce to instances of illicit relations could bring about a drastic increase of spousal infidelity within unhappy marriages (Bernard-Maugiron 2011, 371).

15 Copts 38 is not the only Coptic civil society organization able to mobilize supporters with loud voices after the revolution. At the end of April 2013, a Coptic movement called "Protection of the Faith" demonstrated outside the Coptic cathedral in the centre of Cairo. They raised banners saying "No negotiation about the holy secrets!", "We will only be governed by our Book!", and "No divorce except for *zina*!" See Fares 2013b.

Conclusion

In this chapter I have shown that in the context of a centralizing state *where Islamic* shari'a *is the general law,* the authority of the Orthodox Copt Church has been limited. the authority of the Orthodox Coptic Church has been limited. Its jurisdiction was transferred to national courts that ruled on family cases involving both Muslims and non-Muslims, and which are predominantly presided over by Muslim judges. While the state has gained authority and influence through the establishment of a unitary judicial system in 1956, we have seen that the church has become stricter in an attempt to bring courts under the authority of the church and to limit conversions. In the process I have highlighted some of strengths and weaknesses in Ehrlich's work. The chapter has argued that he did not take sufficient account of normative disagreement and agency in the creation of the norms that govern social associations central to living law. On the other hand, his treatment of state law contains a significant element of agency from litigants and adjudication by judges. This chapter has emphasized that the church, the laity, and the state are not monoliths. Although many members of the Coptic community acquiesce in the Church's rules of divorce, they have been contested by some members of the clergy and the laity who circumvent them by converting to other communities and denominations, or to Islam in order to be subject to the Muslim law of personal status purportedly based on Islamic *shari'a.*

In my exploration of court practice, I have shown the presence of divergent rulings with regard to judicial divorce due to *zina.* The practical implementation of the 2008 amendment also bears witness to challenges by Muslim judges who interpret Coptic divorce law in line with Muslim personal status law. In pursuing this line of inquiry I have also highlighted how Muslim judges' interpretation of Orthodox Coptic personal status law continues to be influenced by the general law of the state, Islamic shari'a. In addition, judicial discourse is shaped by social norms reflecting entrenched societal views that discriminate against women. While it is difficult to establish empirically the origin of these norms, the data available to the author suggests that they are commonly held by both Muslims and Christians. I have used the situation of Orthodox Copts seeking divorce to highlight the fact that the living law is not only characterized by a considerable degree of agency, but also by interaction between state law and informal norms and values. This demonstrates that the relationship between law and society is characterized not just by the superimposition of law, but also by the interplay of social norms with judicial practice in this field.

I have also drawn attention to the attempts by Coptic activists to renegotiate their citizenship rights in a period of political upheaval when new constitutional norms were being articulated. Copts 38 navigated between the church and Islamic law in its role as the general law of the state, in an attempt to renegotiate citizenship rights. In this contribution I have considered the plurality of normative repertoires invoked, while taking into consideration the limitations on political interplay. Although the 2011 revolution opened up a political space for new political actors, normative plurality is constrained by the constellation of a hegemonic Islamic repertoire and a moralistic discourse centered on fighting *zina*. After the 2012 constitution was ratified, Copts 38 quickly changed their strategy and tried to change the system from within the church. In so doing, they formulated their struggle for increased divorce rights in terms of fighting *fitna* or disorder arising from uncontrolled lust, which also shapes the normative approach of the Orthodox Coptic Church.

References

Al-Ahram Online (2012), Coptic Christians Call for Divorce Law Relaxation, 23 April 2012. http://english.ahram.org.eg/NewsContent/1/64/39993/Egypt/Politics-/Coptic-Christians-call-for-divorce-law-relaxation.aspx (Accessed 20 June 2013)

Al-Sanhuri, Muhammad (2013), The Ministry of Justice Forms Two Committees for the Purpose of Making Legislative Amendments Pertaining to Personal Status for Non-Muslims and the Family. *Al-masry al youm*, 14 March 2013. http://www.almasryalyoum.com/node/1567306 (Accessed 3 April 2013)

Berger, Maurits (2001), Public Policy and Islamic law: the Modern Dhimmi in Contemporary Egyptian FamilyLaw. *Islamic Law and Society* 8:88-136.

Berger, Maurits (2002), Conflicts Law and Public Policy in Egyptian Family Law: Islamic Law through the Backdoor. *The American Journal of Comparative Law* 50:555-594.

Bernard-Maugiron, Nathalie (2011), Divorce and Remarriage of Orthodox Copts in Egypt: the 2008 State Council Ruling and the Amendment of the 1938 Personal Status Regulations, *Islamic Law and Society* 18:356-386.

Copts 38 Manifesto (2012), Manifesto of Copts 38 (on file with author).

Dupret, Baudouin (1999), Legal Pluralism, Normative Plurality, and the Arab World. In: Baudouin Dupret (ed.), *Legal pluralism in the Arab World*. Hague: Kluwer Law International, pp. 29-40

Dupret, Baudouin (2007), What Is Islamic Law? A Praxiological Answer and an Egyptian Case. *Theory of Culture Society* 24:79-100.

Egypt Independent (2013), The Role of the Church is Spiritual, Pope says, 12 June 2013. http://www.egyptindependent.com/news/role-church-spiritual-pope-says (Accessed 13 June 2013)

Ehrlich, Eugen (1922), The Sociology of Law. *Harvard Law Review* 36:130-145.

Ehrlich, Eugen (1975), *Fundamental Principles of the Sociology of Law*, translated by Walter L. Moll. New York: Arno Press.

El-Alami, Dawoud (1992), *The Marriage Contract in Islamic Law*. London: Brill.

El-Gergawi, Sherry (2012), Greek Orthodox Leader to AO: Church Alone will Govern Christians' Personal-Status Issues. *Ahram Online*, 27 September 2012. http://english.ahram.org.eg/NewsContent/1/64/54049/Egypt/Politics-/Greek-Orthodox-leader-to-AO-Church-alone-will-gove.aspx (Accessed 3 October 2012)

Fares, Mikail (2013a), Youm al-saba' Exclusively Publishes the New Personal Status Regulations for Orthodox Copts, 5 April 2013. http://www1.youm7.com/News.asp?NewsID=1006356&SecID=12#.UxuQhdJWGP8 (Accessed 7 April 2013)

Fares, Mikail (2013b), Dozens Demonstrating Against Second Marriage Outside the Cathedral before the Patriarch's Sermon. *Youm al-saba'*, 24 April 2013. http://www.youm7mobile.com/661fb48d0db26fa7b5a2e2fcea82ae2e (Accessed 4 May 2013)

Freedom and Justice Party (2011), Election Program. Retrieved from: http://www.fjponline.com/uploads/FJPprogram.pdf (Accessed August 2012).

Hatem, Mervat (2000), The Pitfalls of the Nationalist Discourses on Citizenship in Egypt. In: Suad Joseph (ed.), *Gender and Citizenship in the Middle East*. Syracuse, New York: Syracuse University Press, pp. 33-57.

Ibrahim, Ekram (2010), Admin Court Suspends Conversion Case. *Al-Masry al-Youm*, 27 April 27 2010. http://www.almasryalyoum.com/en/node/37640 (Accessed 4 June 2013)

Joseph, Suad (2000), Gendering Citizenship in the Middle East. In: Suad Joseph (ed.), *Gender and Citizenship in the Middle East*, Syracuse, New York: Syracuse University Press, pp. 3-30.

Kamal, Karima (2006), *Talaq al-Aqbat*, Cairo: Dar Merit.

Kholoussy, Hanan (2005), The Nationalization of Marriage in Monarchical Egypt. In Arthur Goldschmidt, Amy J. Johnson and Barak A. Salmoni (eds.), *Re-envisioning Egypt 1919-1952*. Cairo: The American University in Cairo Press, pp. 317-350.

Kholoussy, Hanan (2010), *For Better, For Worse: the Marriage Crisis that Made Modern Egypt*. California: Stanford University Press.

Lawrence, Bruce (2013), Citizen Ahmad Among the Believers. In Mohammad Hassan Khalil (ed), *Between Heaven and Hell: Islam, Salvation, and the Fate of Others*. Oxford, New York: Oxford University Press, pp. 288-313.

Leila, Reem (2010), Church and State. *Al Ahram Weekly*, 3 – 9 June 2010, no. 1001. http://weekly.ahram.org.eg/2010/1001/eg7.htm (Accessed 6 June 2012).

Lindbekk, Monika (2013), Enforcement of Personal Status Law by Egyptian Courts. In: Elisa Giunchi (ed.), *Adjudicating Family Law in the Muslim Courts: Experiences from the Muslim Contemporary World*. New York: Routledge, pp. 87-106.

Lindbekk, Monika and Nadia Sonneveld (2014, forthcoming), A Counter-Revolution in Egyptian Family Law? Egypt's Pre-And Post-Revolutionary Period (2011-2013) Compared, *New Middle Eastern Studies*.

Mahmood, Saba (2001), Feminist Theory, Embodiment, and the Docile Agent: Some Reflections on the Egyptian Islamic Revival, *Cultural Anthropology* 16: 202-236.

Melcangi, Alessia (2012), Before and After the Revolution: a Spring also for the Copts of Egypt? BRISMES Graduate Section Annual Conference 2012 London School of Economics and Political Science (LSE) London, United Kingdom, 11 June 2012.

Nelken, David (1984), Law in Action or Living Law? Back to the Beginning in Sociology of Law, *Legal Studies* 4:157-174.

Osman, Ahmed Zaki (2013), Roots of Religious Violence Lie in Both State and Society. *Egypt Independent*, 13 March 2013. http://www.egyptindependent.com/news/roots-religious-violence-lie-both-state-and-society (Accessed 9 May 2013).

Shaham, Ron (2010), Communal Identity, Political Islam and Family Law: Copts and the Debate over the Grounds for Dissolution of Marriage in Twentieth-Century Egypt, *Islam and Christian–Muslim Relations* 21:409-422.

Shams El-Din, Mai (2012), For Copts, Marriage in the Church May Mean Marriage to the Church. *Egypt Independent*, 5 September 2012. http://www.egyptindependent.com/news/copts-marriage-church-may-mean-marriage-church (Accessed 1 October 2012)

Sezgin, Yüksel (2011), Women's Rights in the Triangle of State, Law and Religion: a Comparison of Egypt and India, *Emory International Law Review*, 25:1007-1028.

Sonneveld, Nadia (2012), *Khul' Divorce in Egypt. Public Debates, Judicial Practices, and Everyday Life*. Cairo: The American University in Cairo Press.

Tadros, Mariz (2013), *Copts at the Crossroads: the Challenges of Building Inclusive Democracy in Egypt*. Cairo: American University Press in Cairo.

Vogl, Stefan (2009), Eugen Ehrlich's Linking of Sociology and Jurisprudence. In: Marc Hertogh (ed.), *Living Law: Reconsidering Eugen Ehrlich*. Oxford: Hart, pp. 95-123.

Webber, Jeremy (2009), Naturalism and Agency in the Living Law. In: Marc Hertogh (ed.), *Living Law: Reconsidering Eugen Ehrlich*. Oxford: Hart, pp. 201-221.

Rethinking Corruption in Post-Soviet Uzbekistan: Ethnography of "Living Law"

Rustamjon URINBOYEV and Måns SVENSSON

Introduction

During the first period of ethnographic fieldwork in *Shabboda*[1] – a village located in rural Ferghana in Uzbekistan, we attended a *nikoh toi* (wedding ceremony) arranged by a local farmer. The *nikoh toi* starts at five o'clock in the morning with *nahor oshi* (a morning pilaf[2] feast) at the groom's house. Joyful sounds of *karnay* and *surnay* (traditional Uzbek musical instruments) can be heard from far away and signal to the whole *mahalla* (local community) that the wedding ceremony has begun. On the threshold of the house, the head of the family himself greets each guest on arrival with a handshake or embrace, after which the guests are politely offered seats at the guest tables. Each guest gives *toyana* (gifts such as carpets or cash) while shaking hands with the head of the family. The singer entertains the party with Uzbek classical songs while the guests enjoy what is spread before them: bread, different candies, fruits, nuts, platters of *pilaf*, pots of tea, locally produced beverages, and a bottle of vodka. Guests leave the tables as soon as they have finished their *pilaf*, and the tables are hurriedly cleaned up to welcome new arrivals. We sit at a nicely decorated table with the *oqsoqol* (informal leader of the *mahalla*) and *mahalla* residents, eating *pilaf* and talking about the role and importance of weddings in the lives of Uzbeks. Spontaneously, the *oqsoqol* begins to tell an anecdote related to weddings:

"There is an anecdote widely circulated in Uzbek society. Three men – an American, a Japanese, and an Uzbek – meet in a restaurant for dinner. After some drinks, they all start boasting about their countries and cultures. The American says arrogantly that life in the United States is very good; every month, he earns $10,000 and can buy a new car each month. The Japanese man laughs sarcastically and says that the United States is nothing compared to Japan's hi-tech society where robots

1 The name of the village has been changed to protect the anonymity of informants.

2 Pilaf is a festive Uzbek rice.

carry out all tasks. He adds that he earns $15,000 a month and has a robot at home that does all the housework. When it is the Uzbek's turn to describe his country, he modestly says that the majority of people in Uzbekistan earn $200 a month, but can spend more than $10,000 a month. The Uzbek man also adds that even poor people in Uzbekistan are able to invite up to 1,000 guests to their weddings, while in the United States and Japan, only rich people can afford such events. These statements leave both the American and the Japanese wondering how Uzbeks can spend more than they earn, and have such expensive weddings when the average monthly salary does not exceed $200."

The last phrase was accompanied by loud laughter and nodding, showing mahalla residents' awareness of the 'making-ends meet' philosophy slyly hinted at in the anecdote. The anecdote, true or not, indicates that there is a plethora of 'hidden' informal transactions in Uzbek society that are widespread but mystifying to outsiders. There are different versions of this anecdote, but they all give us a clue to the existence of informal rules and practices (living law) in Uzbekistan that dominate everyday life and help individuals 'get things done.' The anecdote also chimes with the central view of international reports and policy documents that characterize Uzbekistan as one of the most corrupt countries in the world. According to the 2012 Corruption Perceptions Index, released annually by Transparency International (TI 2012), Uzbekistan is among the ten most corrupt countries in the world. Much of the scholarly literature too, especially anthropological accounts, demonstrates that the laws and symbols of the state are virtually absent from everyday life, while 'informality' is an omnipresent phenomenon in both 'state' and 'non-state' arenas[3]. The anecdote thus begs the questions whether there is a 'living law' in Uzbekistan, and if so, how it works, how it can be studied empirically, and what implications it has for understanding corruption in the local context. What are the relations between formal and informal structures with regard to corruption in Uzbekistan? In which ways do these relations manifest themselves in everyday life? This study seeks to address these questions.

Our paper aims to explore the multifaceted meaning, logic, and morality of informal transactions, in order to better understand the social context that informs the meaning of corruption and bribery in Uzbekistan. We accept and use the working definition of corruption presented by Transparency

---

3 See e.g. Wegerich 2006; Ilkhamov 2007; Kandiyoti 2007; Trevisani 2007; Markowitz 2008; Rasanayagam 2011.

International (TI): "corruption is the abuse of entrusted power for private gain." However, when applying this concept, we question the validity of the Western-centric interpretations of the definition, hereinafter 'Western-centric interpretations', (e.g. Becker 2004; Kaufmann *et al.* 2004; TI 2012; World Bank 2012), and emphasize the need to take into consideration critiques from scholars such as Tanzi (1998, 8-10), who notes that the meaning of the word 'abuse' varies according to local legal and cultural standards (see also Gupta 1995; Werner 2000; Humphrey 2002; Polese 2008). To use this definition correctly, we argue the necessity to consider local context, and thereby aim to provide additional tools for interpreting the definition of corruption through the concept of 'living law'. In this study we argue that Western-centric interpretations cannot satisfactorily explain the nuances of corruption in Uzbekistan, and that there is a need to consider the 'living law' of everyday life through which informal transactions are carried out. A theoretically-founded hypothesis is that informal transactions in Uzbek society reflect different cultural and functional meanings to a greater degree than in most of the Western world. The more the focus moves from Western-centric interpretations to ethnographic (contextual) analyses of everyday life and socio-economic conditions, the more it becomes discernible that the bulk of informal transactions in Uzbek society are simply manifestations of coping (survival) strategies, deeply embedded social norms, and traditions. Hence we argue that there is a need to make a distinction between the informal practices of kleptocratic elites, which have nothing to do with 'survival', and the informal coping strategies of ordinary citizens and low-level officials (i.e. 'the corruption of the weak'). If this is true, there may be reasons to re-evaluate the relevance of international legal definitions of corruption and bribery in the context of Uzbekistan, and possibly in that of other Central Asian countries too.

Methodology

This paper is based on three periods of field research carried out between 2009 and 2012 in the Ferghana Province of Uzbekistan. The first field research was conducted during April-May 2009, the second lasted for three months between June-August 2010, and the last was undertaken during June-July 2012. The field site was chosen on the basis of contacts and social networks available to the authors. The first author, being native Uzbek, had the advantage of knowing the language and possessing a pre-existing understanding of local conditions, whereas the second author, being from Sweden (non-native), added an external perspective to the study. Both authors arrived in Uzbekistan for the first period in 2009 and stayed in the field site together. The first author was alone for the second and third field trips in 2010 and 2012. We used participant observation and informal interviews as our data collection strategy.

During the field research we observed eight wedding ceremonies that were hosted and attended by different social groups ranging from local elites to ordinary farm workers. Our observations frequently took the form of informal chats and conversations that arose on the spur of the moment. The weddings took place in the Fergana region of Uzbekistan, during April 2009 – July 2012. Apart from observing weddings, during the second and third field trips we conducted two informal interviews with a traffic policeman and a minibus driver. These key informants were selected on the basis of their daily involvement with the law and/or state officials, their knowledge, their willingness to talk, and their communicability. These interviews were more free-flowing, and focused on such questions as the role of law in everyday life, people's perceptions of bribery, local definitions and interpretations of the 'licit' and 'illicit', everyday coping strategies, values and moral obligations, and the perceived role of the state in everyday life. Questions were mainly used as a guide and were adapted according to the pace of the interview. The interviews lasted from 45 minutes to two hours.

The rest of the chapter is organized in the following manner: The next section, part two, focuses on previous research that situates this study within 'corruption' research and presents an analytical framework for understanding our perspective on corruption. Part three provides the theoretical framework of the study by using Eugen Ehrlich's concept of 'living law.' It will be argued that Ehrlich's theory of 'living law' was informed by the clashes and interactions of the different legal cultures he experienced in Bukowina, and that his theory remains a useful tool for studying corruption in social settings such as Uzbekistan, where society is mostly based on informal economy, kinship, neighbourhood ties, and patron-client networks. In part four, we present the results of our ethnographic fieldwork conducted between 2009-2012 in rural Ferghana, Uzbekistan, in which we explore the 'living law' in 'state' and 'non-state' arenas with reference to ethnographic data on wedding ceremonies, two informal interviews, and our participant observation. Finally, part five draws out the implications of the ethnographic material for Western-centric interpretations, and highlights the most important findings of the study.

Previous research

Corruption has become, without any doubt, a fashionable research topic in the literature on post-Soviet societies[4]. Much of the scholarly literature concerning it focuses on the 'economy of favours' that became a popular term for conceptualizing a wide range of illicit practices such as bribery, kickbacks, nepotism, patronage, cronyism, and so forth. As Humphrey (2012, 23) describes, one idea common to this entire body of literature is that these informal ways of conducting economic activity are carried out through "personal connections" that somehow naturally give rise to favours. However, Humphrey (2012) in her recent anthropological work shows how the 'economy of favours' may also manifest cultural and moral values, and suggests that favours can also be understood as ways of enabling actors to enhance a sense of self-worth within relevant social circles, and as sources of esteem for ordinary people in social settings such as Russia and Mongolia. Humphrey's work thus leads to the view that economic transactions may reflect different cultural and functional meanings depending on the local context.

A 'diverse economies' perspective developed by Gibson-Graham and her collective (The Community Economies Collective 2001; Gibson-Graham 2006, 2008) has been influential in promoting the understanding of the multifarious nature of economic activities. The central claim Gibson-Graham make is that many studies addressing informal economy and corruption issues tend to disregard the heterogeneity of informal activities (in all their diversity) undertaken in different parts of the world. They have demonstrated that monetary transactions do not necessarily include or explain economic activity. Other studies also similarly concluded that the meaning of goods and money is significantly determined by local cul-

[4] E.g. Gleason 1995; Holmes 1997; Ledeneva 1998, 2009; Kurkchiyan 2000; Mandel and Humphrey 2002; Ries 2002; Humphrey and Sneath 2004; Ilkhamov 2004, 2007; Knack 2006; Trevisani 2007; Humphrey 2012. Corruption was also a central topic in the literature about the Soviet Union (Simis 1982; Critchlow 1988; Srubar 1991; Zemtsov 1991; Staples 1993).

ture, political use, and context (Parry and Bloch 1989; Thomas 1991). For example, in African societies, monetary exchanges may just be the modern equivalent of gift exchanges. Therefore corruption in Africa has been seen by some social scientists as a mere infusion of a culture of traditional gift-giving into the bureaucracy (Harrison, 1999; Hydén 2006). In the context of India, Akhil Gupta (1995 cited in Polese 2008) has shown that the 'practice' of bribe-giving is not simply an economic transaction, but a cultural practice that requires a great degree of performative competence. One possible inference from these studies is that Western-centric interpretations need to be re-contextualized when talking about corruption in non-Western societies.

Many of these insights have been confirmed in analysis of post-Soviet societies. Anthropological studies have demonstrated the existence of local perceptions of moral codes and values present in informal transactions that significantly differ from Western morality and standards[5]. This literature is based upon a theoretical understanding of money, gifts, and the morality of exchange (Mauss 1924; Parry and Bloch 1989; Thomas 1991), as well as on empirical studies concerned with different kinds of transactions between citizens and state officials. At first glance, many of these transactions may look like bribes; however, the research shows that if the cultural context is taken into consideration, these transactions may well be considered to be morally acceptable gifts. Caroline Humphrey (2002) conveys the multifaceted morality of various illegal transactions by means of numerous examples of customs and police officers involved in dubious transactions. This leads her to argue for rethinking bribery in some spheres in Russia. In the context of Russia, Ledeneva (2009) has also showed that there is a need to differentiate between 'supportive' and 'subversive' functions of informal practices: from sociability, safety nets, survival kits, and forms of social capital to means of access, diversion of resources, bridging formal organisations, and subverting formal procedures. Similar patterns have been observed in other post-Soviet states as well (e.g. Werner 2000; Polese 2008; Rasanayagam 2011).

Despite the great diversity of scholarly explanations for, and approaches to, the nature and causes of corruption in post-Soviet societies, one question

---

5 E.g. Abramson 2000; Werner 2000; Kurkchiyan 2000; Humphrey 2002, 2012; Wanner 2005; Sneath 2006; Markowitz 2008; Polese 2008; Ledeneva 2009; Rasanayagam 2011; Urinboyev 2011; Urinboyev and Svensson 2013.

commonly raised is whether there is a need to re-evaluate Western-centric interpretations when talking about (or measuring) corruption in post-Soviet societies. In this chapter, we acknowledge the scholarly context described above; however, our aim is not to offer a new definition of 'corruption', nor to establish a strict boundary between licit (legal) and illicit (illegal) practices. Instead, utilizing the concept of 'living law', we aim to provide additional tools for re-contextualizing corruption, thereby demonstrating the importance of local perceptions, social norms, and moral codes (living law) to better understand *what makes a practice corrupt or illegal.* This task, in turn, requires the creation of a suitable theoretical framework. For this reason, in the next section we will draw on Eugen Ehrlich's concept of 'living law' to build a theoretical framework.

There is another scientific field of importance to our study that has to do with the specific choice of weddings as the social arena that we focus on in our empirical studies. Weddings are considered to be very much concerned with money and gift exchange and therefore of great interest when understanding different aspects of socio-economic structures[6]. We will elaborate on this literature in the analysis section.

Theoretical framework – Ehrlich's 'living law'

Eugen Ehrlich (1862-1922) was an Austrian legal scholar. Although Ehrlich wrote his book "Grundlagen einer Soziologie des Rechts" a century ago in a time of dramatic political and social turmoil in Europe, his ideas are still relevant to current academic debates, as evidenced by a growing body of literature focusing on 'living law'[7]. As Ziegert (2002) describes, Ehrlich's life and work mirrors dramatic cultural and political changes in Europe in the pre-World War I period. Ehrlich was born in Czernowitz (today Cernovitsi in Ukraine), which at the time was a part of the Austro-Hungarian Empire and the capital city of the province of Bukowina. Ehrlich provides an example of the living law of Bukowina, a multicultural society where Armenians, Germans, Jews, Russians, Ruthenians, Ukrainians, Slovaks, Hungarians,

6 E.g. Mauss 1924; Barnett 1938; Bates 1974; Annaklychev 1984; Borozna 1984; Peters 1990; White 1994; Mundy 1995; Kandiyoti 1998; Yalçin-Heckmann 2001; Agadjanian and Makarova 2003; Kandiyoti and Azimova 2004.

7 E.g. O'Day, 1966; Nelken, 1984, 2008; Teubner, 1997; Hertogh, 2009; Larsson, 2013; Svensson, 2013; Urinboyev, 2013.

and Gypsies lived side-by-side (Eppinger, 2009, 28; Ehrlich 1912/1967, 43). The normative order that Ehrlich observed in Bukowina was mostly based on informal rules, while the law imposed from Vienna had a limited meaning in everyday life. As Deflem (2008, 90) notes, the experiences of multiculturalism and political instability had a great impact on Ehrlich in the development of his concept of 'living law'.

Ehrlich (2002)[8] presents three major concepts besides 'living law', namely, 'the inner order of associations', 'rules of conduct', and 'norms for decision'. These form the basis of his concept of 'living law'. According to Ehrlich, there are various types of and names for 'rules of conduct', such as rules of law, of morals, of religion, of ethical custom, of honour, of decorum, of tact, of etiquette, of fashion. These rules are an ever-present part of society and emanate from the social forces that are operative in society. Not all laws can develop into 'rules of conduct'; only those that become part and parcel of social life do so. Laws that are effective only in very rare cases of legal controversy are a mere doctrine, norms for decision, dogma, or theory. Ehrlich calls the laws that only apply in very few cases as 'norms for decision', whereas he refers to 'rules of conduct' that guide everyday social behaviour as 'living law.' From this perspective, Ehrlich claims that the 'living law' is not directly linked to the state or its legal system but rather to the inner order of various social groups or associations. By 'the inner order of associations', Ehrlich means the society's reflexive web of expectations that give power and meaning to norms. It is not state coercion, but mainly society's reflexive web of expectations, or the inner order of associations that makes law work and brings about social order. By making a distinction between '(social) associations' and their 'inner order', Ehrlich asserts that there is a living law that governs everyday life, and that everyday life runs smoothly because the living law works. In this regard, Ehrlich (2002, 493) states that "the living law is the law which dominates life itself, even though it has not been posited in legal propositions. The source of our knowledge of this law is the modern legal document, secondly, direct observation of life, of commerce, of customs and usages, and of all associations, not only those that the law has recognized but also those that it has overlooked and passed by, indeed even those that it has disapproved." In this connection,

8 Unless otherwise indicated, all references to Ehrlich in this paper refer to Ehrlich (2002).

Ehrlich alludes to the entirety of law dominating social life as 'living law', whereas he refers to legal propositions as 'juristic law.'

The central claim Ehrlich (2002, Foreword) makes is that "At the present as well as at any other time, the center of gravity of legal development lies not in legislation, nor in juristic science, nor in judicial decision, but in society itself." For Ehrlich, the law is not the only regulator of political, social, intellectual, and economic life, and there are many other normative orders that influence social behaviour more effectively than the law. Norms for decision created by the state can be alien to the daily life of society. They often do not spread beyond court premises, and become rules of conduct only in court decisions. For Ehrlich, society consists of a multitude of (social) associations, (among which the state is one), each with its own inner order. In this context, the state is not the only association that determines the main parameters of everyday social behaviour. There are many other (social) associations with their own inner order that make certain demands on individuals in exchange for what they offer; further, the social norms which dominate in these associations influence individuals' social behaviour more forcibly than the laws of the state. As a result, it is possible that an individual will conduct himself according to the law only if it is made imperative by his social relations and associations. From this perspective, everyday social interactions and social behaviour, whether temporary or permanent, can be sustained exclusively by living laws that are quite distinct from the state's laws. The social order is in this sense established, maintained, and transformed via the continuous struggles and interplay between various normative orders (social, legal, religious, etc.). Thus, Ehrlich asserts that social life is primarily regulated by the 'living law'.

Another important dimension to Ehrlich's 'living law' is its approach to empirical research, or method broadly conceived. Ehrlich (2002) claims that if we want to reify the 'living law', we should attentively observe everyday life, relations of domination, and people's actual habits, and inquire into their thoughts on the opinions of relevant people in their surrounding environment and on proper social behaviour. Further, he advises that people's feelings and reactions are instructive in for anyone dissecting the social significance of law and other social norms. Ehrlich thus stresses the importance of considering the local context and the informal normative structures when examining the (in-) effectiveness of state law. This is in line with legal ethnography: Geertz (1973) considers the contextualization of phenomena to be the very essence of ethnographic research.

Although Ehrlich developed the 'living law' concept a century ago, it has great relevance for any attempt to understand how formal and informal structures interweave in contemporary societies. Nelken (1984) suggests that Ehrlich's 'living law' should be considered suited not only to settings such as Bukowina, as is commonly asserted, but also useful for understanding the normative pluralism inherent in other working normative orders. Ehrlich's concept of 'living law' was developed in a context comparable to contemporary conditions in Central Asia, since both Bukowina and Central Asian countries seem to share similar socio-political characteristics – multiculturalism, multi-ethnic and multi-faith societies, and the clash of different normative orders. Hence, the 'living law' concept provides useful insights when trying to understand corruption in the context of post-Soviet Central Asia, where there is an interplay of different normative orders. Armed with the concept of 'living law', we might infer that living law guides economic transactions in both 'state' and 'non-state' arenas, and that we cannot satisfactorily explore the nuances of corruption in Uzbekistan without considering the 'living law' through which such transactions are carried out.

The ethnographic fieldwork we conducted in Uzbekistan can be regarded as 'living law informed ethnography', since we were interested in understanding the interweaving of formal and informal structures, systems of values and belief, patterns of social action and regulatory structures, with the aim of identifying the patterns of 'living law' in both 'state' and 'non-state' arenas. More specifically, we observed the role of state law and its interplay with unwritten rules (living law) in everyday life, and directly or indirectly in various social arenas and situations. We observed, for example, how traffic police enforce traffic rules, and to what extent people conform to state law when dealing with state officials. Hence, when exploring the local meaning, logic, and morality of informal transactions, we focused on exchanges between ordinary citizens in wedding ceremonies and informal transactions between citizens and state officials in cases involving traffic violations. The reason for this focus is that these are the two arenas that may inform us how informal regulatory (normative) structures interact and clash with state law. The results of the ethnographic fieldwork will be presented in the next sections.

Living law in 'non-state' arenas

We used the case of wedding ceremonies to illustrate the social meaning and morality of informal transactions in Uzbekistan. The choice of wedding ceremonies for collecting empirical data is based on three main arguments. First, wedding ceremonies embody authentic features of Uzbek culture: traditions, values, collectivism, age and gender hierarchies, social networks and kinship relations, the central role of the *mahalla* (a residential neighbourhood institution), and power and status-based relations. After independence, weddings became central occasions where the return to authentic Uzbek forms was clearly in evidence (Kandiyoti and Azimova, 2004). Second, the arrangement of a marriage in Uzbekistan is a lengthy and costly process involving a complex traditional exchange of gifts and money between the in-laws. Money and gifts are conspicuous features of both the marriage negotiations and the wedding ceremony. Weddings thus display multivocality in the meaning of money and gift exchanges and exhibit a culture of money. Third, the wedding ceremony is the concern of the whole community, as it is arranged with support and resources from the local society and thereby reflects the status and social position of the families that are to be united. In this regard, the wedding involves both formal and informal aspects of the local community in gathering the necessary resources. Weddings are thus arenas where we can find the 'living law' of everyday life.

The entanglement of economy, morality, and materiality: wedding ceremonies in rural Ferghana

Amongst numerous life-cycle rituals, *nikoh toi* (the wedding ceremony) is the most central ceremony in rural Fergana. The *nikoh toi* is often held inside the host family's home. All *mahalla* (local community) residents, relatives, classmates, colleagues, and friends are invited to the wedding ceremony. A *nikoh toi* is on average attended by approximately 200-500 guests, men and women sitting separately at different guest tables. The *nikoh toi* also fulfils a redistributive and risk-reducing function in rural Fergana: it is the social norm that tells each wedding guest to contribute to the wedding with money, gifts, or labour. Thus, by arranging or attending a *nikoh toi*, a household broadens its social networks and engages in reciprocal transactions, since the wedding involves a great deal of exchange and reciprocation of money and material goods within networks of kin and friendship. Consequently, such high levels of transactions during weddings enact the ties of obligations and expectations within kinship and friendship networks, blending the moral aspects of social relations with their material aspects.

The *nikoh toi* starts at five in the morning with the male-only event, *nahor oshi* (morning *pilaf* feast), at the groom's house. An identical *nahor oshi* is arranged at the bride's house. According to the social norms, upon arrival, each guest should give *toyana* (gifts such as carpets or cash) while shaking hands with the head of the family. The *nikoh toi* also illustrates the hierarchical nature of social relations in rural Ferghana, as guests are offered seats based on their socio-economic status and political influence. The best tables are often reserved for the 'people of influence', such as local government officials, police, highly educated people, successful businessmen, and wealthy relatives and friends. The presence of people of influence at the wedding sends an important signal to the *mahalla* that the wedding host is well-connected. Guests with lower socio-economic status are directed to more modest tables.

After the *nahor oshi,* the groom brings the bride from her house to the central mosque for a religious ritual. By tradition, during this ceremony the bride does not initially give her consent to the marriage; the groom therefore then pays some money to the bride's family to gain her consent. Money does not fulfil an economic purpose in this case, but is a ritual payment for the bride's consent.

The bride's arrival in the groom's house is the high point of the wedding party, when she is welcomed with joyful traditional Uzbek songs, and showered with sweets. The main wedding party begins with a *kelin salom* (bride's greeting) ceremony to welcome the bride into the groom's family. In this ceremony, the bride bows to greet everyone, from the groom's parents to neighbours. There is a special Uzbek song for this ceremony in which the singer states the names and type of people to whom the bride should bow. The people who are greeted by the bride are expected to come up to the front and give her money; in this way, the bride receives money every time she greets a guest, or her husband's relatives and friends. Since brides cannot afford to buy new wedding gowns in rural Fergana, they usually hire one from local shops. The money generated from the *kelin salom* ceremony is used to pay for this.

Shortly after the *kelin salom* ceremony, the wedding party continues with very fast Uzbek songs. Traditionally, the *ortakash* (announcer), equipped with a microphone, invites guests individually or in small groups to the front dancing area to give a short speech in honour of the occasion and instructs them to dance to a song played by the *ashulachi* (the singer and musicians). The general audience listens to the speeches and continues to enjoy appetizers and vodka. Although most of the speeches are not listened to attentively, the general audience takes part in the activities by giving money to dancing guests. The custom is that wedding guests give money to those who get up to make a speech and dance to the songs played by *ashulachi.* Other guests come up to the dancers and give them money. This tradition is called *pul qistirish* (giving money). The visibility of the money during the wedding dance is striking; everybody, from children to old people, dances with money in their hands. The amount of money that guests give depends on the age, social status, and occupation of the person dancing. By giving money, someone can express their respect and loyalty to the person who is dancing. If this person is the groom's father, or a local government employee, or a wealthy man, a large number of guests approach him and give money. In such cases, it is possible to see a crowd of people lined up to do this. This is the most central part of the wedding, in which it can be seen how social status and reputation are translated into hard cash. After observing this, it is very easy to compare one person's social status and reputation with that of others. All the money accumulated during the dancing is given to the singer and musicians as payment for their efforts.

The wedding ends with a women-only ceremony called the *yuz ochdi* (unveiling of the bride). During this ceremony, the bride usually wears a white handkerchief to cover her face, until the groom's nephew removes it. Women sing traditional songs, and the groom's family and neighbours give gifts to the bride. Shortly after this ceremony the bride is taken by a *yanga* (female relative of the bride) to the room intended for the young couple, where the bride gets ready to meet the groom. A few hours later, the groom accompanied by his best man appears at the threshold of the room, where the bride is waiting for him. To be allowed access to the bride's room, the groom symbolically bargains for and buys the bride from the *yanga*, and then the *yanga* leaves the young couple alone for the night.

Analysing wedding transactions

Our fieldwork in rural Fergana shows that the practice of giving and taking gifts and money has turned into an institutionalised practice in which economic and social life are permeated by large numbers of informal transactions. Kinship and friendship networks are increasingly mobilized and tied to one another through the exchange and reciprocation of money, material goods, and services. Such aspects of weddings have been widely discussed in the anthropological, theoretical, and ethnographic literature in relation, for example, to Africa, the Middle East, and the Caucasus (Bates 1974; Peters 1990; Mundy 1995; Yalçin-Heckmann 2001), and also in that of Soviet and Western ethnographers in relation to Central Asian societies (Annaklychev 1984; Borozna 1984; Werner 1997; Kandiyoti and Azimova 2004).

The *nikoh toy* provides numerous ritualistic symbols through which individuals and groups can display their social status and power and shape their relations with one another. The public acceptance of social hierarchies, status contestations, and gender divisions becomes clearly articulated in *nikoh toy*. Men and women sit separately at different tables during the wedding. Status contestations and social hierarchies are even reflected in the placement of guests: people of influence are seated at the best tables and served more quickly than others. If an influential person dances during the wedding party, one can observe a crowd hurriedly lining up to give money to them. Few people, however will give money to a dancer who does not belong to the category of people of influence. This is the most central aspect of the wedding, showing the importance of money as a means to display one's social status and prestige. Thus, wedding transactions have non-commercial value and are increasingly geared to displaying one's social status and power. Such features of wedding transactions represent what Gibson-Graham (1996) describe as noncapitalist economic forms.

Although it is always risky to draw parallels between different social contexts, the social hierarchies and gift exchanges that are omnipresent in Uzbek weddings could be comparable to the North West American *potlatch* [9] ceremony in which hierarchical relations within and between clans and villages are created and strengthened through gift exchanges, dance performances, and other ceremonies (see e.g. Mauss, 1924; Barnett, 1938;

---

[9] *Potlatch* is a gift-giving ceremony and informal economic activity practiced by indigenous peoples of the Pacific Northwest Coast of Canada and the United States.

Piddocke, 1965). There are many forms of *potlatch*, such as celebrations of births, rites of passages, weddings, and funerals. It usually involves a feast with music, dance, and spiritual ceremonies. According to *potlatch* culture, each gift is part of a system of reciprocity in which the honour of giver and recipient are engaged; hence gifts are distributed according to the rank of the receiver. The donor, by offering gifts selectively, expresses the esteem in which he holds one recipient compared to another.

The nature of wedding transactions in rural Fergana is consistent with the concept of gift exchange proposed by Marcel Mauss (1924). For Mauss, a distinctive aspect of a gift exchange is that it engages the person in three main obligations: the obligation to give, to receive, and to reciprocate, thereby ensuring communication and establishing a high level of social interaction between individuals. After attending several weddings in rural Fergana we realised that money and gift exchanges are an essential part of social interactions. Even though weddings involve non-commercial practices such as appreciative gift-giving and the fulfilment of moral obligations to help family and friends, it seems that the moral aspects of social relations are blended with their material aspects. Consequently the socialization of individuals in rural Fergana largely takes place in an extremely monetized social environment, where individuals are bound to one another through the amount and type of (cash) gifts they exchange. This observation is similar to Werner's (1997) description of wedding ceremonies in post-Soviet Kazakhstan. As Werner shows, despite the post-Soviet economic collapse, many Kazakhs continue to expend a large amount of financial and labour resources on life-cycle rituals, because they provided a means for social networking and redistributive activities.

Weddings display multivocality in the meaning of money and gift exchanges. The major item on display during the *kelin salom* and wedding dance was – money. Payments made to the bride's family during the religious ritual reveal that the meaning of a monetary transaction is deeply embedded in the cultural practices. The conspicuous presence of money during the wedding dance is to do with fulfilling a ritual role, and serves to enhance the reputation of both the money-giver and the recipient. The visibility of money during the wedding dance shows the deep embeddedness of money in local culture and traditions. From this perspective, the use of money and the morality of exchanges that we observed during weddings are consistent with Parry and Bloch (1989) who argue that the meaning of goods and money is significantly determined by local culture, political use, and context.

As the example of the *nikoh toy* shows, money is not simply a commodity or an economic phenomenon but also plays a very important cultural role in Uzbekistan: it acts as a glue in social interactions and solidarity, a means of carrying out traditions, a part of a traditional dance, a way of paying respect, and much more. Since people dance holding money, the *kelin salom* generates money, hands are shaken with money, and respect is translated into hard cash, money has turned into a social phenomenon: a culture of money. When considering how money and gifts play such a central role in the performance of rituals, it is safe to say that there are informal structures which assign ceremonial and cultural meaning to informal transactions. These findings suggest that there is a need to re-contextualize Western-centric interpretations in such social settings as Uzbekistan, where the relationship between economy, morality, and materiality are intertwined.

Living Law in 'State' Arenas

In this section we present the results of two informal interviews which demonstrate the multifaceted meaning, changing morality and logic of bribery in Uzbekistan. The interviews address informal transactions between traffic police and citizens and thereby exemplify the omnipotence of 'living law' in state arenas. The interviews were conducted during the second (June-August 2010) and third field trips (June-July 2012). The interviews involve the following two actors and issues: (1) the 'survival techniques' of traffic police; and (2) the coping strategies of a minibus driver in dealing with traffic police. Our interview material is thus largely derived from the accounts of two key informants, but in order to enhance the reliability of the data we have cross-checked our findings through informal interviews with other informants. Due to the informants' concerns about safety and confidentiality, we neither took notes nor recorded the interviews. Instead, immediately following an interview, we wrote down our recollections of the substance of what the informants had said. To protect the anonymity of our informants, their names have been changed.

The first interview is centred around *Dilshod*, a traffic policeman in Ferghana province, and the second focuses on *Zokir*, a minibus driver who drives between Oltiariq and Ferghana city on a daily basis. In the following sections, *Dilshod,* and *Zokir* speak in the first person, and the authors' comments are only provided to explain and analyze the context. The sections that are direct comments made by *Dilshod* have [D] at the beginning, *Zokir*'s [Z], and the authors' [A].

'Survival strategies' of the traffic policeman

[D] It is not so easy to work as a traffic policeman in Uzbekistan. We have to communicate with more than a hundred people on a daily basis. We do not have fixed working hours. If you want to get a job with the traffic police, you have to pay a bribe, around 6,000-7,000 USD, to top officials in the traffic police. The biggest problem actually is that we do not get paid a salary for our work. The official salary for traffic policemen is 900,000 soum[10], but in fact, we do not receive any salary. In rare cases, we might receive 10 per cent of this salary, 100,000 soum. Of course, you may wonder how we survive. Here is the reality for you: Instead of paying a salary, our administration provides us with traffic tickets which we can sell to drivers to earn a salary.[11] We usually sell these tickets to drivers who drive without having their seat belt fastened and/or drive cars which do not meet technical safety standards. The price of one traffic ticket is 12,500 soum. So we earn our salary by selling traffic tickets to drivers. Since we do not get any salary, we are not required to return ticket receipts or reports to our administration and can keep the money made from the ticket sales.

This is not the end of the story. Our bosses give us the order (i.e. set the target) to sell at least twenty tickets per day. However, drivers do not violate traffic rules every day. How can we sell twenty tickets per day? If I do not sell twenty tickets per day, I might get a warning from the administration or even lose my job. Under these circumstances, we are under strong pressure to find drivers to sell tickets to. There is also an informal monthly payment called *gruz* (burden) which we have to pay directly into our bosses' pocket. The amount of this monthly payment ranges from 50,000 to 100,000 soums. We have to make this payment if we want to keep our job. These circumstances compel us to sell tickets even to drivers who act legally. Ordinary

10 Soum is the national currency of Uzbekistan. 1 USD was equal to 2,700 soum (black market rate) in June 2012.

11 The expression 'to sell tickets to drivers' is a slang expression widely used among traffic policemen in Ferghana meaning 'to impose a fine on drivers'.

people do not know about these problems and therefore hate us. It is politics. We cannot talk about these problems openly.

I know many people look upon the traffic police as the most corrupt profession in Uzbekistan. Since we do not receive any salary from the state for our work, the money we earn through selling tickets is completely legal. I am an ordinary man, like everybody else; I have a family, kids to feed! Instead of giving us a salary, our bosses force us to earn our salary through selling tickets to drivers. So tell me, how can I feed my kids when the state does not pay me any salary? If I received a normal salary, I would not bother selling tickets to law-abiding drivers.

[A] There are three main points that need to be elaborated on in this context. First, the interview shows the existence of a shared language among traffic policemen that serves to reconstruct the meaning and application of traffic laws. When describing his informal practices, the traffic policeman tends to use the expression 'selling tickets to drivers' rather than saying 'imposing a fine on drivers'. This expression also reveals that traffic police look at traffic tickets as a commodity for earning income rather than a means to enforce the state traffic laws. Thus, the linguistic representation is useful to understand the local context of informal transactions, as it reveals how the absence of formal income-earning opportunities influences the traffic police's moral code and legal culture.

Second, the traffic policeman's reasoning throws light on the functional role and meaning of bribery in Uzbekistan. His illicit practices are completely legal, he claims, since he does not receive any salary from the state for his arduous work. From a legal positivist perspective, these practices fall within the interpretation of corruption adapted from Western moral and juridical codes. Such interpretation is quite normal and legitimate in the context of Western welfare states where public authorities provide formal means of survival. But is it appropriate to interpret the policeman's actions as illicit in the context of Uzbekistan, where the state fails to pay even a basic salary to the traffic policeman? In the light of these problems, one conclusion could be that informal practices allow low-level state officials such as traffic policemen to survive in the absence of decent salaries. This situation reminds us of Abel Polese's (2008) anthropological study on Ukraine in which he concluded that corruption needs to be redefined, at least when dealing with cases in which it helps people to survive.

Third, it is also necessary to acknowledge the fact that corruption has different meanings and logic within different levels of society, and that there is a difference between large numbers of low-level officials on the one hand, and the smaller group of state elites on the other. During the interview, the traffic policeman expressed dissatisfaction with his working conditions and criticized the unreasonable demands of his administration. He frequently mentioned that he has to follow the unwritten rules (or living law in Ehrlich's terms) of his organization in order to keep his job. This leads us to argue that there is a need to distinguish between the informal practices of kleptocratic elites and the survival strategies of low-level officials who are dependent on informal coping strategies in order to survive.

If traffic police work is so risky, morally questionable and financially unrewarding there would seem to be a paradox – why do people bother to pay a 7,000 USD bribe to get a job with the traffic police? We were not able to find the answer to this question during the interview with *Dilshod*, the traffic policeman. To further understand the picture, we interviewed *Zokir*, a minibus driver who described how traffic policemen supplement their salary by 'pardoning' drivers in exchange for a small 'gift.'

Minibus driver: You have to make a distinction between 'good' and 'bad' bribery

[Z] As you know, there are different types of traffic violations such as speeding, red light crossing, driving under the influence of alcohol, etc. According to the law, if I am caught running a red light, the traffic police can fine me around 60,000 soum. If the traffic police stop me for exceeding the speed limit, I have to pay a fine of 100,000 soum[12]. Now I will tell you how I usually avoid paying fines when I am stopped by the traffic police. For example, if I am caught driving too fast, I will, of course, try to not pay the official fine. Instead, I put 15,000 soum into my car documents and hand them to the policeman, and apologize for driving a bit too fast. Obviously, the policeman is more interested in accepting my 'gift' (*kongildan chiqqani* in Uzbek) rather than following the law and giving me a speeding ticket. If

[12] Due to an extremely high inflation rate, Uzbek authorities annually raise the monthly minimum wage. This means that the increase of the monthly minimum wage automatically raises the amount of traffic fines, because fines are determined on the basis of the monthly minimum wage. Since we conducted interviews with informants in June 2012, fine amounts mentioned in this paper reflect the June 2012 levels.

I pay the official fine, all the money goes to the state budget and the policeman does not benefit from this transaction. I have heard they pay at least 5,000 USD in bribes to get a job with the traffic police. Many people say they have to please their bosses with nice gifts every month. They also have to feed their children. Of course, due to these circumstances, they have to earn extra money in order to cover these costs. Therefore the police gladly accept my 'gift' and do not give me a speeding ticket. Now let's work it out: The official fine for speeding is 100,000 soum, but I can get away with 15,000 soum. So this is a win-win situation as I save 85,000 soum and the policeman earns 15,000 soum for his family. As you see, bribery can also be a good thing. I would not use the word *pora* (bribe) in relation to these transactions, because I voluntarily offer a 'gift' to the policeman. So you have to make a distinction between 'good' and 'bad' bribery. An example of bad bribery would be if the police stopped me and forced me to pay when I was not breaking the law, then we can talk about real bribery. In this case, the police are abusing power. This is a bad bribe.

[A] This interview highlights two main issues. First, the minibus driver uses the expression 'gift' when describing his bribe to the policeman. This example indicates that the line between gift and bribe is very fluid in Uzbekistan, since the term 'gift' can be used in relation to the *toyana* that we described at weddings, as well as to informal transactions between state officials and citizens. Unlike in English, there is no single generic term for 'gift' in the Uzbek language, but there are numerous terms that are used depending on the context and type of event, such as *toyana, sovg'a, hadya, ko'rmana, suyunchi,* and *ko'ngildan chiqqani.* The gift-bribe dilemma has also been studied in the context of Ukraine (Polese 2008), Russia (Ledeneva 2009) and Kazakhstan (Werner 2000). For instance, Cynthia Werner's (2000) anthropological work also points to the blurred boundary between gift and bribe in Kazakhstan. She argues that the anti-corruption legislation promoted by powerful global organizations should be sensitive to local settings where gift exchange is an integral part of the culture. In that sense, our research seems to support the findings of previous research, suggesting that Western-centric interpretations should be re-contextualized when dealing with corruption in Uzbekistan and recognize local understandings of gifts, moral codes, and the values of informal transactions.

Second, the minibus driver makes a distinction between 'good' and 'bad' bribery. When making this distinction, he refers to the voluntary nature of the informal payment he makes to the police. According to his moral code, there is no element of bribery if he himself voluntarily offers a 'gift' to the police as compensation for a traffic law violation. As he himself states, this is a win-win transaction for both the driver and the policeman, since the former saves money, while the latter makes extra income for his family. At the same time, the driver uses the word 'bribe' in relation to 'gifts' he is forced to give, even though his actions are in compliance with the law. Nevertheless, both of the transactions described are punishable by law and interpreted as corruption in Uzbekistan's jurisprudence, as well as in Western juridical codes. According to Uzbek law, the voluntary nature of informal transactions between citizens and state officials does not influence their criminal nature. Thus the way the driver distinguishes between 'good' and 'bad' bribery indicates the existence of dual morality in bribery, and reveals the multifaceted meaning and morality of informal transactions in Uzbekistan. A similar situation has also been described in Johan Rasanayagam's study (2011) in which he, through an ethnographic case study of a local teacher in Uzbekistan, showed the clashes between local morality and legal norms where the teacher believed that a 'little corruption' does not hurt anyone.

Previous studies have argued that illicit practices persist in post-Soviet societies because they are deeply embedded in cultural practices and local understandings of esteem and self-worth (e.g. Abramson 2000; Humphrey 2002, 2012; Patico 2002; Wanner 2005; Polese 2008). In the context of Russia, Caroline Humphrey (2002, 146) showed that 'the bribe is not in essence just a payment for a commodity or service but it is also recognition of a person's socio-political nonmarket status.'

These insights have been confirmed during our ethnographic field research in Uzbekistan, in 2009. What follows is a note relating to one incident we experienced in Uzbekistan while travelling by taxi from Tashkent to the Ferghana Valley. There is only route to the Ferghana Valley via a mountain pass called *Kamchik.* Since the *Kamchik* is the only route connecting the Fergana to the rest of Uzbekistan, it is heavily guarded, and there are many checkpoints where police and border officials check passports. A large number of traffic police are also to be seen at the *Kamchik* pass. When we reached the pass, the driver asked us to unbuckle our seat belts, as it was uncommon at that time to use seatbelts, and the traffic police did not impose any fine for driving without seat belts.[13] Thus any use of seat belts by a driver or passengers would be a clear signal that there was a foreigner/non-native in the car, which might easily attract the attention of the traffic police, always seeking reasons to stop cars. In requesting us not to use the seat belts, the driver was actually trying to avoid any unnecessary attention from the police. However, out of concern for his personal safety, Måns Svensson, the second, Swedish author of this paper, did not unfasten his seat belt. As the driver predicted, our car was soon stopped by the traffic police. As usual, they checked the driver's documents. Due to the presence of a foreign citizen in the car, the police also wanted to check the car's luggage compartment. Måns Svensson, suspicious of the actions of the police, demanded that he must be present during the policeman's checks. This was an open challenge to the traffic policeman's traditional authority. Trying to avoid conflict with a foreign citizen, the policeman decided not to check the luggage compartment and politely asked Måns Svensson to sit in the car. The policeman then ordered the driver to follow him to his small office to discuss some minor details in his car documents. After ten minutes, the driver returned to the car with an angry face and told us that he had to pay 15,000 soum because of Måns Svensson's failure to 'show respect' towards the policeman. Not wanting the driver to take the consequences for his action, Måns Svensson later covered his losses.

This incident provides useful insights into local meanings of informal transactions in Uzbekistan. The power of the traffic police is rarely challenged in Uzbekistan, and ordinary people always show absolute obedience when they interact with the police. Unlike in the West, when stopped by the police, citizens in Uzbekistan get out of their car and hand over documents to the policeman, addressing him as 'commander.' Thus relations between the traffic police and citizens are very hierarchical. As we described in previous sections, such hierarchical relations between citizens and state officials can also be observed in non-state arenas such as weddings, where 'people of influence' get the best tables. As a foreigner, Måns Svensson was unaware of local social norms and hierarchies (or 'living law' in Ehrlich's terms). By demanding to be present during the luggage check he challenged the traditional power of the policeman to dictate the rules. According to Uzbek law, Måns Svensson's actions were entirely legal. However, from a

[13] Seat belt use was not mandatory in Uzbekistan until 2010.

'living law' perspective, his actions were not consistent with prevalent social norms and hierarchies, which indirectly resulted in the imposition of a 15,000 soum fine. Consequently this incident may provide a starting point for us to reconsider the nature and context of other informal transactions in Uzbekistan, and to view transactions not so much as illicit, but more as providing insight into the manifestations of social norms, hierarchies, status contestations, and coping strategies. Therefore, when measuring corruption in societies such as Uzbekistan, emphasis should also be placed on the recalcitrant complexity of local social life and hierarchies which assign cultural meaning to informal transactions that may be different from those in the West.

Discussion and conclusions

The aim of this study was to explore the multifaceted meaning, logic, and morality of informal transactions in order to better understand the social context that informs the meaning of corruption and bribery in Uzbekistan. In doing so, we questioned the validity of Western-centric interpretations of corruption and recognized the need to consider local context and moral codes, thereby providing additional tools for re-contextualizing corruption through the concept of 'living law.' The ethnographic data on wedding ceremonies and two informal interviews were analyzed in order to describe and understand the local perceptions of moral codes and the values of informal transactions.

We used evidence from wedding ceremonies to show the local relationship to money and how this could undermine Western-centric interpretations of corruption. Our aim was to show the underlying social norms, moral codes, and local perceptions in order to describe a society where corruption occurs. The wedding example suggests that talking of corruption in a place where money has a different social function may not be appropriate. Accordingly, in a place such as Uzbekistan where money is used with a meaning that may be different from the one in the West, corruption should be re-contextualized.

One could argue that the connection between social practices in weddings, and corruption, is too tenuous. The reader might wish that we had carried out observations of actual corruption in order to note the parallels in structure and meaning, of exchanges at weddings, and corruption in public transactions, thereby demonstrating the relation rather than surmising it. In regard to this, the ethnographic data was complemented with two informal interviews that dealt directly with informal transactions in state arenas. As our results indicate, there is a need to make a distinction between the informal practices of kleptocratic elites, which have nothing to do with 'survival', and the informal coping strategies of the ordinary citizens and low-level officials (i.e. 'corruption of the weak'). In other words, a bribe given to top state officials to keep the monopoly on a sector is not the same as a small payment to a low-level traffic policeman. But they are both classified as corruption by a number of international reports (e.g. TI 2012). We suggest that there may be reasons to re-evaluate the validity of Western-centric interpretations when talking about and measuring corruption in the context of Uzbekistan, and possibly other Central Asian countries.

Our results can be summarised in three points: (a) informal transactions are deeply embedded in cultural practices; (b) not all informal transactions are corrupt; and (c) when talking about, or measuring, corruption, social norms, moral codes, and local perceptions should be considered. If these are not taken into consideration, informal transactions that are not corrupt run the risk of being labelled as illicit. 'Corruption' is an overly general term, which often simply masks the fact that sets of different rules are competing with those of the state. Similar points have been made before by scholars such as Werner (2000), Humphrey (2002) and Polese (2008). In that sense, our research could be said to empirically support the findings of previous research which has called for a more nuanced view at a grass-roots level of informal transactions in developing countries. Our research differs in one respect from previous research by exploring informal transactions in both non-state and state arenas through Ehrlich's concept of 'living law.' By utilizing this concept, we underline the importance of understanding the 'living law' of the society in which corruption is being discussed and/or measured.

Even though the state in Uzbekistan might look omnipotent because of its infrastructural and coercive capacity, our fieldwork suggests that it has limited meaning in everyday life at the local level. The decline of the Soviet-type welfare state has spurred the informalization of state, society, and lifeworlds in Uzbekistan, since both ordinary citizens and state officials in Fergana have become increasingly dependent on informal coping strategies for gaining a livelihood. In the introduction to this chapter, we state that we accept the definition of 'corruption' as Transparency International describes it: 'corruption is the abuse of entrusted power for private gain.' However, we also stress the need to focus on the key word 'abuse' from the point of view of a sociological understanding of the specific cultural context in which corruption is seen. Our study has shown that informal transactions that are considered to be corruption in a Western-centric interpretation have little to do with abuse. Rather, informal coping strategies are incorporated into Uzbek culture as a rational way of 'getting things done.' Hence, anti-corruption measures are not simply a matter of getting people to obey the law. They are, more importantly, about promoting socio-economic change.

References

Abramson, David MacKenzie (2000), Constructing Corruption: Foreign Aid, Bureaucratization, and Uzbek Social Networks. Unpublished paper presented at Harvard University.

Agadjanian, Victor, and Makarova, Ekaterina (2003), From Soviet Modernization to Post-Soviet Transformation: Understanding Marriage and Fertility Dynamics in Uzbekistan. *Development and Change* 34:447-473.

Annaklychev, Shikhberdy (1984), The Wedding Ceremonies of Turkmen Workers. In: Tamara Dragadze (ed.), *Kinship and Marriage in the Soviet Union. Field Studies*. London and Boston: Routledge and Kegan Paul, pp. 15-39.

Barnett, Homer Garner (1938), The Nature of the Potlatch. *American Anthropologist* 40:349-358.

Bates, Daniel G. (1974), Normative and Alternative Systems of Marriage among the Yörük of South-eastern Turkey. *Anthropological Quarterly* 47:270-287.

Becker, Kristina Flodman (2004), *SIDA Fact Finding Study: The Informal Economy*. SIDA: Stockholm.

Borozna, Nella G. (1984), Some Features of the Traditional Wedding Ceremony of the Uzbek-Durmen of the Southern Raions of Tadzhikistan and Uzbekistan. In: Tamara Dragadze (ed.), *Kinship and Marriage in the Soviet Union. Field Studies*. London and Boston: Routledge and Kegan Paul, pp. 60-73.

Critchlow, James (1988), Corruption, Nationalism, and the Native Elites in Central Asia. *The Journal of Communist Studies* 4:142-61.

Deflem, Mathieu (2008), *Sociology of Law: Visions of a Scholarly Tradition*. Cambridge: Cambridge University Press.

Ehrlich, Eugen (1912/1967), Das lebende Recht der Völker der Bukowina. Reprinted in *Eugen Ehrlich, Recht und Leben*, edited by Manfred Rehbinder, Berlin: Duncker & Humblot, pp. 43-60.

Ehrlich, Eugen (2002), *Fundamental Principles of the Sociology of Law*, translated by Walter L. Moll, New Brunswick/London: Transaction Publishers.

Eppinger, Monica (2009), Governing in the Vernacular: Eugen Ehrlich and Late Habsburg Ethnography. In: Marc Hertogh (ed.), *Living Law: Reconsidering Eugen Ehrlich*. Oxford and Portland, OR: Hart Publishing, pp. 21-48.

Geertz, Clifford (1973), *The Interpretation of Cultures*. New York: Basic Books.

Gibson-Graham (Julie Graham and Katherine Gibson) (2006), *The End Of Capitalism (As We Knew It): A Feminist Critique of Political Economy*. Minneapolis, MN: University of Minnesota Press.

Gibson-Graham, Julie Katherine (2008), Diverse Economies: Performative Practices for 'Other Worlds'. *Progress in Human Geography* 32:613-632.

Gleason, Gregory (1995), Corruption, Decolonization and Development in Central Asia. *European Journal on Criminal Policy and Research* 3:38-47.

Gupta, Akhil (1995), Blurred Boundaries: the Discourse of Corruption, the Culture of Politics, and the Imagined State. *American Ethnologist* 22:375-402.

Harrison, Graham (1999), Corruption, development theory and the boundaries of social change. *Contemporary Politics*, 5:207-220.

Hertogh, Marc (ed., 2009), *Living Law: Reconsidering Eugen Ehrlich*. Oxford and Portland, OR: Hart Publishing.

Holmes, Leslie (1997), Corruption and the Crisis of the Post-Communist State. *Crime, Law and Social Change* 27:275-297.

Humphrey, Caroline (2002), *The Unmaking of Soviet Life: Everyday Economies after Socialism*. Ithaca, NY: Cornell University Press.

Humphrey, Caroline (2012), Favors and "Normal Heroes": The Case of Postsocialist Higher Education. *HAU: Journal of Ethnographic Theory* 2, No. 2:22-41.

Humphrey, Caroline and Sneath, David Andrews (2004), Shanghaied By the Bureaucracy: Bribery and Post-Soviet Officialdom in Russia and Mongolia. In: Italo Pardo (ed.), *Between Morality and the Law: Corruption, Anthropology, and Comparative Society*. Aldershot: Ashgate, pp. 85-99.

Hydén, Goran (2006), *African Politics in Comparative Perspective*. New York: Cambridge University Press.

Ilkhamov, Alisher (2004), The Limits of Centralization: Regional Challenges in Uzbekistan. In: Pauline Jones Luong (ed.), *The Transformation of Central Asia. States and Societies from Soviet Rule to Independence*. Ithaca, NY: Cornell University Press, pp. 159-181.

Ilkhamov, Alisher (2007), Neopatrimonialism, Interest Groups and Patronage Networks: The Impasses of the Governance System in Uzbekistan. *Central Asian Survey* 26:65-84.

Kandiyoti, Deniz (1998), Rural Livelihoods and Social Networks in Uzbekistan: Perspectives from Andijan. *Central Asian Survey* 17:561-578.

Kandiyoti, Deniz (2007), Post-Soviet Institutional Design and the Paradoxes of the Uzbek Path. *Central Asian Survey* 26:31-48.

Kandiyoti, Deniz and Azimova, Nadira (2004), The Communal and the Sacred: Women's World of Ritual in Uzbekistan. *Royal Anthropological Institute* 10:327-349.

Kaufmann, Daniel, Kraay, Aart, and Mastruzzi, Massimo (2004), Governance Matters III: Governance Indicators for 1996, 1998, 2000, and 2002. World Bank Policy Research Working Paper No. 3106. Washington D.C: The World Bank.

Knack, S. (2006), *Measuring Corruption in Eastern Europe and Central Asia: A Critique of the Cross-Country Indicators*. Washington, D.C: World Bank.

Kurkchiyan, Marina (2000), The Transformation of the Second Economy into the Informal Economy. In: Alena Ledeneva and Marina Kurkchiyan (eds.), *Economic Crime in Russia*. London: Kluwer Law International, pp. 83-97.

Larsson, Stefan (2013), Sociology of Law in a Digital Society – A Tweet from Global Bukowina. *Societas/Communitas, The Institute for Applied Social Sciences, University of Warsaw* 15,, 1.

Ledeneva, Alena (1998), *Russia's Economy of Favors: "Blat", Networking and Informal Exchange*. Cambridge: Cambridge University Press.

Ledeneva, Alena (2009), From Russia with Blat: Can Informal Networks Help Modernize Russia? *Social Research: An International Quarterly* 76:257-288.

Mandel, Ruth and Humphrey, Caroline (2002). *Markets and Moralities: Ethnographies of Postsocialism*. Oxford: Berg.

Markowitz, Lawrence P. (2008), Local Elites, Prokurators and Extraction in Rural Uzbekistan. *Central Asian Survey* 27:1-14.

Mauss, Marcell. (1924), *The Gift: Forms and Functions of Exchange in Archaic Societies*. London: Routledge.

Mundy, Martha (1995), *Domestic Government. Kinship, Community and Polity in North Yemen*. London and New York: I.B. Tauris.

Nelken, David (1984), Law in Action or Living Law? Back to the Beginning in Sociology of Law. *Legal Studies* 4:157-174.

Nelken, David (2008), Eugen Ehrlich, Living Law, and Plural Legalities. *Theoretical Inquiries in Law* 9:443-471.

O'Day, James F. (1966), Ehrlich's Living Law Revisited –Further Vindication for a Prophet without Honor. *Western Reserve Law Review* 18:210-231.

Parry, Jonathan and Bloch, Maurice (1989), *Money and the Morality of Exchange*. Cambridge: Cambridge University Press.

Patico, Jennifer (2002), Chocolate and Cognac: Gifts and the Recognition of Social Worlds in Post-Soviet Russia. *Ethnos* 67:345-368.

Peters, L. Emrys, Goody, Jack, and Emanuel, Marx (1990), *The Bedouin of Cyrenaica. Studies in Personal and Corporate Power*. New York: Cambridge University Press.

Piddocke, Stuart (1965), The Potlatch System of the Southern Kwakiutl: A New Perspective. *Southwestern Journal of Anthropology* 21:244-264.

Polese, Abel (2008), "If I Receive It, It Is a Gift; If I Demand It, Then It Is a Bribe": On the Local Meaning of Economic Transactions in Post-Soviet Ukraine. *Anthropology in Action* 15, No. 3:47-60.

Rasanayagam, Johan (2011). Informal Economy, Informal State: The Case of Uzbekistan. *International Journal of Sociology and Social Policy* 31 No. 11/12:681-696.

Ries, Nancy (2002), "Honest Bandits" and "Warped People": Russian Narratives about Money, Corruption, and Moral Decay. In: Carol J. Greenhouse, Elizabeth Mertz, and Kay B. Warren (eds.), *Ethnography in Unstable Places: Everyday Lives in Contexts of Dramatic Political Change*. Durham, NC: Duke University Press, pp. 276-315.

Simis, K.M. (1982), *USSR: The Corrupt Society*, translated by Jacqueline Edwards and Mitchell Schneider. New York: Simon and Schuster.

Sneath, David Andrews (2006), Transacting and Enacting: Corruption, Obligation and the Use of Monies in Mongolia. *Ethnos* 71:89-112.

Srubar, I. (1991), War der Reale Sozialismus modern? Versuch einer strukturellen Bestimmung. *Kölner Zeitschrift für Soziologie und Sozialpsychologie* 43:415-432.

Staples, John (1993), Soviet Use of Corruption Purges as a Control Mechanism: The Uzbekistan Case. *Past Imperfect* 2:29-48.

Svensson, Måns (2013), Norms in Law and Society: Towards a Definition of the Socio-Legal Concept of Norms. In: Matthias Baier (ed.), *Social and Legal Norms*. Farnham: Ashgate.

Tanzi, Vito (1998), *Corruption Around the World: Causes, Consequences, Scopes and Cures*. Washington DC: International Monetary Fund.

Teubner, Gunther (1997), Global Bukowina: Legal Pluralism in the World-Society. In: Gunther Teubner (ed.), *Global Law without a State*. Brookfield: Dartmouth, pp. 3-28.

The Community Economies Collective (2001), Imagining and Enacting Non-capitalist Futures. *Socialist Review* 28 No. 3:93-135.

Thomas, Nicholas (1991), *Entangled Objects: Exchange, Material Culture, and Colonialism in the Pacific*. Cambridge, Mass: Harvard University Press.

Transparency International (2012), Corruption Perceptions Index 2012. Available from: http://www.transparency.org/cpi2012/results#myAnchor2 [Accessed 23 January 2012].

Trevisani, Tommaso (2007), After the Kolkhoz: Rural Elites in Competition. *Central Asian Survey* 26:85-104.

Urinboyev, Rustamjon (2011), Law, Social Norms and Welfare as Means of Public Administration: Case Study of Mahalla Institutions in Uzbekistan. *The NISPAcee Journal of Public Administration and Policy*, 4, No. 1:33-57.

Urinboyev, Rustamjon (2013), Living Law and Political Stability in Post-Soviet

Central Asia. A Case Study of the Ferghana Valley in Uzbekistan. Ph.D. Dissertation, Lund University, Lund.

Urinboyev, Rustamjon, and Svensson, Måns (2013), Corruption in a Culture of Money: Understanding Social Norms in Post-Soviet Uzbekistan. In: Matthias Baier (ed.), *Social and Legal Norms*. Farnham: Ashgate.

Wanner, Catherine (2005), Money, Morality and New Forms of Exchange in Post-socialist Ukraine. *Ethnos* 70:515-537.

Wegerich, Kai (2006), "A Little Help from My Friend?" Analysis of Network Links on the Meso Level in Uzbekistan. *Central Asian Survey* 25:115-128.

Werner, Cynthia Ann (1997), Women and the Art of Household Networking in Rural Kazakstan. *The Islamic Quarterly* 61, No. 1: 52-68.

Werner, Cynthia Ann (2000), Gifts, Bribes, and Development in Post-Soviet Kazakstan. *Human Organization* 59:11-22.

White, Jenny B. (1994), *Money Makes Us Relatives: Women's Labor in Urban Turkey*. Austin, TX: University of Texas Press.

World Bank (2012), Workers in the Informal Economy. Available from: http://web.worldbank.org/WBSITE/EXTERNAL/TOPICS/EXTSOCIALPROTECTION/EXTLM/0,,contentMDK:20224904$\sim$menuPK:584866$\sim$pagePK:148956$\sim$piPK:216618$\sim$theSitePK:390615,00.html [Accessed 3 August 2012].

Yalçin-Heckmann, Lale (2001), The Political Economy of an Azeri Wedding. *Max Planck Institute for Social Anthropology Working Papers*, No. 28.

Zemtsov, Ilya (1991), *Encyclopedia of Soviet Life*. Transaction Publishers.

Eugen Ehrlich's Passion

Ehrlich's Passion: Bukovina Traditional Textiles

Olga LITVINOVA

As we know so little about Eugen Ehrlich's private life, it is all the more interesting to look at those details we have. One aspect of the life of the creator of the "Living law" theory was his passion for collecting traditional Bukovina embroidery and tapestry (Rottleuthner 1992, 2). The objects had great value for him. During the First World War, when Chernivtsi, then part of the Austrian-Hungarian Empire, was suddenly threatened by the Russian advance, Ehrlich took his collection to his new home and kept it there for the rest of his life. He was very anxious that it should be in safe hands after his death. Strong evidence for this is the fact that in his will, he invited a certain person "to choose something from my embroidery collection" after his death (Ehrlich 1999, 2)[1]. Since the collection is mentioned along with his savings and his library, which were also to go to his heirs, it can be assumed that all three things had a similar to value for Ehrlich as he lay on his deathbed.

Unfortunately Ehrlich's collection of Bukovina traditional textiles was dispersed long ago. It would seem impossible to know which of the items he had collected were his favourites and how many he had. Nevertheless, if we define in general terms the characteristics of the local textiles and their role in traditional life, we can understand the most significant features of this cultural phenomenon. This will throw additional light on their admirer and collector, Eugen Ehrlich, who lived in Chernivtsi a century ago. It will give us a clearer idea of his social environment.

The XIXth century Bukovina traditional textiles collected by Eugen Ehrlich and others, were ornamented. Ornaments are defined as symbols "based on a developed semantic system derived from the repetition of signs with or without a composition centre" (Naiden and Selivachov 1993, n.p.). While in the Middle Ages ornamented costumes were a sign the wearer belonged to the privileged class (Rybakov 1987, 22), in XIXth century Bukovina ornament became a feature of everyday peasant cloth (Kozhol-

[1] Translations from German, Ukrainian and Russian sources by the author, Olga Litvinova.

janko 2010, n.p.). Although in general terms Ukrainian and Romanian people in Bukovina had the same traditional costume (Kupchanko 1875, 63; Lagov 1915, 67; Vovk 1928, 166), there were some distinguishing features in the details of the way they were embellished. A common characteristic of all traditional shirts and dresses was the prevalence of elaborate embroidery on the textile object. This is a case, which Wassily Kandinsky's (1908/1977, 47) words fit perfectly: "the power of ornament is expressed with such effort, that it seems the object itself is 'dissolving' in it".[2]

The most outstanding is the clothes ornamentation of the Carpathian Hutsul subethnos. Irrespective of how they are woven and embroidered, the garments display the following geometric motifs: even, angular or zigzag lone or parallel lines, single crosses and combined crosses, squares with 8-ray stars or crosses inside, or rhombuses with crosses or circles (Franko 1985, 475). The most common Hutsul decorations look like "XOX" or "OXO" or some variation of these (Shukhevych 1908, 230). The patterns usually combine crosses with a circle shape, "O". The "O" and "X" signs were used by pagans for protective purposes and also to invoke spiritual forces (Gonzales-Wippler 2001, 147 and 150). "O" very likely meant the sun, "colo", a cult object for all ancient Slavs (Ivanova 1983, 106).

While Carpathians adorned textiles with geometrical motifs only, the peasants on the Bukovina plains added to these plant, animal or anthropomorphic motifs (Kobaljchinsjka 2008, 88). The proportion of geometrical and non-geometrical motifs in the embellishment of clothes and rugs, and the emphases of the motifs differed from area to area. However, there is a motif that appears everywhere: rhombuses with small symmetric hooks on the up and down corners, which were called "the little sheep horns" (Fediv 2013, n.p.).

Of particular interest were the traditional embroidered non-geometrical images – namely flowers, butterflies, birds and leaves – which were always clearly recognisable (Mozdalevskij 1918, 19). The usual motif on the embroidered ritual towels was and still is the mythical Arbor Vitae (tree of

[2] In the summer of 1889 Wassily Kandinsky, the founder of modern abstract painting, was a student of law and ethnography and studied customary law in the Northern Russian Vologda province (Duechting 1991, 9). As Nina Kandinsky (1999, 35) records, he was fascinated by the wealth of magnificent folk ornaments that he encountered during the expedition, and this was a key factor in his decision to change his career.

life), "symbolizing life binding together Heaven, Earth and Netherworld" (Lehner and Lehner 1960, 20).

Up to the 1960s home-made Bukovina wool yarn was dyed with natural pigments found locally (Zhuk 1966, 23). The colour most frequently used, whether on textiles or, for example, on Easter eggs, is cherry red. Besides red, the commonest colours have always been blue, green, orange-yellow, yellow, intense pink, lemon yellow, sand, terracotta, purple, dark or pale grey, brown and black (Kupchanko 1875, 18; Tkachuk 2013, n.p.).

If we assume that in 1914 the people living in those 396 Bukovina villages inhabited by Ukrainians or Romanians (Baladyzhenko 1915, 14) all had their own local embroidery or weaving designs and that on top of that, every artisan had her own taste and style, there must have been a considerable number of embroidery patterns. Residents of various Bukovina towns and areas had recognizable embroidery designs, which exhibited at the same time a "need for integration", and a "need for separation," defined by Ehrlich's contemporary Simmel (1905/1997, 191) as two contradictory functions of any fashion. Today the records of the past (postcards and period photographs) show how differently Bukovinians dressed[3].

Ancient Bukovina folk songs, particularly those edited by Jury Fedkovych (1865, reprint 1968) and Alexander Lonachevskij (1875) convey information about embroidery and tapestry customs and design. For example, one song describes three traditional embroidery techniques used on men's shirts (Lonachevskij 1875, 90-91). About 120 different stitches were used in the embroideries on dresses (Semchuk 2007, n.p.), more than a quarter of the 449 existing around the world (Eaton 1986, 169). Ehrlich demonstrated his knowledge of the techniques when he likened two different legal codes to plain canvas and completed embroidery (Rehbinder 1986, 17).

Every artisan had her own special embroidery design (Mozdalevskij 1918, 18; Musatova 2008, 186; Jakovleva 2006, 34). Typical distinguishing features of embroidery and tapestry patterns were references to the social group – to the people of an area, ethnos or town, and also to the gender, age, family status and other characteristics of a particular person (Konovalova 2009, n.p.). Nowadays as in the past, Bukovinians embellish clothing with typical "male" and "female" motifs.[4] Thus each embroidered object

[3] See for example the website of the Czernowitz-L Discussion Group: http://czernowitz.ehpes.com/, last accessed 7 June 2014.

[4] Oak leaves and acorns, cornflowers, wine, images of hops etc. for men's clothes and

can be seen as an individual social logogram of its owner. In addition, the embroidery may depend on the purpose of the embellished object and on the meaning of the motifs, known to locals and hidden to the outsider.

What is common to all the needlework of the area is the tasteful combination of colours and the highest level of technical perfection. So, Ehrlich's collection would have contained ornamented textiles: woven and embroidered. It is highly likely that he was given some as presents by his Bukovina friends. Without doubts Ehrlich, a native of Chernivtsy, met every day people wearing picturesque costumes and headdresses. He could have got information about the design, origin and meaning of embroidery first hand from the people who owned it, or those who made it. For Ehrlich (1936/2002, 26), society consisted of associations. In his writings, Ehrlich contrasts the paucity of codified state law with the richness of the living law which people actually develop to organize the life of their associations. On the streets of Chernivtsy the associations were visible in their ornamented clothes and accessories.

In Ehrlich's time special decorated textiles were used by Bukovina locals in all significant family events. Weddings are a prime example. Ehrlich never married (Rehbinder 1986, 16) and lived with his mother, but must have known about the picturesque and noisy local weddings. According to Vovk (1928, 283), for the three-day wedding festivity, the local church and all the rooms in the groom's house were decorated with embroidered artefacts and ritual flowers, twigs and herbs. The bride and groom wore homemade embroidered wedding clothes that had special significance. About 40 ornamented ritual towels, each 3.5 metres long, were used in various ways: icons were decorated with them; the couple returning from church were greeted with bread and salt on one of them; they were also draped cross-wise over the shoulders of the most honoured guests: parents, grandparents, siblings, godparents, best friends, friends, and a designated relative whose function it was to keep order and morals during the festivities. At the wedding the bride distributed ornamented textiles among the guests: handkerchiefs, tablecloths, bed linen, headdresses etc. In the Bukovina, a richly ornamented carpet was laid in front of the altar, on the spot where the priest declared the couple husband and wife. The carpet was either made by the

viburnum, roses, hollyhocks, lilies etc. for women's clothes (Marusik-Zhmendak 2009, n.p.).

bride herself or inherited (Pezhansjkij 1925, 14). "Standing on the carpet" was used as synonym for marriage in Bukovina folk poetry. Instead of exchanging rings, the couple on the carpet had their elbows bound together by the priest with an embroidered towel (Fedkovych 1865/1968, 23). Again, this was a synonym for marriage in local songs (Fedkovych 1865/1968, 118-120).

Making ornamental items for her future family kept the girl busy throughout her childhood and adolescence (Vovk 1928, 250). After the wedding, the rooms were decorated with tapestry, and embroidered towels – "ryshnyk" – covered the home icons (Osadcha 2010, n.p.). Ornamented carpets and towels are still used today in Ukrainian and Romanian ceremonies.

Like other Christian rituals, baptisms were marked by much use of embroidered textiles. For example, the child's special robe was embroidered by the godmother. The godfather also wore a newly embroidered shirt given by the child's mother (Marusik-Zhmendak 2009, n.p.). Instead of money, the church was given a richly ornamented towel or carpet. As these were later put on permanent display in the church, every family tried to outdo its neighbours. It was sincerely believed that, family and friends would be rewarded by God for producing finely made artefacts for the church (Lonachevskij 1875, 206; Grinchenko 1900, 6).

Embellished textiles also had a prominent place in traditional funerals. If a peasant passed away, the open coffin was put on display in front of the home altar's icons, on a table covered with an ornamented kylym (a flat-woven wool tapestry). The body was dressed in traditionally ornamented clothes, and lay on a cushion embroidered with crosses. An ornamented wool runner was placed under the feet. Tkachuk (2013, n.p.) explains that it symbolized a "safe bridge to the peaceful hereafter". When the coffin was finally carried out it was also covered by an embellished tapestry (Golubezj 1936, 5). If an unmarried Hutsul male died, his horse was covered with an ornamented kylym and led to the grave behind the funeral procession (Shukhevych 1908, 122). When going out of the house to the cemetery the last person in the funeral procession fixed the gate with an embroidered towel "to prevent the dead body from coming back" (Vovk 1928, 71). On the way to the cemetery, the large wooden crucifix carried in front of the procession was decorated with a long white linen towel depicting an Arbor Vitae. If it was a woman's funeral, this towel was often her own needlework (Grinchenko 1900, 28). During the funeral, the coffin was lowered into the grave on two embroidered linen towels, each of them up to 20 metres long. Finally the linen towels were cut up, and the mourners wore pieces around their upper arms when they returned to the home of the dead person for the ritual meal (Vovk 1928, 175).

Obviously, in the past, every Bukovina peasant family needed a great many decorated textiles. There were however, certain calendar limitations on weaving, sewing and embroidering. On Fridays and Sundays during the two weeks between New Year and the Orthodox Christmas, at Easter, and on other important holy days, it was absolutely taboo to do any needlework. If the prohibition was violated, the work would be poor and, therefore, resources would be wasted (Grinchenko 1900, 39). People even believed that bad weather could result when badly made textiles were sacrificed to the gods of the elements (Grinchenko 1900, 32 and 6).

The abundant use of ornamented objects in Bukovina Christian rituals is plausibly explained by scholars as a reflection of pagan beliefs in the magic power of ornaments (Shukhevych 1908, 124; Vovk 1928, 173-174). The Orthodox Church had no option but to allow them. By contrast Judaism, excluded any ornamentation, because of its strict monotheism, observed since ancient times (Riegl 1899/2004, 312). Ehrlich grew up in his parents' Jewish house, but he later converted to Catholicism[5]. This may have heightened his attention to cultural differences.

As the theorist of the "living law", Ehrlich's attention was also drawn to customs. Bukovina pagan customs were intimately connected with the use of ornamented textiles by the peasantry. For example, a key function was given to ornamented cloth in the Ukrainian pagan ritual performed when a newly-bought cow was led to the farm. The lady of the house had to take off an ornamented apron or head scarf and lay it down for the cow to walk over into the yard. Krasikov (2010, n.p.) says the ornamented cloth symbolizes the bridge to a new, peaceful home, and the fact that the cow will be treated like a member of the family. The Hutsuls have a similar ritual at the start of the grazing season: when the young calves and lambs are moved to the meadows for the first time, they are led over an ornamented wool runner in order "make them wish to return" (Grinchenko 1900, 70).

At the beginning of the XXth century the Bukovina peasantry firmly be-

[5] Rehbinder 1986, 14, Ehrlich's Jewish background is further discussed in Hanne Petersen's article in this volume.

lieved in the magic power of their traditional ornaments. Thus the wooden beams of the stables, and door frames were carved with protective ornamental "XOX" signs (Vlad 1983, 5). Even in recent years, this "XOX" pattern is seen woven into and embroidered on textiles or painted on Easter eggs. The pattern is even pressed onto pieces of home-made butter or cheese taken to the church on Easter Sunday to be blessed (Gajova 2013, n.p.). It is interesting to note the desire for double security: that of the pagan ritual ornamentation followed by Christian blessing. There is other evidence of the persistence of pagan pre-Christian rituals, for example cattle, pets and even family members being led through "sacred smoke" on New Year morning to keep away "dark powers." Even in recent times some people in Ukrainian and Romanian Bukovina villages carry on with the pagan ritual (Moisej 2009, 188).

Ancient peoples have seen female sex appeal as analogical to the fertility of the soil (Tokarev 1983, 98). Similarly Bukovinians believed soil fertility increased, through the erotic attraction of women in which ornamented costume played a part. In 1859, a local explained to an ethnographer that women visiting their husbands working in the fields would take care to wear beautifully decorated clothes in order to maximize the grain or flax yield (Grinchenko 1900, 16). Other horticultural rituals also show pagan belief in the magic power of ornamenttation to increase yields. In Ukrainian and Romanian mythology, all plants, particularly trees, have souls and an experienced gardener assisted by a small grandchild would threaten underperforming trees with a "tree frightening" ritual. The child climbed high up the tree while the gardener abused the tree at length for being infertile despite his good care. Wielding an axe, he then threatened to cut the tree down. Impersonating the soul of the tree, the grandchild would start crying, begging to be spared, and promising full performance in the next harvest. As if it were going to be crucified, the tree had long nails hammered into its trunk, or was slightly cut with the axe. Finally, the gardener and the child together bandage the wounds with an ornamented scarf (Voropai 1958, 111-112).

A great many ornamented textiles were needed in the "Green week" before the Trinity festivities. Female spirits of the waters, fields and forests, "rusalki", hidden at other times of the year, had embroidered cloths sacrificed to them (Grinchenko 1900, 116-118). The "rusalki" were believed to be the embodied souls of virgins who had died on the eve of their marriage

(Shukhevych 1908, 199). According to folklore, "rusalki are young, tall, seductively beautiful … At night during the 'Green Week' they swim naked or walk on land in long white robes. They … do their utmost to attract real living males, because they are very bored without them" (Dalj 1880, 58). For forest and water maids, "living" in the tree tops or in the water, embroidered cloths, 80 cm wide and several metres long, were hung down from the tips of tree branches. They would to be used at night by the maidens who would swing on them, jump to the ground and then walk around the villages (Grinchenko 1900, 117; Vovk 1928, 68). During the "Green week" the field maidens, who according to Ukrainian legend plant wild flowers in spring, received food served on beautifully decorated towels at the edges of fields (Voropai 1959, 258). The village girls hoped to encounter the mysterious maidens at night and to ask them for beauty (Gozaljuk 2008, n.p.). Young men also wished to see the wonderful creatures, although they were told that the female spirits, while liking to make love to them might also tickle them to death or drown them (Grinchenko 1900, 118; Gozaljuk 2008, n.p.). As a protective measure men were warned not to go into the forest or along the river alone. If they encountered an amorous "rusalka" they were advised to immediately turn their shirt inside out, so that the embroidered side was next to the skin (Vlad 1983, 16). A local ethnographer gives another example of the protective use of an ornamented textile by Hutsul forestry workers in a similar situation. They often spent nights in the woods, the supposed dwelling place of the seductive female spirits ("nichnyzy") which caused the erotic nightmare. The advice given to any young man suffering from erotic nightmares during the lonely night in the forest was that he should "firstly, immediately wake up, if he was asleep, sniff the sprig of oregano, which men always had tucked into their belts, and then, in the morning, before the cockerels began to crow, he should savagely beat his own legs with his ornamented Hutsul belt" (Shukhevych 1908, 199). Ornamented items were thus both the means to attract mythical spirits and also to escape their power.

Even in legal disputes the power of ornaments was assumed to be beneficial. When Ehrlich was in the Bukovina, there were such Hutsul customs as that of visiting a church the day before a court hearing. There a man would tear up his embroidered shirt. Another way of ensuring that one appeared believable in court was to tear up red wool yarn in front of the altar (Shukhevych 1908, 228). In the past, the traditional ornaments of pieces of clothing functioned as personal amulets. Embroideries were used in the Eastern Carpathians alongside other physical amulets, for example, the dried remains of a snake that just had swallowed a frog. The amulet was kept in the pocket to help one's performance during a trial, or when facing other types of state authorities (Grinchenko 1900, 54).

During the 1880s, Ivan Franko researched legal customs in the Carpathian area. Like many scholars, he encountered evidence within the Bukovina peasantry for widespread belief in a plethora of spirits. At the turn of the century, Shukhevych (1908, 199-214) counted up to 20 different local spirits, beasts and wizards, both male and female, that people believed to exist. Vampires are the ones best known in Western culture. In 1886 Franko published his research on the burning of "vampires" in several Hutsul villages in 1831. Peasants had burnt neighbours as "vampires" because they believed that they would spread cholera. Where the disease had not killed the local priests, they could stop the killings. When put on trial the villagers were acquitted as they said they had acted according to their customary law (Franko 1886/1980a, 578-579). When analysing rulings of a village court from 1867 to 1873 in the Carpathian town of Dobryvljany, Franko noticed that the harshest punishments were meted out in cases of alleged witchcraft against village neighbours. The fines were ten times those for insulting state authorities (Franko 1882/1980b, 472). A similar study on witchcraft as it figured from the seventeenth to the nineteenth century in the peasant courts of Bukovina, Northern Ukraine and Poland was published by Petr Efimenko (1893, 374-401). This is another aspect of the culture which produced the ornamented textiles.

Conclusion

Eugen Ehrlich's experience of the Bukovina familiarized him with a colourful culture characterised by a truly remarkable artistic expression of traditional life. Bukovina ornamented textiles were the objects Eugen Ehrlich collected while working on his "Living law" theory. They were marked by the close relation local people had with nature and ancient traditions. Each piece of ornamented cloth was a personal logogram and amulet for its owner. In XIXth century Bukovina ornaments were a socio-cultural attribute mirroring peasant fears of bad luck, spirits, wizards, diseases, hunger, death, the elements and even misfortune in courts of law.

References

Baladyzhenko, Konstantin (1915), *Bukovina (Zelena Rusj) i ee proshloe.* Petrograd: Tipografija br. V. i I. Linnik.

Dalj Vladimir I. (1880), *O poverjakh, sueverijakh i predrassudkakh russkogo naroda.* Izdanije 2. Sankt Peterburg, Moscow: Tipografija M.O. Voljfa.

Duechting, Hajo (1991), *Wassily Kandinsky. 1866-1944. A Revolution in Painting.* Kőln: Benedict Taschen.

Eaton, Antony (1986), *The Complete Stitch Encyclopaedia. Over 700 Unique Full-colour Step-by-step Photographs.* London: Ward Lock.

Efimenko, Petr (1893), Sud nad vedjmami. *Kievskaja Starina* 11:374-401.

Ehrlich, Eugen (1936/2002), *Fundamental Principles of the Sociology of Law*, translated by Walter L. Moll. New Brunswick/London: Transaction.

Ehrlich, Eugen (1992), Testament. *Zeitschrift für Rechtssoziologie* 11:1-2.

Fediv, Iryna (2013), Odjag, tkaniny ta vychyvka. *Chernovitzkij oblastnoj khudozhestvennyj musej.* http://www.karpaty.info/ru/uk/ch/co/chernivtsi/museums/art (Accessed 24 March 2014).

Fedkovych, Yuriy (1865/1968), *Narodny pisni Bukovyny v zapisakh Yuriya Fedkovycha.* Kiev: Muzychna Ukraina.

Franko Ivan (2006), Podilsjki kylymy. *Visnyk Ljvivsjkogo Universitetu* 6:212-219.

Franko, Ivan (1886/1980a), Sozczchennie upyrej v Naguevichakh v 1831 g. In: Ivan Franko. *Zibrannja tvoriv u 50-i tomakh,* Vol. 46. Kiev: Naukova dumka, pp. 565-581.

Franko, Ivan (1882/1980b), Sud gromadsjkij v sili Dobrivljanakh. In: Ivan Franko. *Zibrannja tvoriv u 50-i tomakh*, Vol, 26. Kiev: Naukova dumka, pp. 198-204.

Franko, Ivan (1985), Etnografichna vystavka u Ternopoli. In: Ivan Franko. *Zibrannja tvoriv u 50-i tomakh,* Vol. 1. Kiev: Naukova dumka, pp. 469-479.

Gajova, Evgenja (2013), Sorochki Zakarpattja. *Nazionaljnyj musej narodnoj arkhitektury ta pobutu Ukraini m. Kiev.* http://pyrohiv.com.ua/ua/articles/read/224/sorochki-dolinjan-zakarpattja (Accessed 24 December 2013).

Golubezj, Mykola (1936), *Ukrainsjkij kylym: druga vystava. Hutsuljsjke misteztvo v Kosovi.* Ljviv: Z drukarni Naukova tovarstva im. Shevchenka u Ljvovi.

Gonzalez-Wippler, Migene (2001), *The Complete Book of Amulets & Talismans.* St. Paul, Minnesota: Llewelyn Publication.

Gozaljuk, Alla (2008), Ukrainsjka svjata ta obrjadova dijstva vesnjano-litnjogo ziklu. *Ukrainoznavstvo* 4(29). http://www.ualogos.kiev.ua/fulltext.html?id=1425 (Accessed 20 December 2013).

Grinchenko, Boris D. (1900), *Iz ust naroda: malorusskie rasskazy, skazki i pr.* Chernigov: Biblioteka Istorii.

Ivanova, Julia (1983), Sledy soljarnogo kuljta. In: Sergej Tokarev (ed.) *Kalendarnyje obychaji i obrjady v stranach zarubezhnoj Evropy. Istoricheskije korni i razvitije obychajev.* Moscow: Nauka, pp. 105-116.

Jakovleva, Olga (2006), Ruchnyk jak symvol u kognytivnoj modeli svitu praukrainzjiv. *Narodna tvorchistj ta etnografija* 3:30-35.

Kandinsky, Nina (1999), *Kandinsky und ich. Mein Leben mit einem grossen Künstler.* Munich: Knaur.

Kandinsky, Wassily (1908/1977), The Language of Form and Colour. In: Wassily Kandinsky. *Concerning the Spiritual in Art.* New York: Dover Publication, pp. 27-45.

Kobaljchinsjka, Romana (2008), Bukovynsjkij kostjum kinzja XIX-XX stolittja u kolekzii Derzhavnogo museju narodnoj arkhitekturi ta pobutu NAN Ukrainy. In: Romana Kobaljchinsjka (ed.), *Muzejnyj zbirnyk naukovykh prazj*, Vol. 8. Kiev: IMFE im. M.T. Ryljsjkogo, pp. 87-91.

Konovalova, Olga (2009), Ukrainsjka narodna ornamentyka jak kulturnij kod nazii. In: Olga Konovalova (ed.), *Ukrainsjke misteztvoznavstvo: materili, doslidzhennja, rezensii*, Vol. 9. Kiev: IMFE im. M.T. Ryljskogo. http://archive.nbuv.gov.ua/portal/Soc_Gum/Ukrmyst/2009/_private/Konovalova.htm (Accessed 24 December 2013).

Kozholjanko, Georgij (2010), Dopovnjuvaljni elementy tradizijnogo kostjuma ukrainziv Bukovyny. *Narodna tvorchistj ta etnografija,* Vol. 1. http://archive.nbuv.gov.ua/portal/Soc_Gum/NTE/2010_1/kozholjanko.html (Accessed 20 March 2013).

Krasikov, Mykchailo (2010), Ukraininjskij narodnij zvychaji, povjazani z kupivlej korovy: suchastna magichna praktyka. *Narodna tvorchistj ta etnografija*, Vol. 6. http://archive.nbuv.gov.ua/portal/Soc_Gum/NTE/2010_6/krasykov.htm_(Accessed 23 December 2013).

Kupchanko, Georgij (1875), *Nekotoryje istoriko-geograficheskie svedenija o Bukovine*. Kiev: Tip. M.P. Friza.

Lagov, Nikolaj (1915), *Galichina, ee istorija, priroda, naselenije, bogatstva, dostoprimechateljnosti*. Petrograd: Izdanije N.P. Karabastikova.

Lehner, Ernst, and Lehner, Johanna (1960), *Folklore and Symbolism of Flowers, Plants and Trees. All Times and Countries. Legendary Stories and Secret Meanings*. New York: Tudor Publishing Company.

Lonachevskij, Alexander (1875), *Sbornik pesen bukovinskogo naroda. Iz materiala, dostavlennogo G.I. Kupchakom v Yugo-Zapadnyj otdel Imperatorskogo Russkogo Geograficheskogo Obscchestva.* Kiev: Tip. M.P. Friza.

Marusik-Zhmendak, Nastasia (2009), Vidy ta symvolyka vyshyvkovogo ornamentu. *Chasi Podii.* http://www.chasipodii.net/article/5610/_(Accessed 25 December 2013).

Modzalevskyj, Vadim (1918), *Osnovni rysy ukrainsjkogo misteztva.* Chernigiv: Druk. G.M. Veseloj.

Moisej, Antonij (2009), Skladovi etnokulturnoj identifikazii v ukrainsjko-rumuno-moldavsjkij prikordonnoj zony (na prikladi ukrainzev Suchavsjkogo povitu

Rumunii ta skhidnoromansjkogo naselenja Chernivizjkoj oblasti Ukrainy). *Bukovynsjkij Zhurnal* 1-2:157-191.

Musatova, Iryna (2008), Arkhaichni rushnyky Pivdnja Ukrainy (sjuzhety i semantyka). In: Olga Konovalova (ed.), *Ukrainsjke misteztvoznavstvo: materialy, doslidzhennja, rezensii*, Vol. 8. Kiev: IMFE im. M.T. Ryljsjkogo, pp. 186-189.

Naiden, Oleksander and Selivachov, Mykhailo (1993), Ornament. In: Volodymyr Kubilovic and Danylo Hussar Struk (eds.), *Internet Encyclopedia of Ukraine, Vol. 1. Canadian Institute of Ukrainian Studies.* http://www.encyclopediaofukraine.com/pages%5CO%5CR%5COrnament.htm (Accessed 14 April 2014).

Nesen, Iryna (2009), Pokhovaljni ta pominaljni obrjadi v seredovishchi "okolochnoj" shljachty Zhitomirshchiny (kinezj XIX-XX stolittja). *Visnyk Ljvivsjkogo Universitetu* 44:241-264.

Osadcha, Olena (2010), Khatna ikona v vyrovannjakh i obrjadakh. *Narodna tvorchistj ta etnografija*, Vol. 6. http://archive.nbuv.gov.ua/portal/Soc_Gum/NTE/2010_6/osadcha.htm (accessed 25 December 2013).

Pezhansjkij, Volodymyr (1925), *Davni kylymy Ukrainy*. Lviv: Dilo.

Rehbinder, Manfred (1986), *Die Begrűndung der Rechtssoziologie durch Eugen Ehrlich.* 2nd edition. Berlin: Dunker & Humblot.

Riegl, Alois (1899/2004), Worldview. In: Alois Riegl, *Historical Grammar of the Visual Arts*, translated by Jacqueline B. Jung. New York: Zone Books, pp. 303-340.

Rottleuthner, Hubert (1992), Redaktionelle Vorbemerkung. *Zeitschrift für Rechtssoziologie.* 11:1-2.

Rybakov, Boris A. (1987), *Jazychestvo Drevnej Rusi.* Moscow: Nauka.

Semchuk, Lesja (2007), Rostashuvannja vyshyvok na komponentakh odjagu etnografichnikh grup ukrainziv Karpatsjkogo regionu: porivnjaljnyj aspect. In: Olga Konovalova (ed.), *Ukrainsjke misteztvoznavstvo: materialy, doslydzhennja, rezensii*, Vol. 7. Kiev: IMFE im. M.T. Riljsjkogo. http://archive.nbuv.gov.ua/portal/Soc_Gum/Ukrmyst/2007/_private/Semchuk.htm (accessed 24 December 2013).

Shukhevych, Volodymyr (1908), *Hutsuljshchina. Napysav Volodymyr Shukhevych*, Vol. V, Ljviv: Zagaljna drukarnja.

Simmel, Georg (1905/1997), The Philosophy of Fashion. In: David Frisby and Mike Featherstone (eds.), *Simmel on Culture*. London, New Delhi: Sage Publications, pp. 187-206.

Tkachuk, Jaroslava (2013), Hutsuljsjkij kylym ta karpatsjkij lyzhnik. *Viche Boruslava.* http://viche-boruslava.org.ua/index.php/ukrainskyi-rid/13-tradytsiia/173-hutsulskyy-kylym-ta-karpatskyy-lizhnyk (accessed 25 March 2014).

Tokarev, Sergej A. (1983), Eroticheskije obychai. In: Sergej Tokarev (ed.) *Kalen-*

darnyje obychaji i obrjady v stranach zarubezhnoj Evropy. Istoricheskije korni i razvitije obychajev. Moscow: Nauka, pp. 98-105.

Vlad, Maria (1992), *Sritenne: Knizhka hutsuljsjkikh zvychaiv i viruvanj.* Kiev: Ukrainsjkij pysjmennik.

Voropai, Oleksa (1958), *Zvychai nashogo harodu. Etnografychnyj naris.* Munich: Ukrainsjke vydavnitztvo.

Vovk, Fedir (1928), *Studii z ukrainsjkoj etnografii ta antropologii.* Praha: Legiografija.

Zhuk, Adam (1966), *Ukrainsjki narodni kylymy.* Kiev: Naukova dumka.

Contributors

Franz von Benda-Beckmann was a head of the Project Group Legal Pluralism at the Max Planck Institute for Social Anthropology in Halle, Germany. He was also an honorary professor at the Universities of Leipzig and Halle. He did fieldwork in Malawi, West Sumatra, and the Moluccas. His academic work was devoted to legal pluralism, and he published widely on theoretical issues, on property, inheritance, natural resource management, social (in)security, law and religion, and decentralization in Indonesia. He edited: with Keebet von Benda-Beckmann and Anne Griffiths (2009), The Power of Law in a Transnational World, Oxford: Berghahn; with Keebet von Benda-Beckmann and Anne Griffiths (2009), Spatializing Law, Farnham: Ashgate; with Keebet von Benda-Beckmann and Julia Eckert (2009), Rules of Law and Laws of Ruling, Farnham: Ashgate; with Keebet von Benda-Beckmann, Martin Ramstedt and Bertram Turner (2013), Religion in Disputes, New York/Basingstoke: Palgrave/Macmillan. He wrote, with Keebet von Benda-Beckmann (2013), Political and Legal Transformations of an Indonesian Polity, Cambridge: Cambridge University Press.

Keebet von Benda-Beckmann is professor emeritus and was head of the Project Group Legal Pluralism at the Max Planck Institute for Social Anthropology in Halle, Germany. She is also an honorary professor at the Universities of Leipzig and Halle. She has done fieldwork in West Sumatra, the Moluccas, and in the Netherlands. Her fields of interest are legal pluralism, dispute management, social (in)security, law and religion, natural resource management, and decentralisation in Indonesia. Her recent publications include edited books: with Franz von Benda-Beckmann and Anne Griffiths (2005) Mobile People, Mobile Law, Aldershot: Ashgate; with Franz von Benda-Beckmann and Melanie G. Wiber (2006) Changing Properties of Property. Oxford: Berghahn; with Franz von Benda-Beckmann (2006) Dynamics of Plural Legal Orders. Special Issue of the Journal of Legal Pluralism; with Martin Ramstedt and Melanie G. Wiber (2014) Temporalities of Law, Special Issue of the Journal of Legal Pluralism. She wrote with Franz von Benda-Beckmann (2013) Political and Legal Transformations of an Indonesian Polity, Cambridge: CUP.

Anne Hellum is a lawyer and anthropologist holding a Doctor Juris Degree from the University of Oslo. She is professor at the Department of Public and International Law at the University of Oslo and Director of the Rights, Culture and Society Program (RICS) at the Faculty of Law. She is visiting professor at the Southern and Eastern African Centre of Women's Law (SEARCWL) at the University of Zimbabwe, and has had visiting appointments at the Human Rights Study Centre at the University of Peshawar and the Department of Anthropology at Michigan State University. Her research has generally focused on the relationship between human rights, gender and legal pluralism in Zimbabwe, South Africa and Norway, with a focus on family and reproduction, the right to land and water, and access to law. Among her publications are Paths with Julie Stewart et al. (2007), Human Rights, Gendered Realities and Plural Legalities, Harare: Weaver Press, with Anne Griffiths and Shaheen Sardar Ali (2011) From Transnational Relations to Transnational Laws: Northern European Laws at the Crossroads, Farnham: Ashgate, with Bill Derman and Kristin Sandvik (2013), Worlds of Human Rights: Ambiguities of Rights Claiming in Africa, Leiden: Brill, with Henriette Sinding Aasen (2013), Women's Human Rights: CEDAW in International, Regional and National Law, Cambridge: Cambridge University Press; with Patricia Kameri-Mbote (2015, in press), Water is Life: Women's Human Rights in National and Local Water Governance in Southern and Eastern Africa. Harare: Weaver Press.

Monika Lindbekk is a doctoral research fellow at the Institute of Criminology and Sociology of Law at the University of Oslo. Her PhD research focuses on divorce law in Egypt before and after the revolution in 2011. She has published articles and book chapters dealing with debates about Islamic family law and its application by Egyptian state courts. Her most recent publications include: The Enforcement of Personal Status Law by Egyptian Courts. In: Elisa Giunchi (ed., 2013), Adjudicating Family Law in Muslim Courts. New York: Routledge. She has also co-authored A Counter-Revolution in Egyptian Family Law? Egypt's Pre-And Post-Revolutionary Period (2011-2013) Compared, New Middle Eastern Studies. Lindbekk is also among the editors of and contributors to a forthcoming book on female judges in Muslim majority countries (Women Judges in the Muslim World: Discourse and Practice. Leiden: Brill).

Olga Litvinova holds a doctorate in the Sociology of Culture and is a Honorary Research Fellow in the School of Social Sciences, Bangor University, Wales. Her research interests are connected with systems theories and to the areas of sociology of culture, law and education. She has worked as a sociologist at the power plant constructor TKZ (Taganrog, South Russia), as the deputy head of a secondary school, and as a lecturer and researcher at the Pedagogical University and the Southern Federal University in Rostov on Don, Russia. Her publications include: (2007), Sistema i sreda sociologii Niklasa Lumanna Moscow: Alfa-M (The System and Environment of Niklas Luhmann's Sociology); with Stefan Machura and

Dmitrij Donskow (2003), Ehrenamtliche Richter in Südrussland, Munster: Lit (People's Assessors in South Russia); with Stefan Machura (2005), Krieg und Gesellschaft: Mehrebenenanalyse der amerikanischen und sowjetischen Verfilmungen von Tolstojs Roman "Krieg und Frieden". In: Stefan Machura and Rüdiger Voigt (eds.), Krieg im Film, Munster: Lit, pp. 103 – 132 (War and Society. Multi-Level Analysis of the American and Soviet Films of Tolstoy's Novel "War and Peace"); with Machura, Stefan (2007). Lay Judges in Rostov Province. In: Ferdinand Feldbrugge (ed.), Russia, Europe, and the Rule of Law, Leiden: Martinus Nijhoff Publishers, pp. 109 – 127.

Stefan Machura, Dr. rer. soc., Dr. rer. pol. habil., is Senior Lecturer in Criminology and Criminal Justice at Bangor University. From 1992 to 2006, he taught Sociology of Law and Political Science at the Ruhr-Universität Bochum, Germany. The publications he has edited include: with Knut Papendorf and Kristian Andenæs (2011), Understanding Law in Society, Zürich/Berlin: Lit; with Ralf Walkenhaus, et al. (2006), Staat im Wandel. Festschrift für Rüdiger Voigt, Stuttgart: Steiner; with Stefan Ulbrich (2003). Recht, Gesellschaft, Kommunikation. Festschrift für Klaus F. Röhl, Baden-Baden: Nomos; with Peter Robson (2001), Law and Film, Oxford: Blackwell; (1998), Special issue "Procedural Justice", Law and Policy, 20:1; with Klaus F. Röhl (1997), Procedural Justice, Aldershot: Ashgate. Other books: (2006), Ehrenamtliche Verwaltungsrichter, Munster: Lit (Lay Judges in Administrative Courts), (2005), Politik und Verwaltung, Opladen: VS-Verlag für Sozialwissenschaft (Politics and Public Administration); (2001). Fairneß und Legitimität, Baden-Baden: Nomos; (1993). Die Kontrolle öffentlicher Unternehmen, Wiesbaden: Deutscher Universitätsverlag (The Control of Public Enterprises).

Knut Papendorf, dr. phil., is professor at the Department of Criminology and Sociology of Law, University of Oslo. He has published books and articles related to criminal policy, sociology of law, comparative law and control politics. His recent publications are Rett for alle? Rettsliggjøring og rettsfjerne personers mulighet til å mobilisere retten. Novus forlag: Oslo (2012); Schadensregulierung bei fehlerhafter Behandlung von Patienten in Norwegen. In: Josef Estermann (ed.), Der Kampf ums Recht, Vienna/Beckenried: Lit/Orlux, 2012, pp. 281 – 292 and The Politics of Abolition: Effects on the Criminal Sociology and Criminal Policy Debate in West Germany. In: Thomas Mathiesen, The Politics of Abolition, London: Routledge, 2014, pp. 256 – 262.

Hanne Petersen has been professor of legal cultures at the University of Copenhagen since 2009. She was Jean Monnet Scholar at the European University Institute in Florence 1993-94, professor of jurisprudence and sociology of law at University of Greenland, Ilisimatusarfik 1995-99, professor of Greenlandic sociology of law at University of Copenhagen 2001-2006. From 2007-2012 she was adjunct professor of law at University of Tromsø, Norway, and from 2011-2012 she was Hedda Andersson guest professor at Lund University, Sweden, as this university's commitment to Gender Equality. She has participated in a number of national and international research projects. Recent publications: (Petersen 2014), Demokratiske stemmer og visioner – før og nu. In: Helle Krunke et al. (eds.), Rettens magt og Magtens ret. Festskrift til Henning Koch. Jurist- og Økonomforbundets forlag, pp. 309-320; (with José Maria Lorenzo Villaverde and Ingrid Lund-Andersen), Contemporary Gender Relations and Changes in Legal Cultures, Copenhagen: Djøf / Jurist- og Økonomforbundet; (Petersen 2012), On-Stage and Off-Stage European and Global Scenes. In: Kjell Åke Modéer and Martin Sunnquist (eds.). Legal Stagings: The Visualization, Medialization and Ritualization of Law in Language, Literature, Media, Art and Architecture. Copenhagen: Museum Tusculanum, pp. 25-49; (Petersen 2011), Justice, Benevolence, and Happiness: Encounter and Challenges in Global Legal Culture. In: Michal Tomásek and Guido Mühlemann (eds.) Interpretation of Law in China – Roots and Perspectives. Prague: Karolinum; (Petersen 2006), Retspluralisme i praksis – grønlandske inspirationer. Copenhagen: Ilisimatusarfik & Jurist- og Økonomforbundet.

Måns Svensson, Associate Professor of Sociology of Law at Lund University in Sweden, director of the Centre for Work, Technology and Social Change at Lund University and Head of Research at Lund University Internet Institute. From a socio-legal perspective Svensson conducts research in areas such as Internet and Society, work-life in transition, and economic security. A selection of recent publications include: with S. Larsson et al. (2014), The Digital IP Challenge Revisited – File-sharing and Copyright Development in Hungary. The WIPO Journal 6(1): 1-20; (2013). Norms in Law and Society: Towards a Definition of the Socio-Legal Concept of Norms. In: Matthias Baier. (ed.), Social and Legal Norms, Aldershot: Ashgate; with Rustamjon Urinboyev and K. Åström, (2012). Welfare as a Means for Political Stability: a Law and Society Analysis. European Journal of Social Security 14(2): 64-85.

Rustamjon Urinboyev is Research Fellow at the Department of Sociology of Law at Lund University, Sweden. He is currently a visiting scholar at Cambridge Central Asia Forum, University of Cambridge. Rustamjon has a PhD in sociology of law (2013) from Lund University; his research focuses on state-society relations, pre-Soviet (Islamic) governance structures in Central Asia, legal pluralism, corruption, ethnography of the state with regional focus on Central Asia, and migration governance in post-Soviet societies. Urinboyev's current (postdoc) research examines the interlinkages between migration and legal cultures in post-Soviet societies, specifically focusing on migration flows from Uzbekistan to Russia and the roles of informal structures and the internet in shaping these migratory processes.

Klaus A. Ziegert, Professor in Jurisprudence, Honorary Affiliate University of Sydney, Sydney, Australia. Studies in law, sociology, communication and media research (Publizistik), Nordic and Slavonic languages and literature, at the University of Frankfurt, Germany (1966-1967) and the University of Münster, Germany (1967-1973); awarded Dr. phil. by the University of Münster, Germany, 1975; DAAD-Research Fellow at the Institute for Sociology of Law at the University of Lund, Sweden 1973-1974; Research Fellow at the Centre for Interdisciplinary Research (ZiF), University of Bielefeld, Germany, 1974-1975; Senior Research Officer at the Max-Planck-Institute for International and Comparative Private Law in Hamburg/FRG, 1975-1982; Lecturer in Jurisprudence (appt. Assoc. Professor in Jurisprudence 1989); in the Department of Jurisprudence, University of Sydney; Head of Department of Jurisprudence from January 1988 to January 1999; Dean of the Faculty of Law, University of Sydney, 1992-1993; Director of the Centre for Asian and Pacific Law at University of Sydney (CAPLUS) 1998-2002.

Gesellschaft und Recht

hrsg. von Dr. Dr. habil. Stefan Machura und Prof. Dr. Klaus F. Röhl

Franziska Prinz
Der Bildgebrauch in gedruckten Rechtsbüchern des 15. bis zum Ausgang des 18. Jahrhunderts
Mit CD-ROM
Dieses Buch dokumentiert und kommentiert den Bestand an Illustrationen in gedruckten Rechtsbüchern von der Mitte des 15. bis zum Ausgang des 18. Jahrhunderts. Es zeigt auf, wie sich der Gebrauch von Bildern seit der Erfindung des Buch- und Bilddrucks in qualitativer und quantitativer Hinsicht verändert hat, welche bildlichen Darstellungen Eingang in juristische Bücher fanden und wie sich diese in ihrer Häufigkeit, Gestaltung und Thematik im Untersuchungszeitraum entwickelt und verändert haben. Die beigefügte Bildsammlung auf CD-Rom enthält 1.045 Illustrationen.
Bd. 5, 2006, 248 S., 24,90 €, gb., ISBN 3-8258-9703-6

Gesellschaft und Recht

hrsg. von Dr. Dr. habil. Stefan Machura und Prof. Dr. Klaus F. Röhl

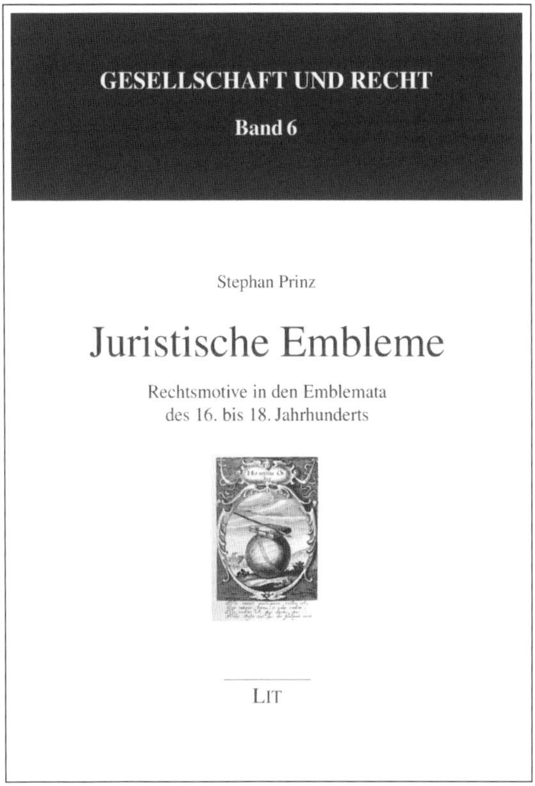

Stephan Prinz
Juristische Embleme
Rechtsmotive in den Emblemata des 16. bis 18. Jahrhunderts
Dieses Buch dokumentiert und kommentiert den Bestand an Emblemen mit juristischen Inhalten. Es zeigt auf, wie sich der Gebrauchs von rechtlichen Inhalten im Rahmen der Emblemkunst entwickelt hat, in welchen unterschiedlichen Bereichen juristische Inhalte vorkommen und wie unterhaltsam und zeitlos gerade die Embleme sich mit immer wiederkehrenden Fragestellungen des Rechts auseinandersetzen. Die beigefügte Emblemsammlung auf CD-Rom enthält über 400 Embleme und deren Beschreibung.
Bd. 6, 2009, 200 S., 24,90 €, br., ISBN 978-3-643-10133-4

LIT Verlag Berlin – Münster – Wien – Zürich – London

Auslieferung Deutschland / Österreich / Schweiz: siehe Impressumsseite